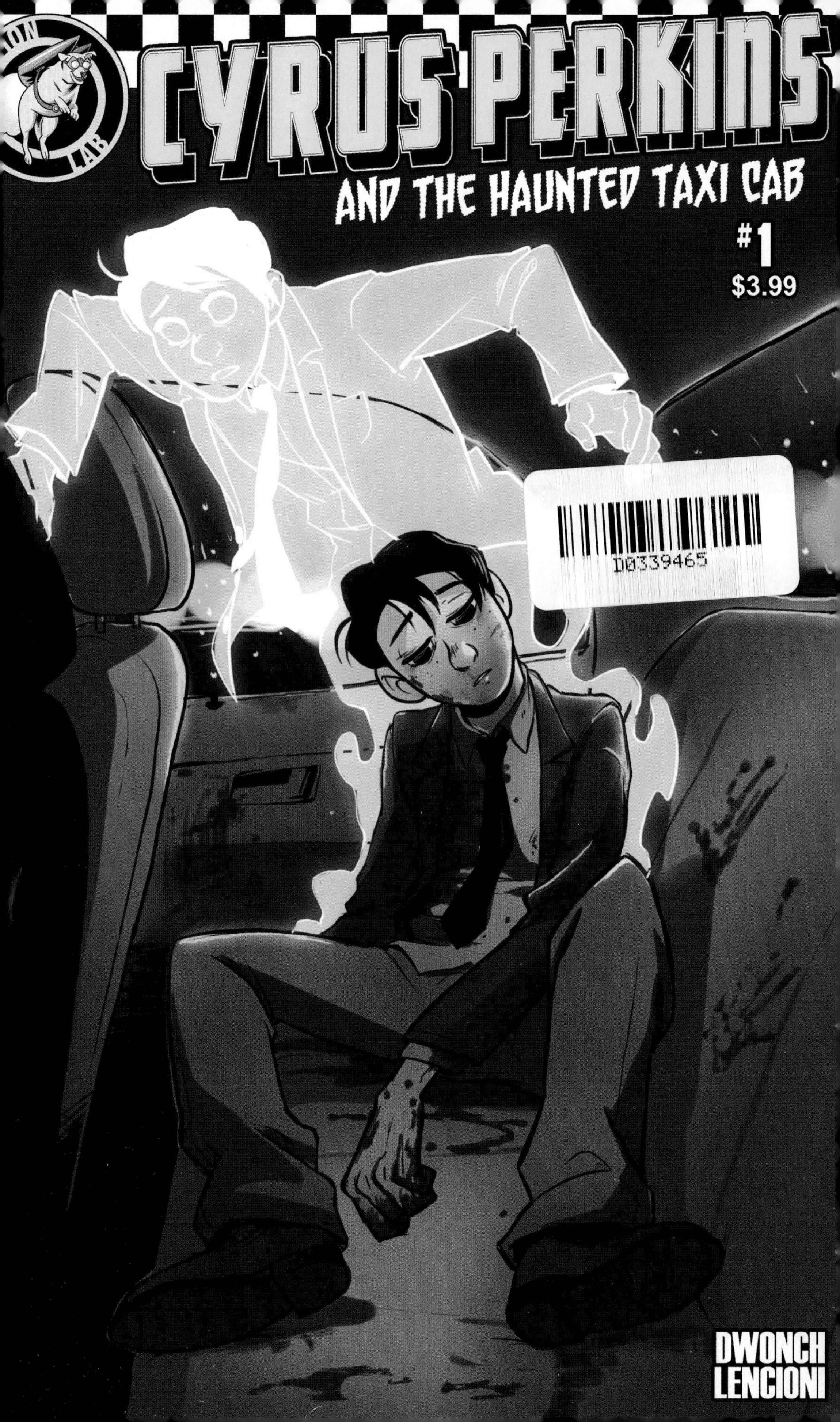
CYRUS PERKINS
AND THE HAUNTED TAXI CAB
#1
$3.99
DWONCH
LENCIONI

CYRUS PERKINS
AND THE HAUNTED TAXI CAB!

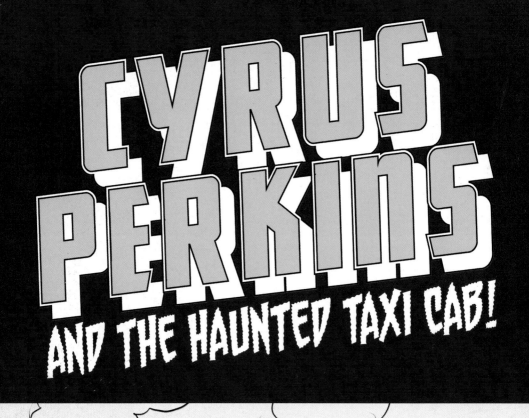

DAVE DWONCH
STORY/LETTERS/COLORS

ANNA LENCIONI
ART/TONES

BRYAN SEATON: PUBLISHER   KEVIN FREEMAN: PRESIDENT
DAVE DWONCH: CREATIVE DIRECTOR   SHAWN GABBORIN: EDITOR IN CHIEF
JAMAL IGLE: VICE-PRESIDENT OF MARKETING
VITO DELSANTE: DIRECTOR OF MARKETING
JIM DIETZ: SOCIAL MEDIA DIRECTOR
CHAD CICCONI: HAUNTS THE OFFICES

"LISTEN
TO ME."

CYRUS.

"YOU- YOU'RE
GOING TO BE OKAY.
YOU JUST NEED TO
STAY AWAKE, YOU
HEAR ME?"

"YOU HEAR
ME, KID?"

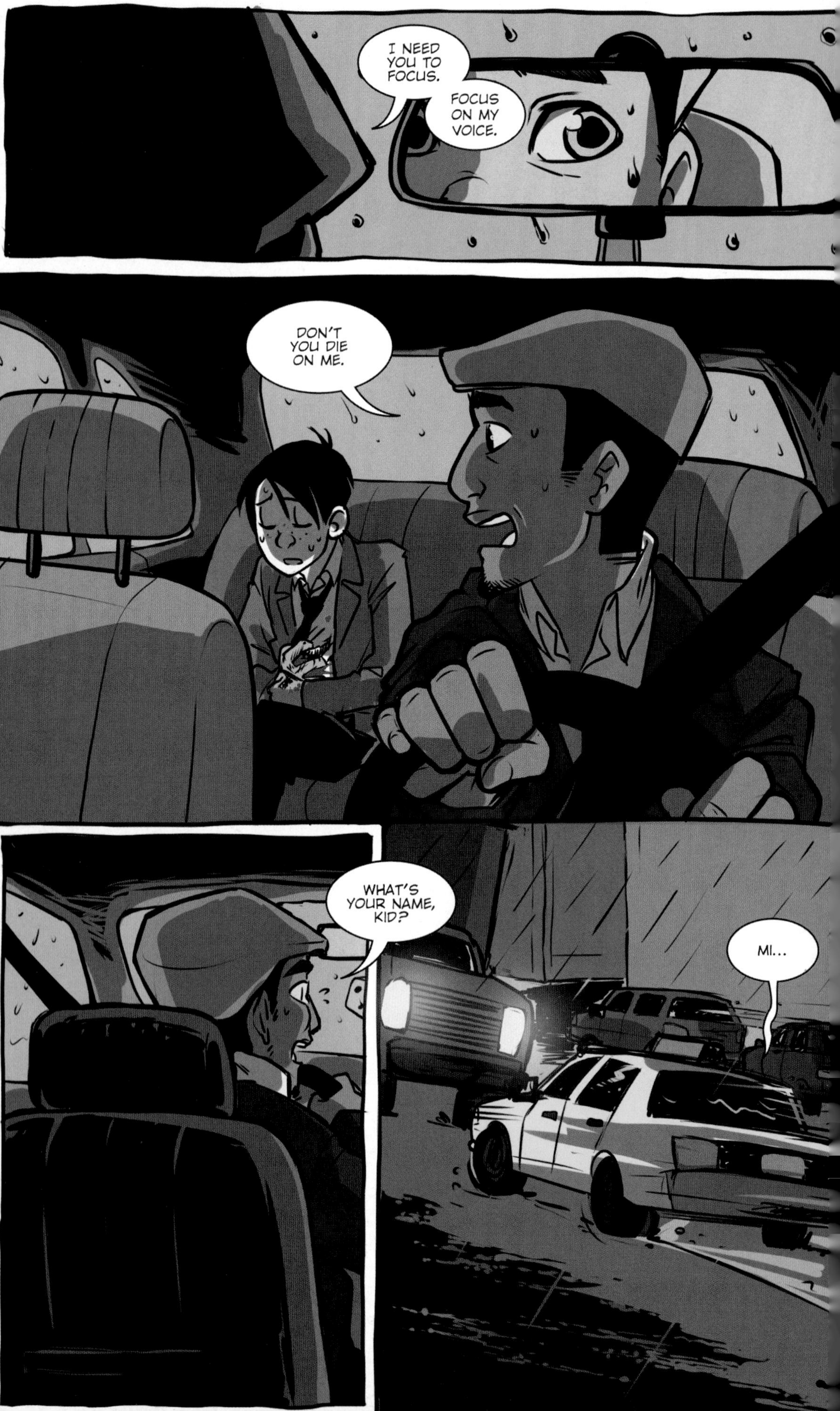
I NEED YOU TO FOCUS.
FOCUS ON MY VOICE.
DON'T YOU DIE ON ME.
WHAT'S YOUR NAME, KID?
MI...

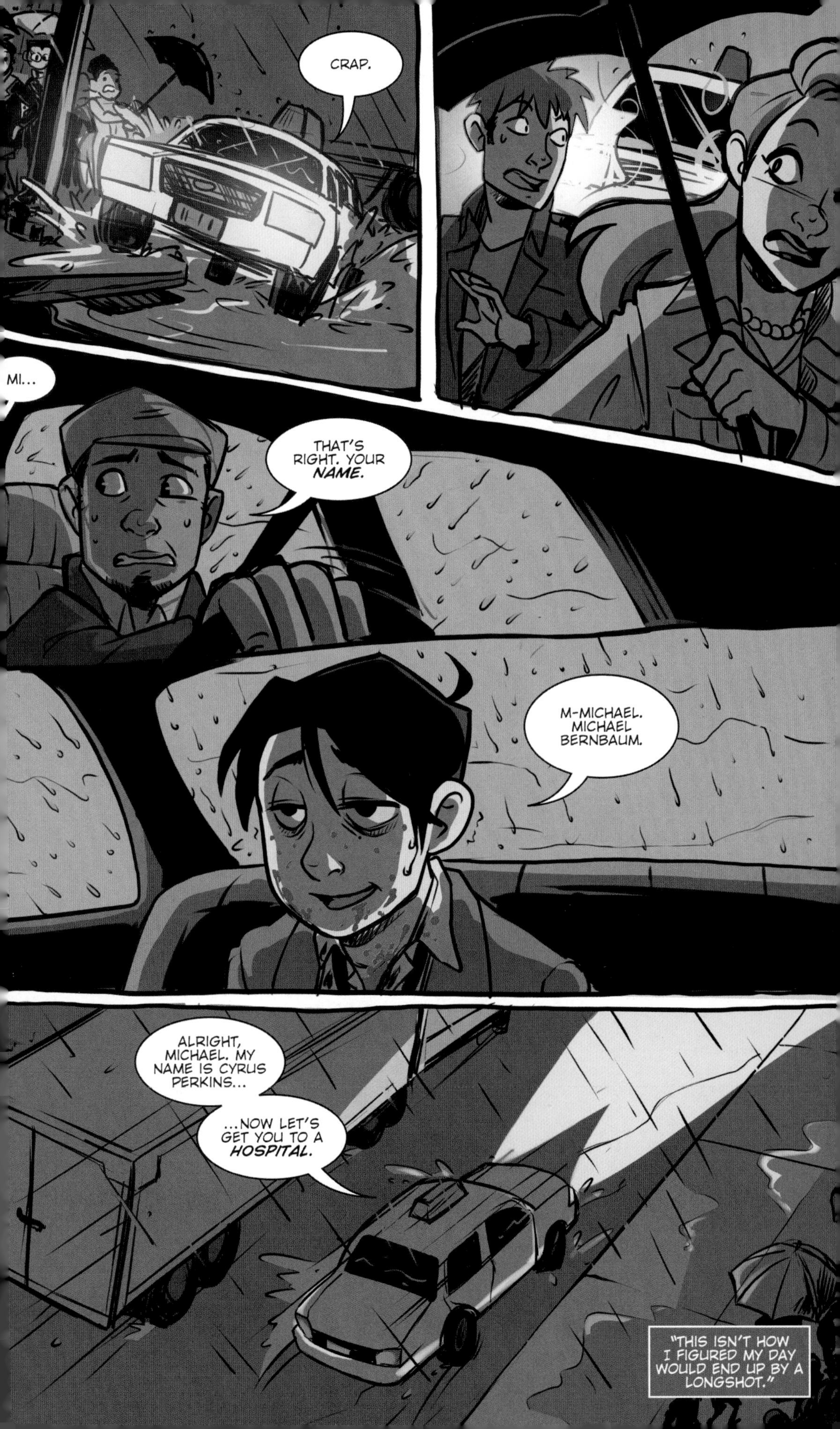
CRAP.
MI...
THAT'S RIGHT. YOUR *NAME.*
M-MICHAEL. MICHAEL BERNBAUM.
ALRIGHT, MICHAEL. MY NAME IS CYRUS PERKINS...
...NOW LET'S GET YOU TO A *HOSPITAL.*
"THIS ISN'T HOW I FIGURED MY DAY WOULD END UP BY A LONGSHOT."

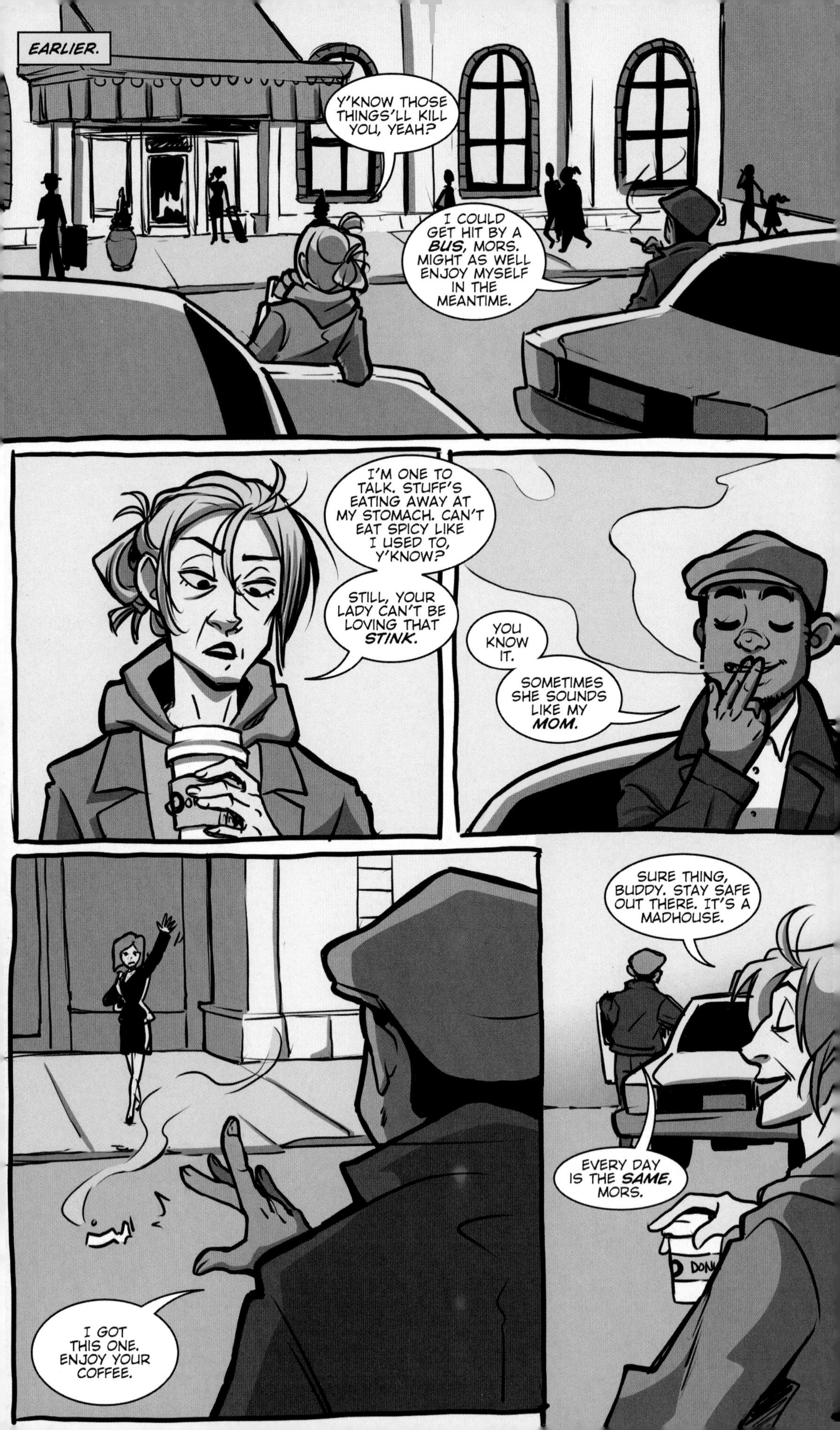
EARLIER.
Y'KNOW THOSE THINGS'LL KILL YOU, YEAH?
I COULD GET HIT BY A BUS, MORS. MIGHT AS WELL ENJOY MYSELF IN THE MEANTIME.
I'M ONE TO TALK. STUFF'S EATING AWAY AT MY STOMACH. CAN'T EAT SPICY LIKE I USED TO, Y'KNOW?
STILL, YOUR LADY CAN'T BE LOVING THAT STINK.
YOU KNOW IT.
SOMETIMES SHE SOUNDS LIKE MY MOM.
I GOT THIS ONE. ENJOY YOUR COFFEE.
SURE THING, BUDDY. STAY SAFE OUT THERE. IT'S A MADHOUSE.
EVERY DAY IS THE SAME, MORS.

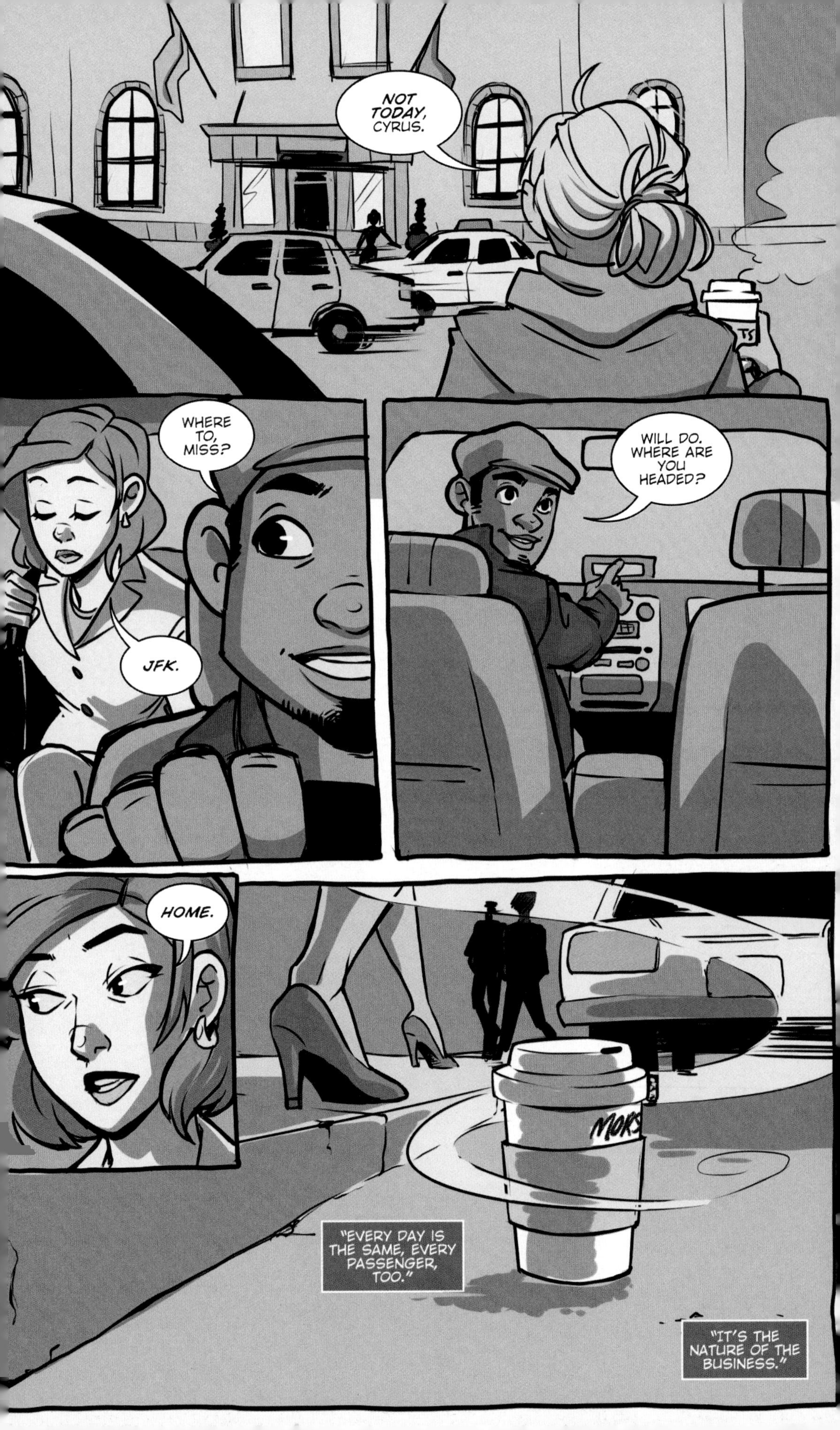

NOT TODAY, CYRUS.
WHERE TO, MISS?
JFK.
WILL DO. WHERE ARE YOU HEADED?
HOME.
"EVERY DAY IS THE SAME, EVERY PASSENGER, TOO."
"IT'S THE NATURE OF THE BUSINESS."

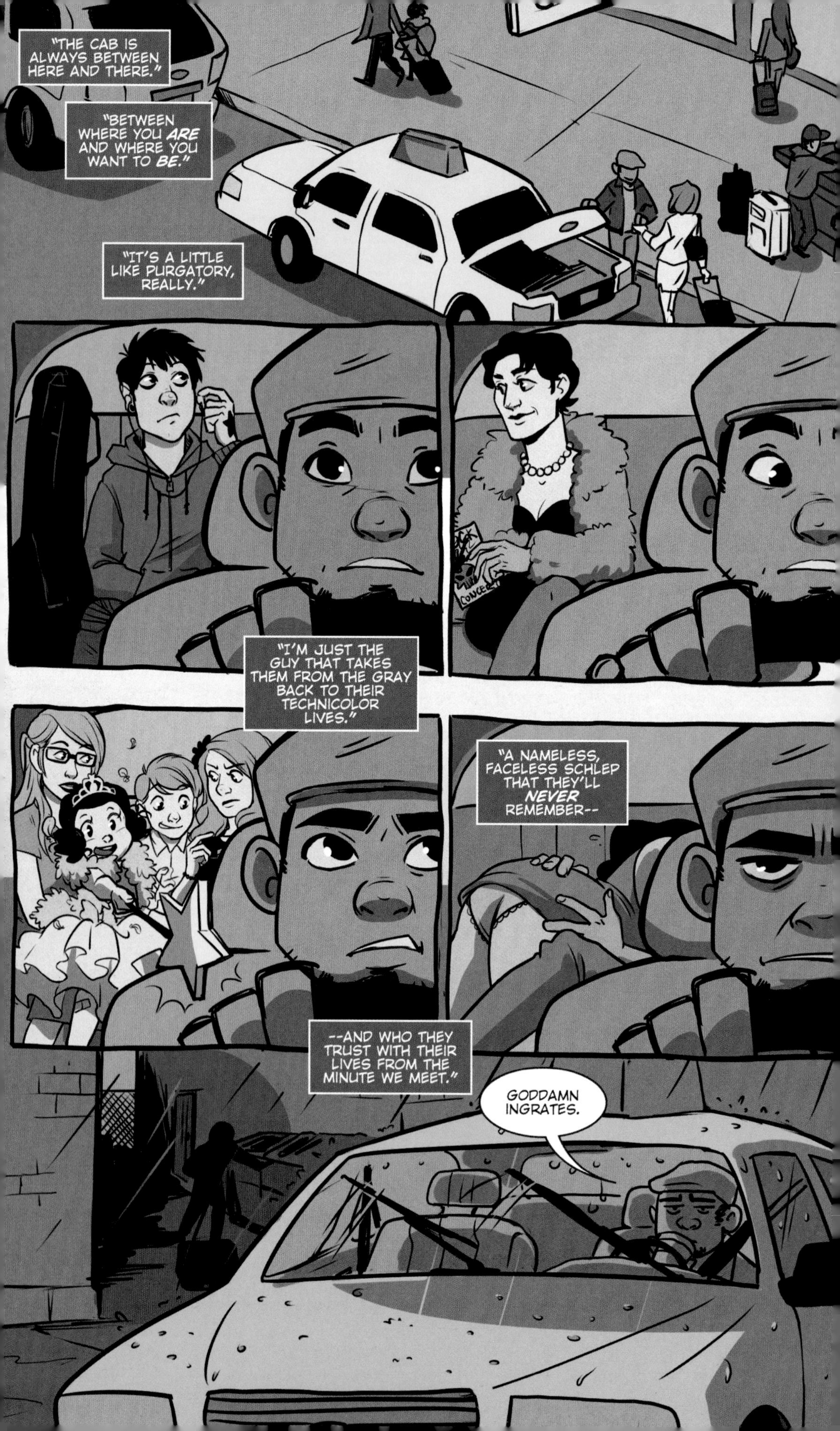
"THE CAB IS ALWAYS BETWEEN HERE AND THERE."
"BETWEEN WHERE YOU *ARE* AND WHERE YOU WANT TO *BE*."
"IT'S A LITTLE LIKE PURGATORY, REALLY."
"I'M JUST THE GUY THAT TAKES THEM FROM THE GRAY BACK TO THEIR TECHNICOLOR LIVES."
"A NAMELESS, FACELESS SCHLEP THAT THEY'LL *NEVER* REMEMBER--
--AND WHO THEY TRUST WITH THEIR LIVES FROM THE MINUTE WE MEET."
GODDAMN INGRATES.

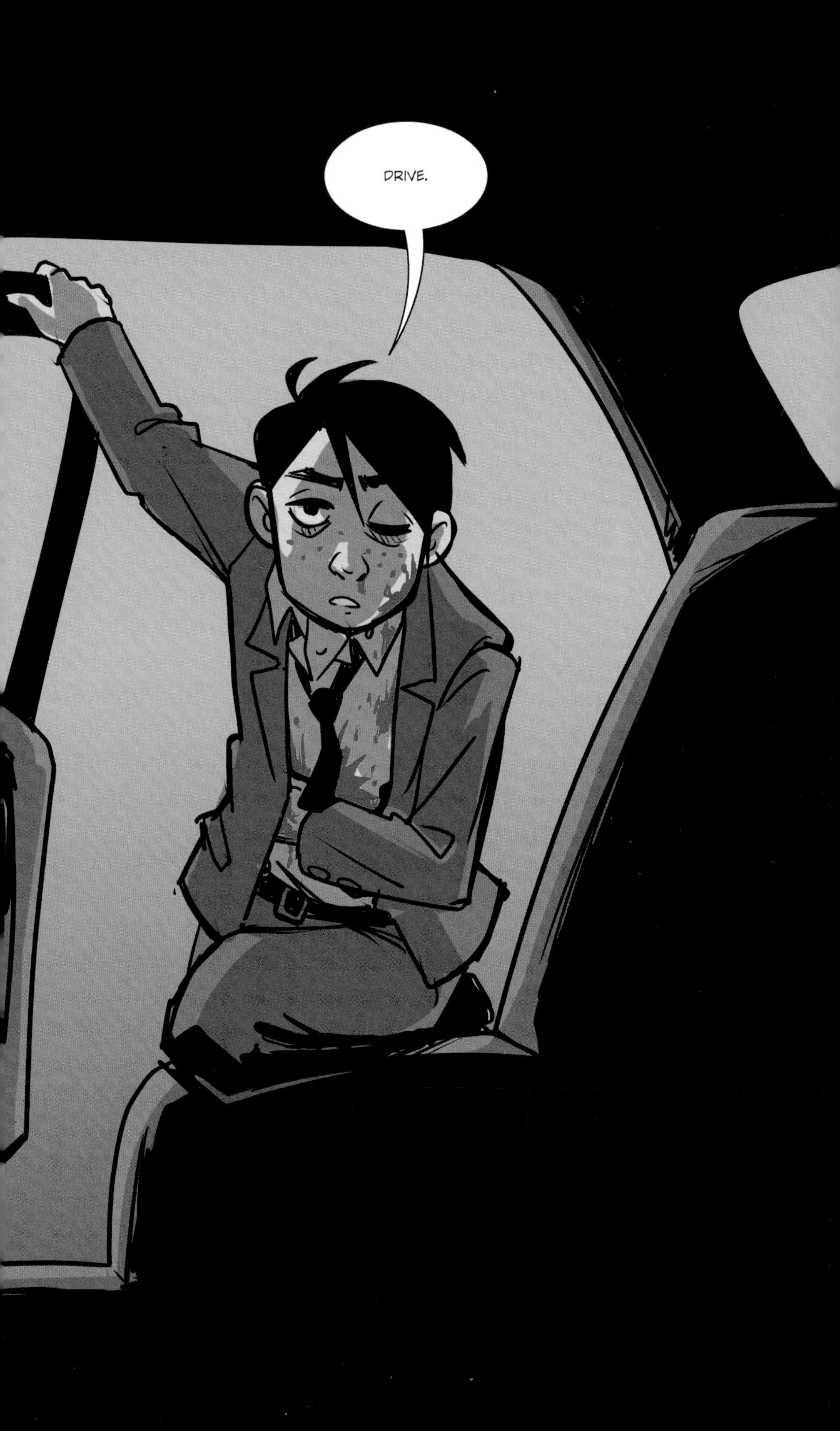
DRIVE.

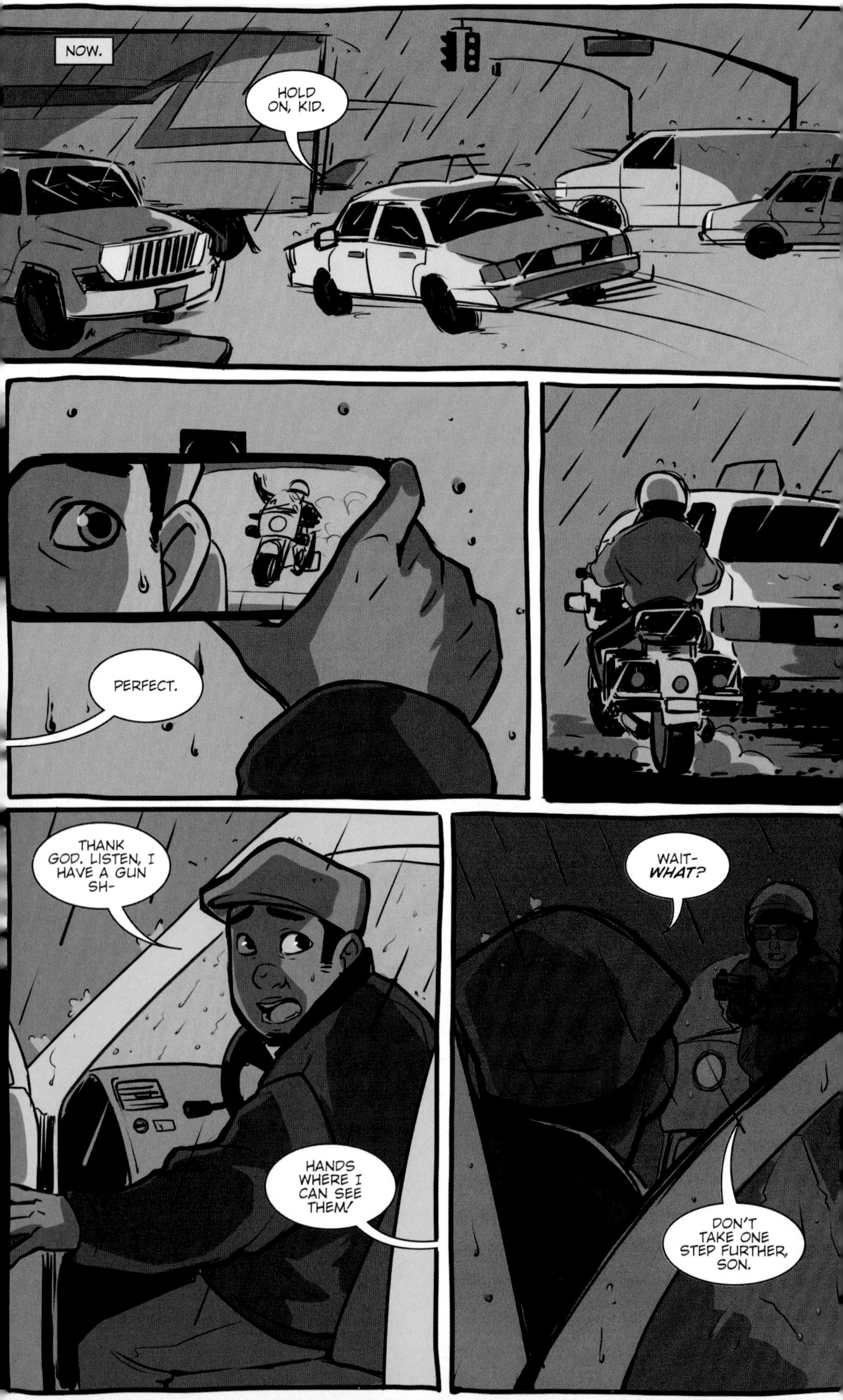
NOW.
HOLD ON, KID.
PERFECT.
THANK GOD. LISTEN, I HAVE A GUN SH-
HANDS WHERE I CAN SEE THEM!
WAIT- *WHAT?*
DON'T TAKE ONE STEP FURTHER, SON.

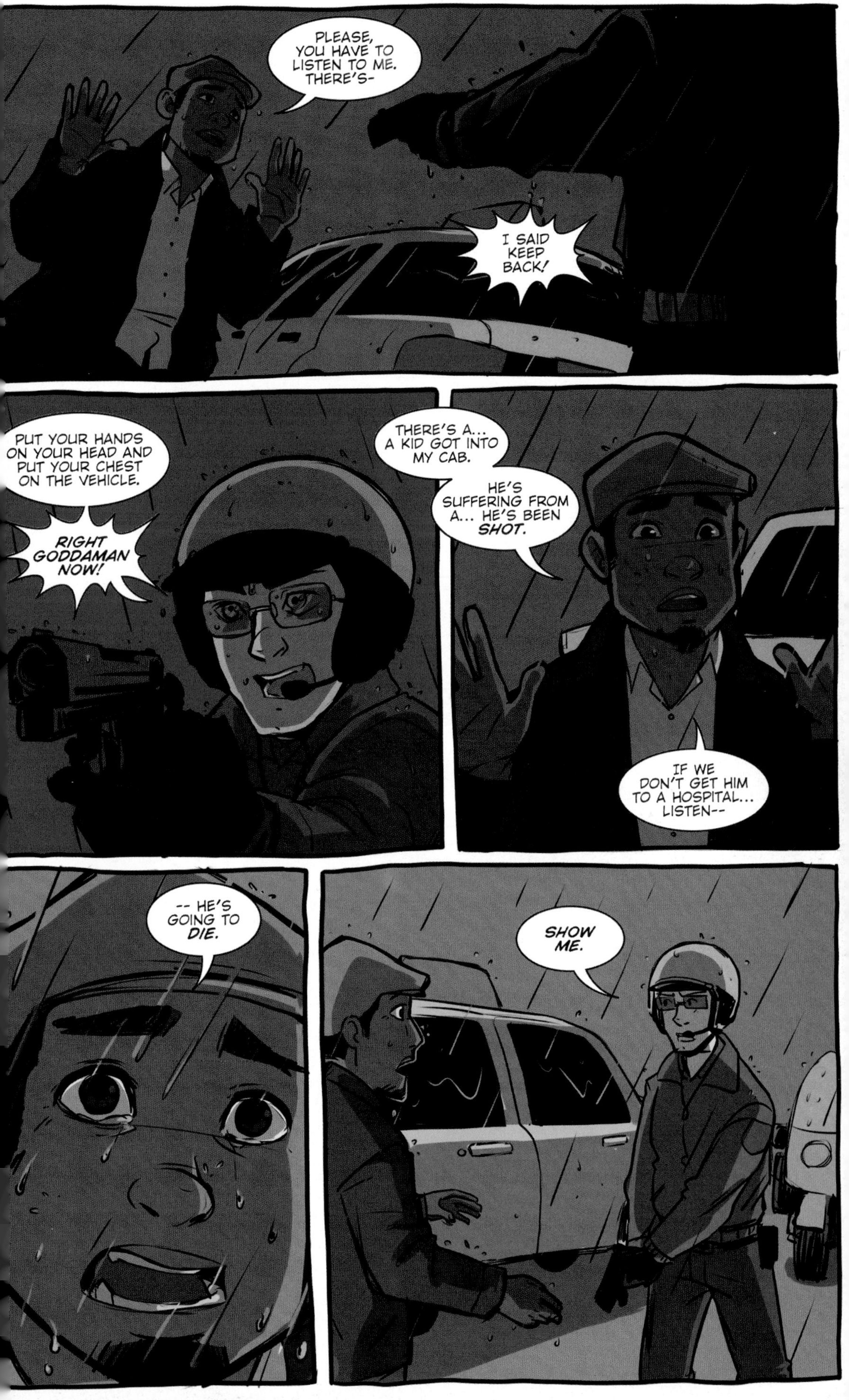
PLEASE, YOU HAVE TO LISTEN TO ME. THERE'S-
I SAID KEEP BACK!
PUT YOUR HANDS ON YOUR HEAD AND PUT YOUR CHEST ON THE VEHICLE.
RIGHT GODDAMAN NOW!
THERE'S A... A KID GOT INTO MY CAB.
HE'S SUFFERING FROM A... HE'S BEEN SHOT.
IF WE DON'T GET HIM TO A HOSPITAL... LISTEN--
-- HE'S GOING TO DIE.
SHOW ME.

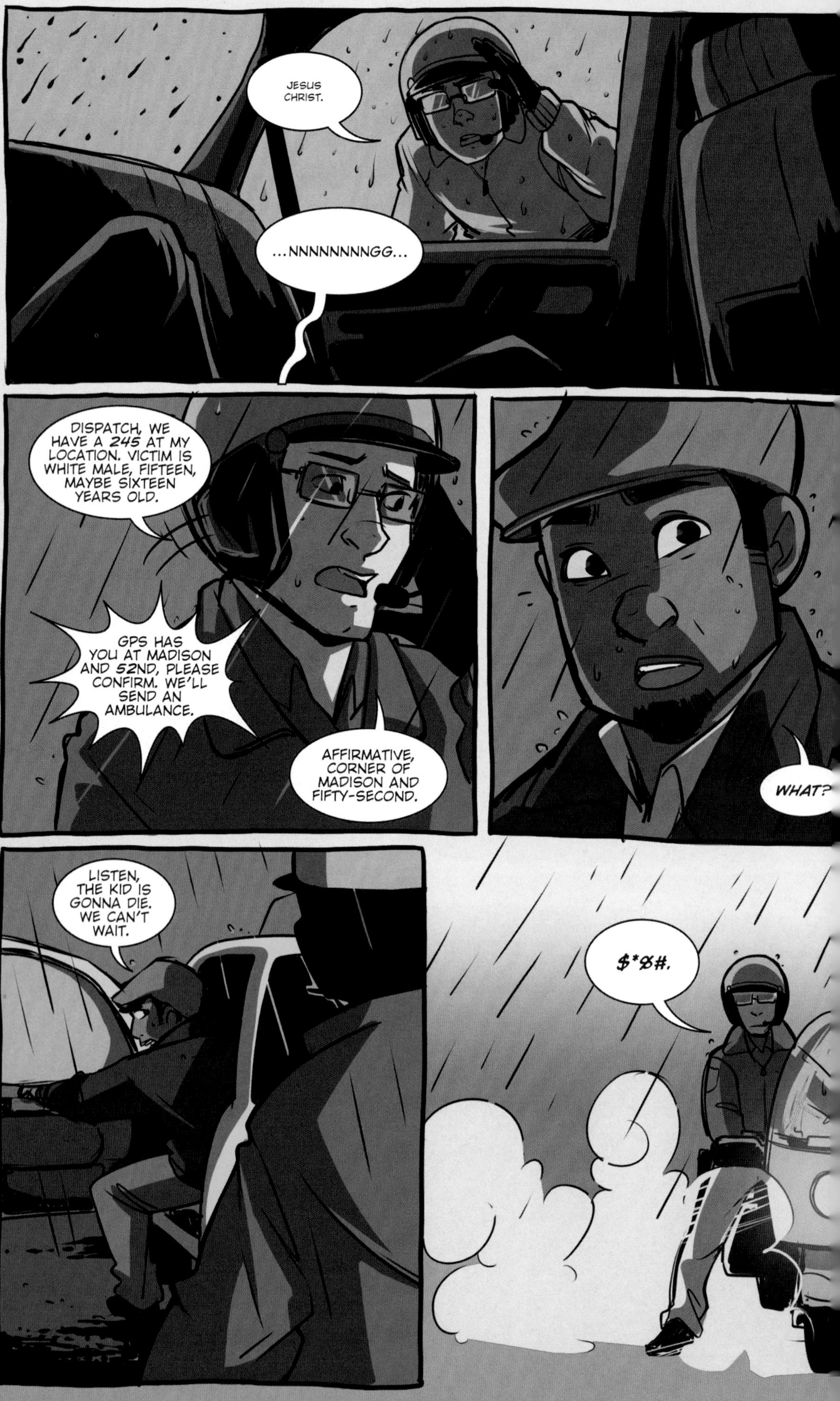
JESUS CHRIST.
...NNNNNNNNGG...
DISPATCH, WE HAVE A 245 AT MY LOCATION. VICTIM IS WHITE MALE, FIFTEEN, MAYBE SIXTEEN YEARS OLD.
GPS HAS YOU AT MADISON AND 52ND, PLEASE CONFIRM. WE'LL SEND AN AMBULANCE.
AFFIRMATIVE, CORNER OF MADISON AND FIFTY-SECOND.
WHAT?
LISTEN, THE KID IS GONNA DIE. WE CAN'T WAIT.
$*&#.

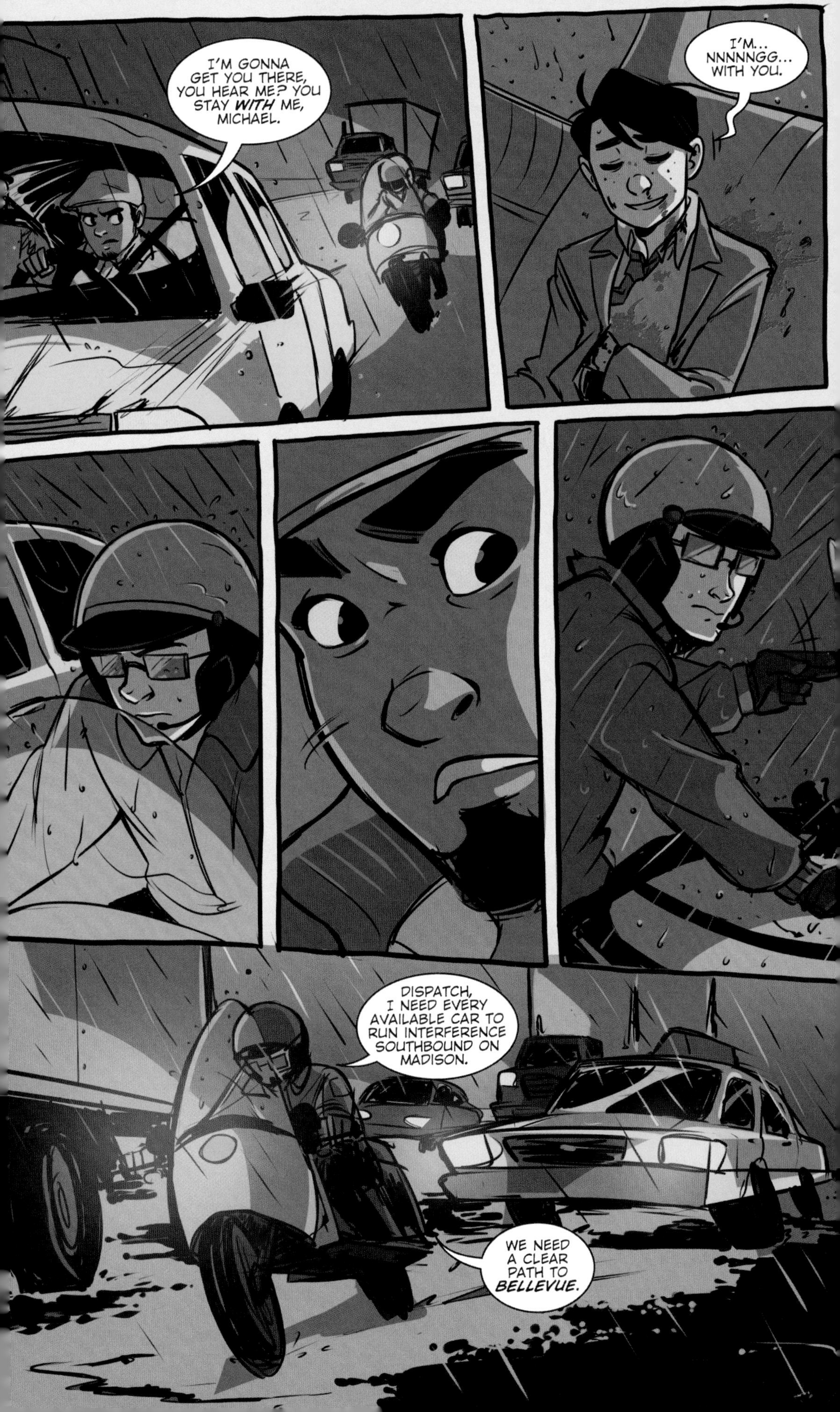
I'M GONNA GET YOU THERE, YOU HEAR ME? YOU STAY *WITH* ME, MICHAEL.
I'M... NNNNNGG... WITH YOU.
DISPATCH, I NEED EVERY AVAILABLE CAR TO RUN INTERFERENCE SOUTHBOUND ON MADISON.
WE NEED A CLEAR PATH TO *BELLEVUE*.

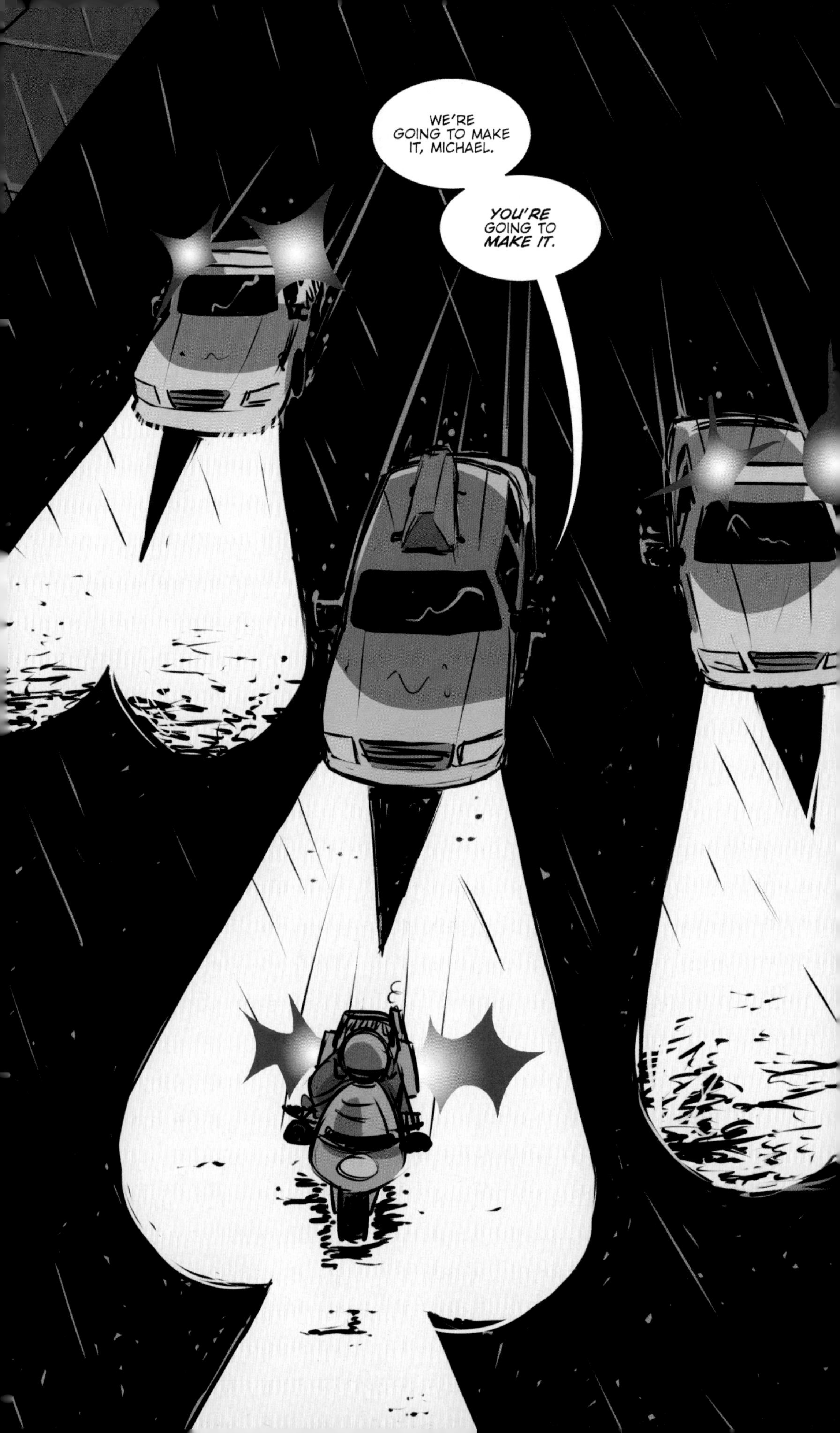
WE'RE GOING TO MAKE IT, MICHAEL.
YOU'RE GOING TO *MAKE IT.*

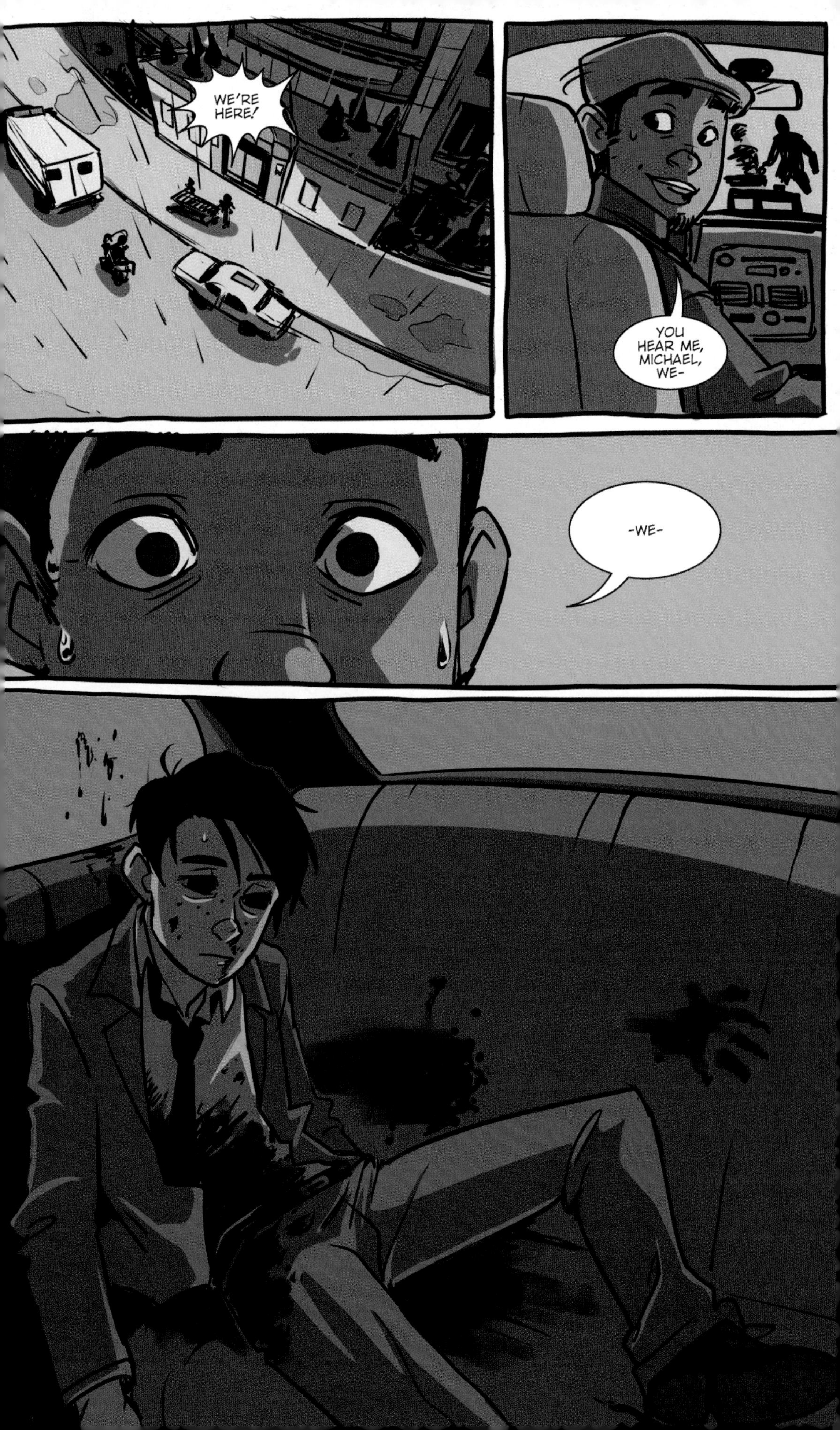
WE'RE HERE!
YOU HEAR ME, MICHAEL, WE-
-WE-

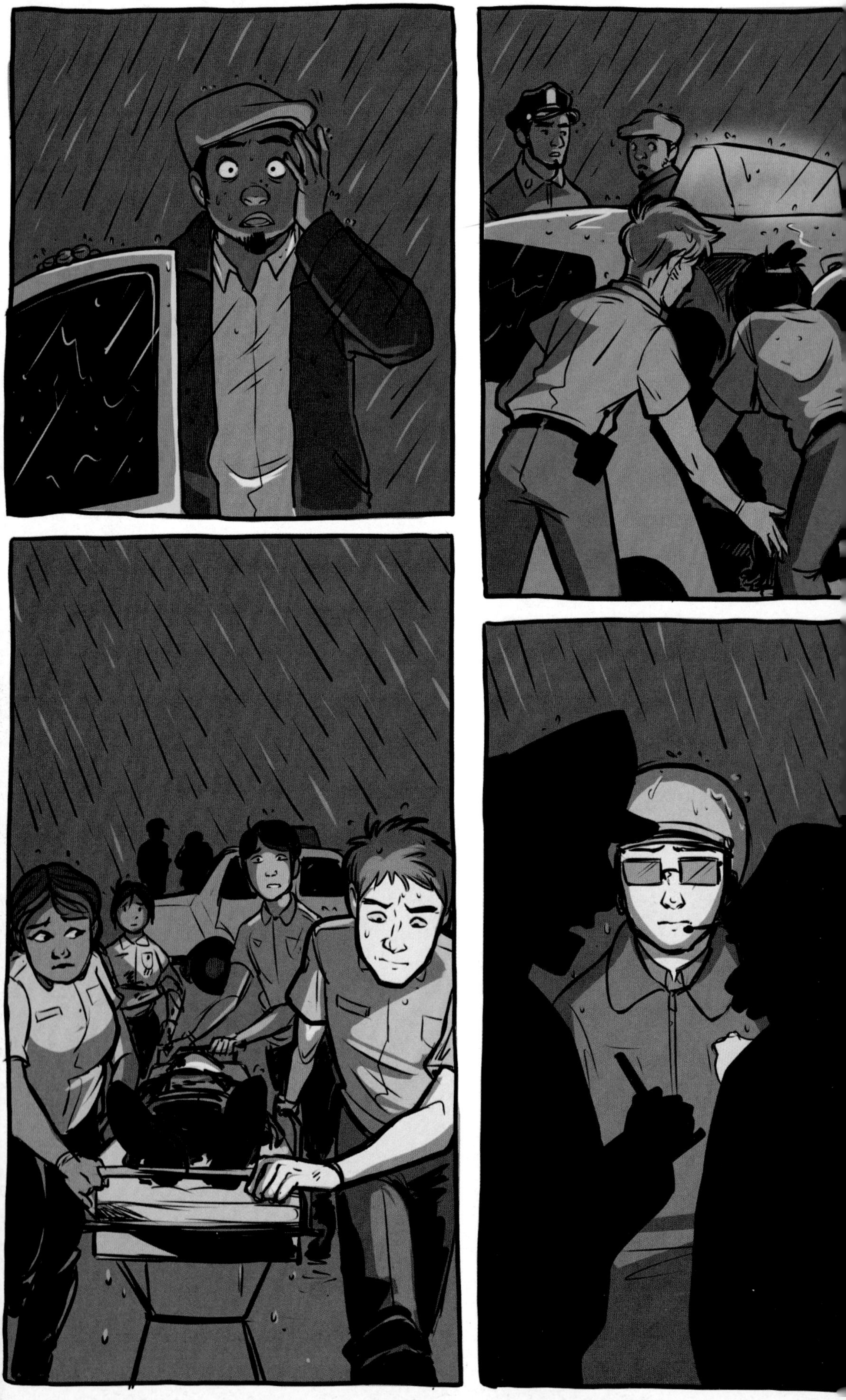

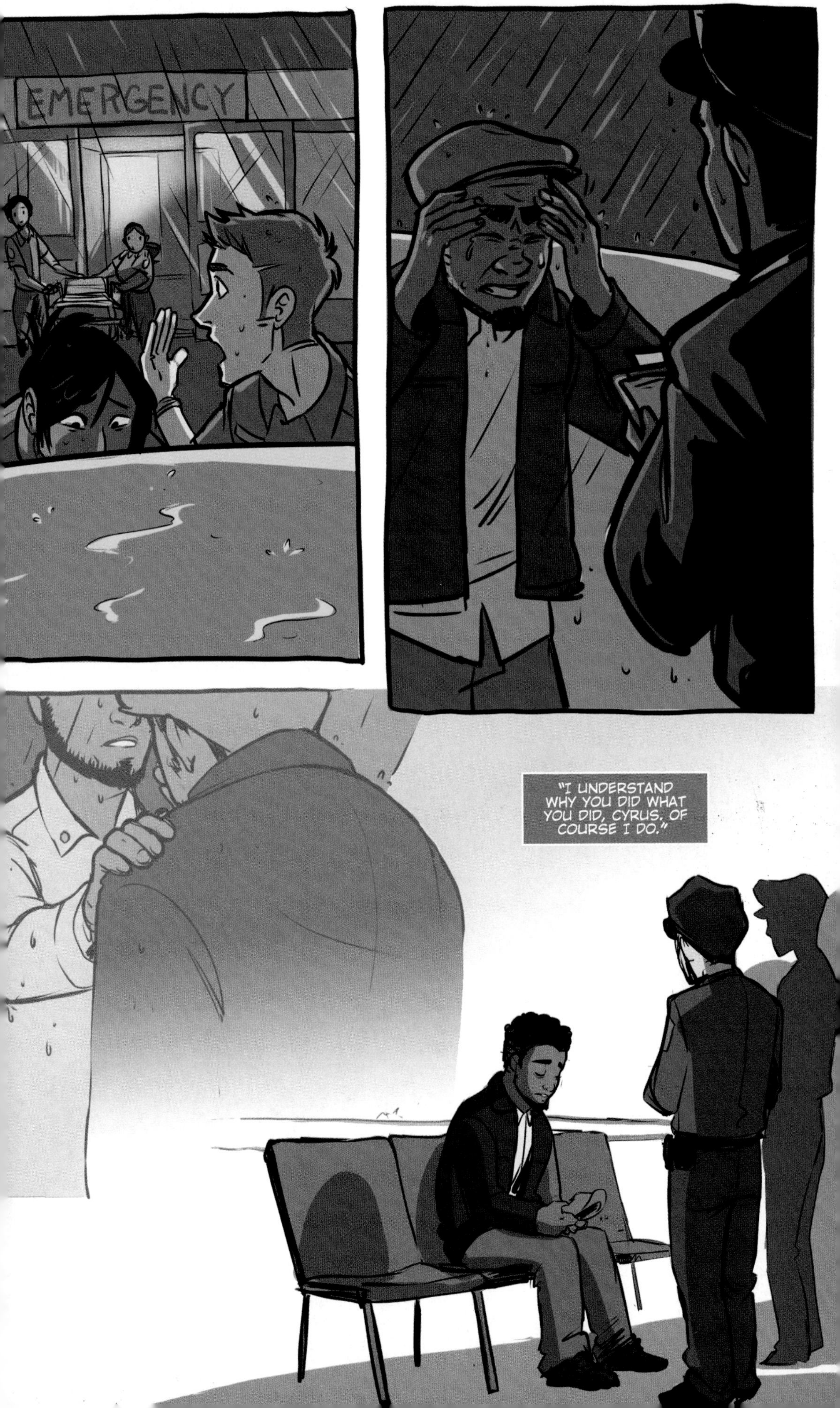
EMERGENCY
"I UNDERSTAND WHY YOU DID WHAT YOU DID, CYRUS. OF COURSE I DO."

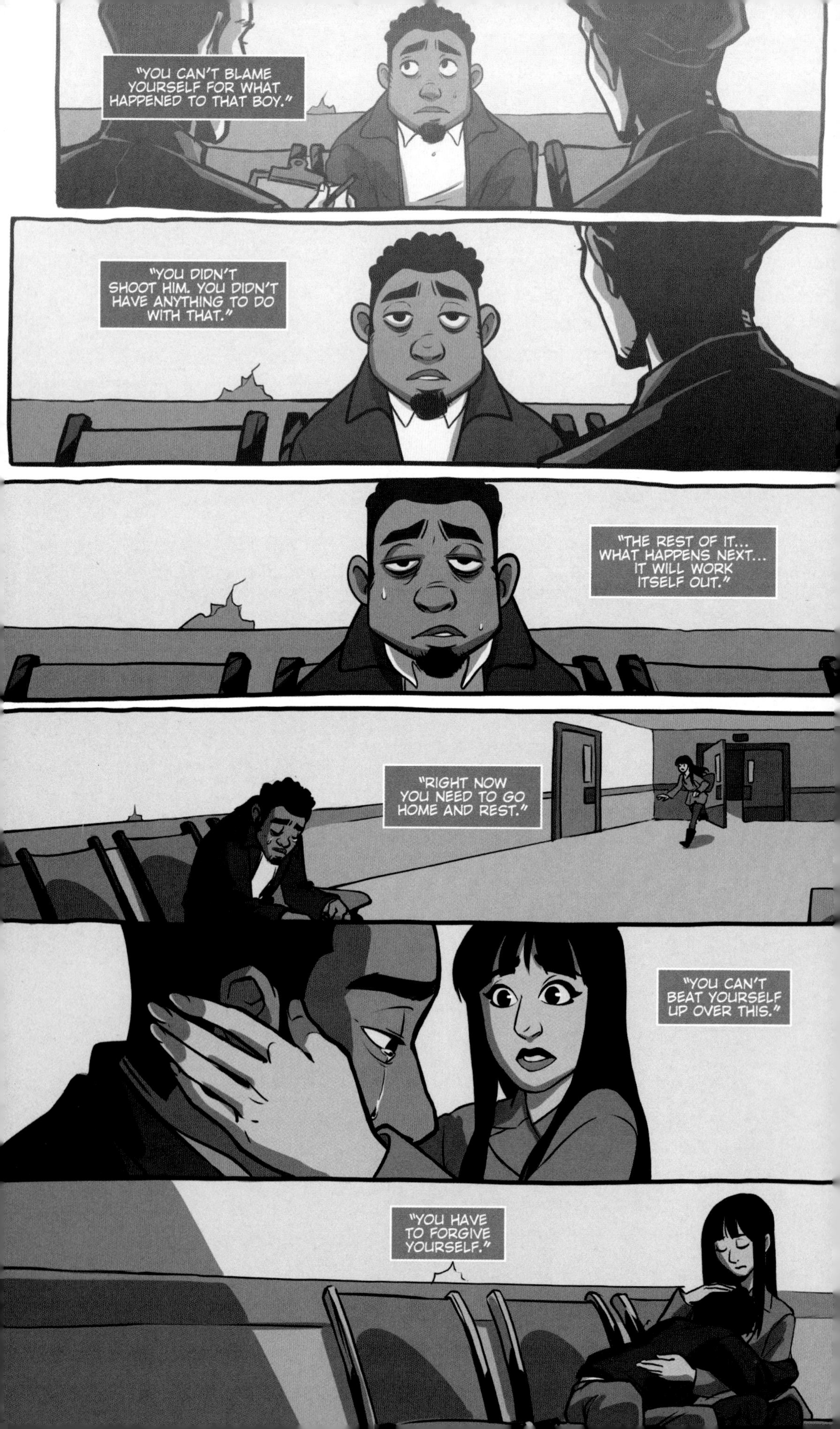
"YOU CAN'T BLAME YOURSELF FOR WHAT HAPPENED TO THAT BOY."
"YOU DIDN'T SHOOT HIM. YOU DIDN'T HAVE ANYTHING TO DO WITH THAT."
"THE REST OF IT... WHAT HAPPENS NEXT... IT WILL WORK ITSELF OUT."
"RIGHT NOW YOU NEED TO GO HOME AND REST."
"YOU CAN'T BEAT YOURSELF UP OVER THIS."
"YOU HAVE TO FORGIVE YOURSELF."

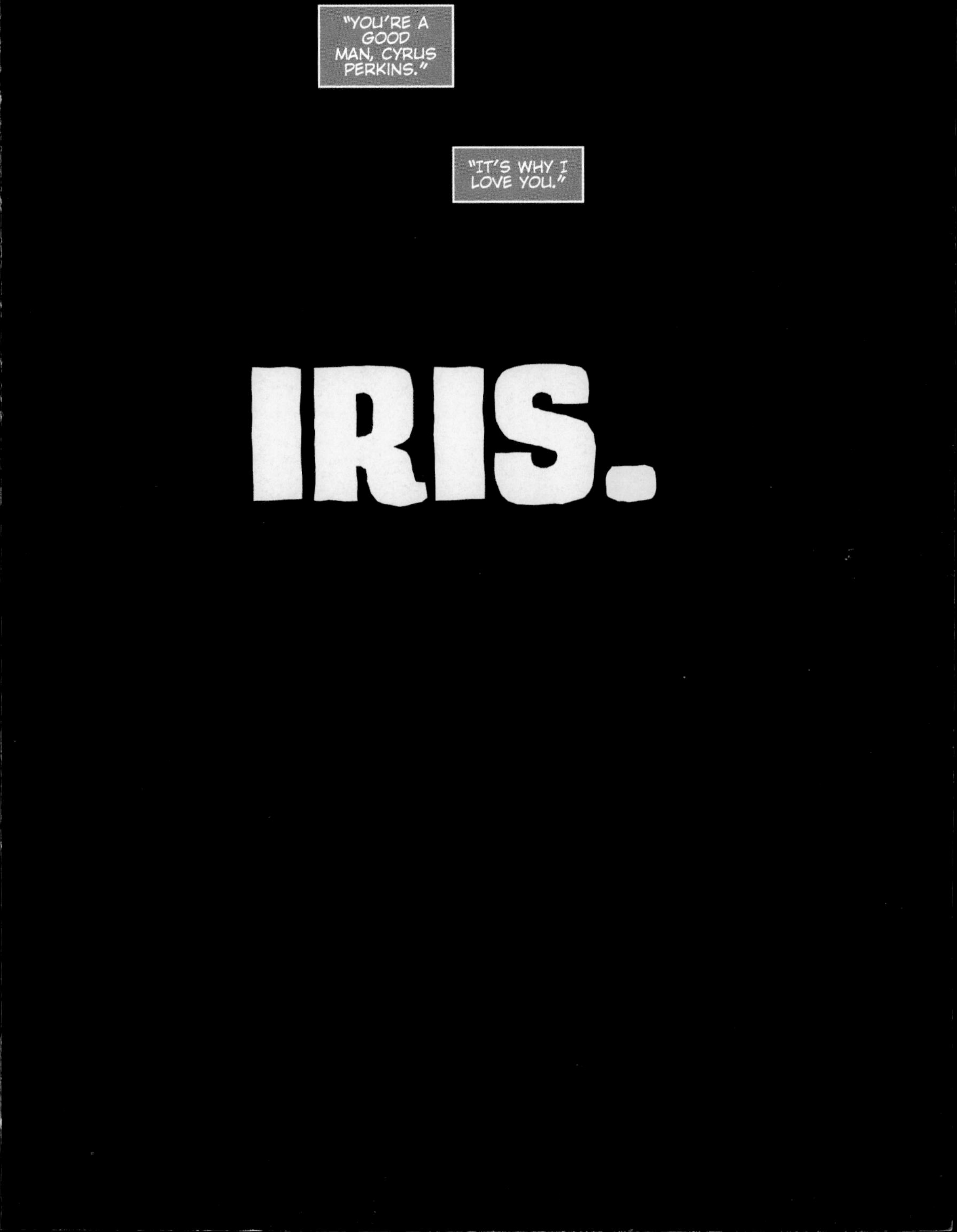
"YOU'RE A GOOD MAN, CYRUS PERKINS."
"IT'S WHY I LOVE YOU."
IRIS.

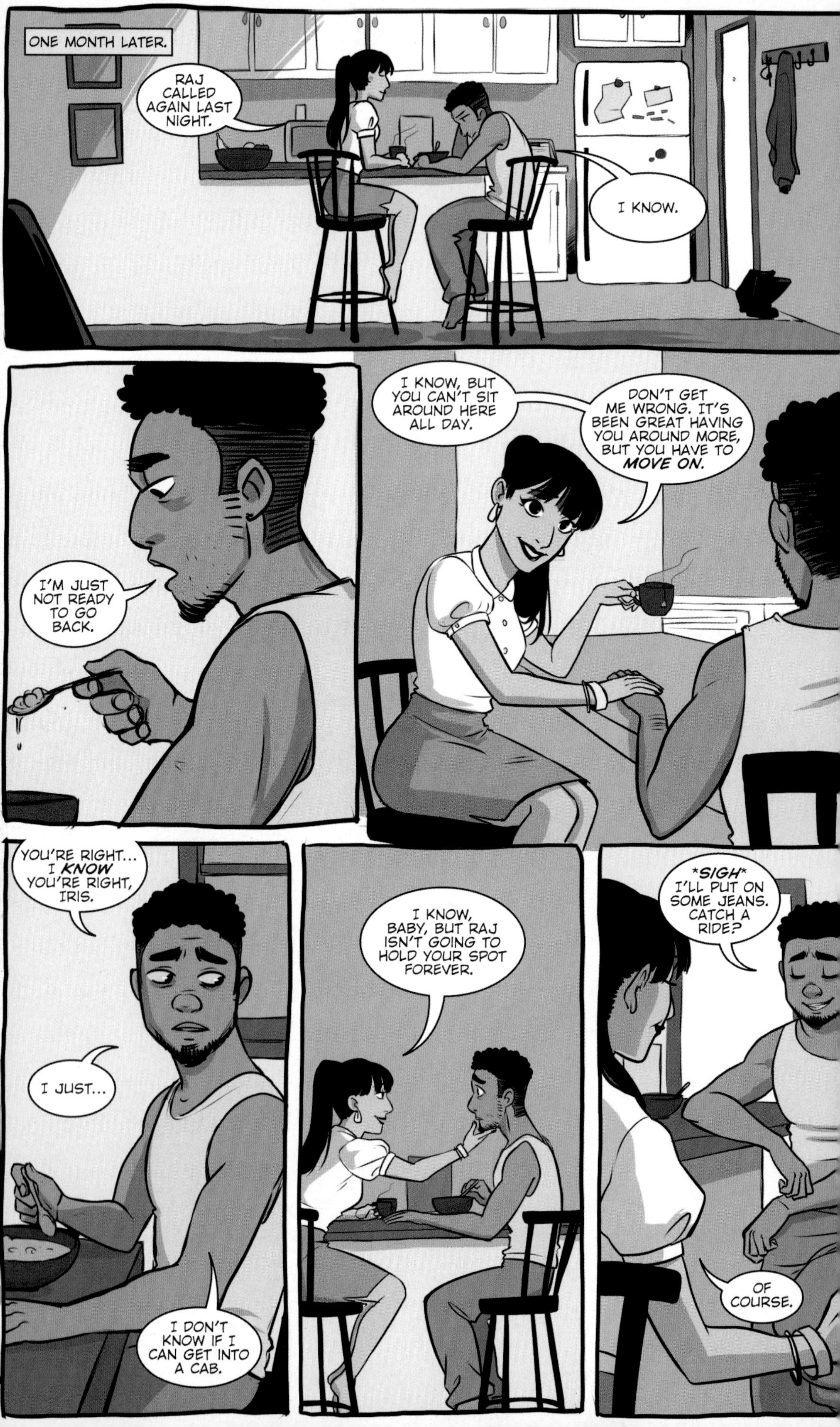
ONE MONTH LATER.
RAJ CALLED AGAIN LAST NIGHT.
I KNOW.
I'M JUST NOT READY TO GO BACK.
I KNOW, BUT YOU CAN'T SIT AROUND HERE ALL DAY.
DON'T GET ME WRONG. IT'S BEEN GREAT HAVING YOU AROUND MORE, BUT YOU HAVE TO MOVE ON.
YOU'RE RIGHT... I KNOW YOU'RE RIGHT, IRIS.
I JUST...
I DON'T KNOW IF I CAN GET INTO A CAB.
I KNOW, BABY, BUT RAJ ISN'T GOING TO HOLD YOUR SPOT FOREVER.
SIGH I'LL PUT ON SOME JEANS. CATCH A RIDE?
OF COURSE.

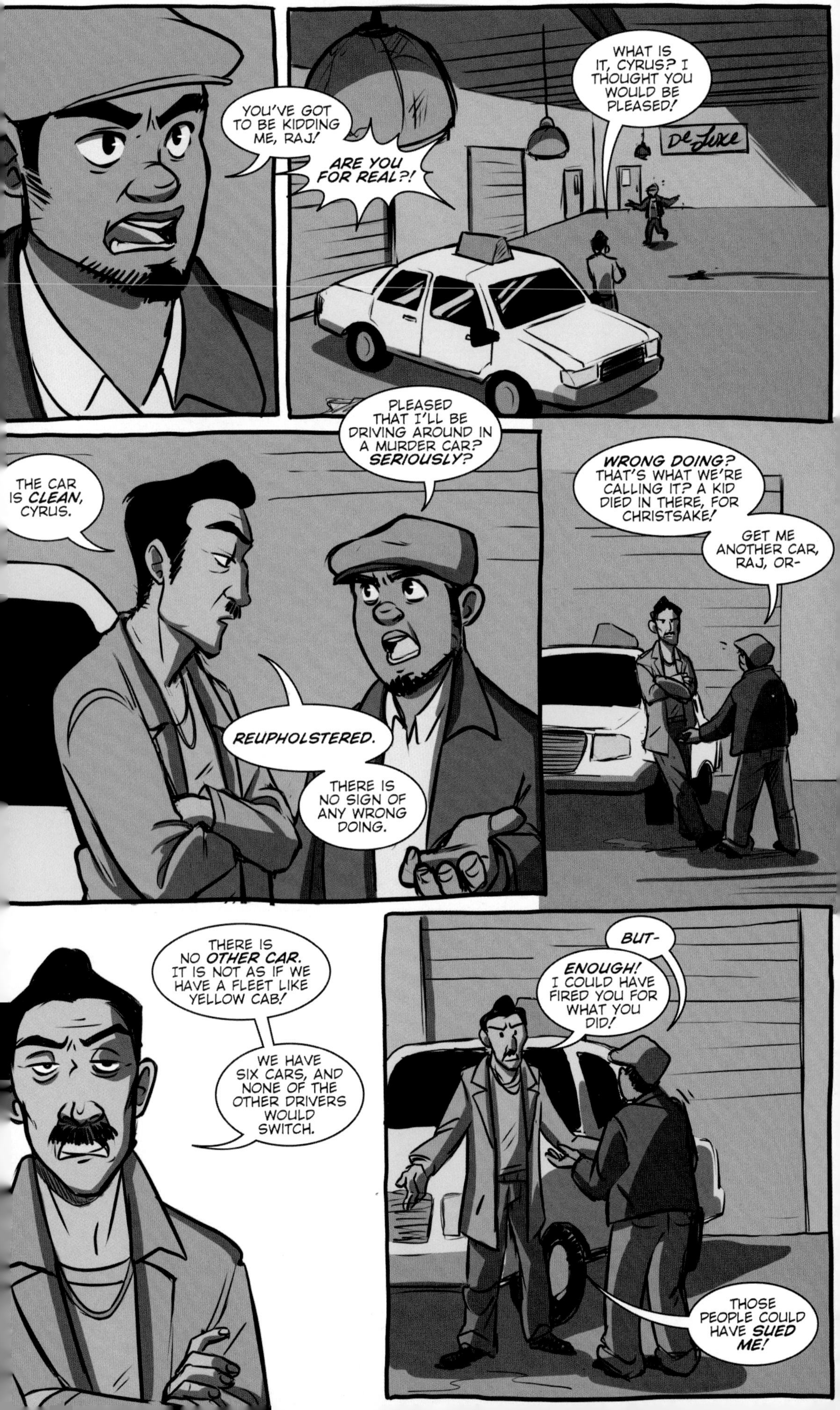

YOU'VE GOT TO BE KIDDING ME, RAJ!
ARE YOU FOR REAL?!
WHAT IS IT, CYRUS? I THOUGHT YOU WOULD BE PLEASED!
De Luxe
PLEASED THAT I'LL BE DRIVING AROUND IN A MURDER CAR? SERIOUSLY?
THE CAR IS CLEAN, CYRUS.
REUPHOLSTERED.
THERE IS NO SIGN OF ANY WRONG DOING.
WRONG DOING? THAT'S WHAT WE'RE CALLING IT? A KID DIED IN THERE, FOR CHRISTSAKE!
GET ME ANOTHER CAR, RAJ, OR-
THERE IS NO OTHER CAR. IT IS NOT AS IF WE HAVE A FLEET LIKE YELLOW CAB!
WE HAVE SIX CARS, AND NONE OF THE OTHER DRIVERS WOULD SWITCH.
BUT-
ENOUGH! I COULD HAVE FIRED YOU FOR WHAT YOU DID!
THOSE PEOPLE COULD HAVE SUED ME!

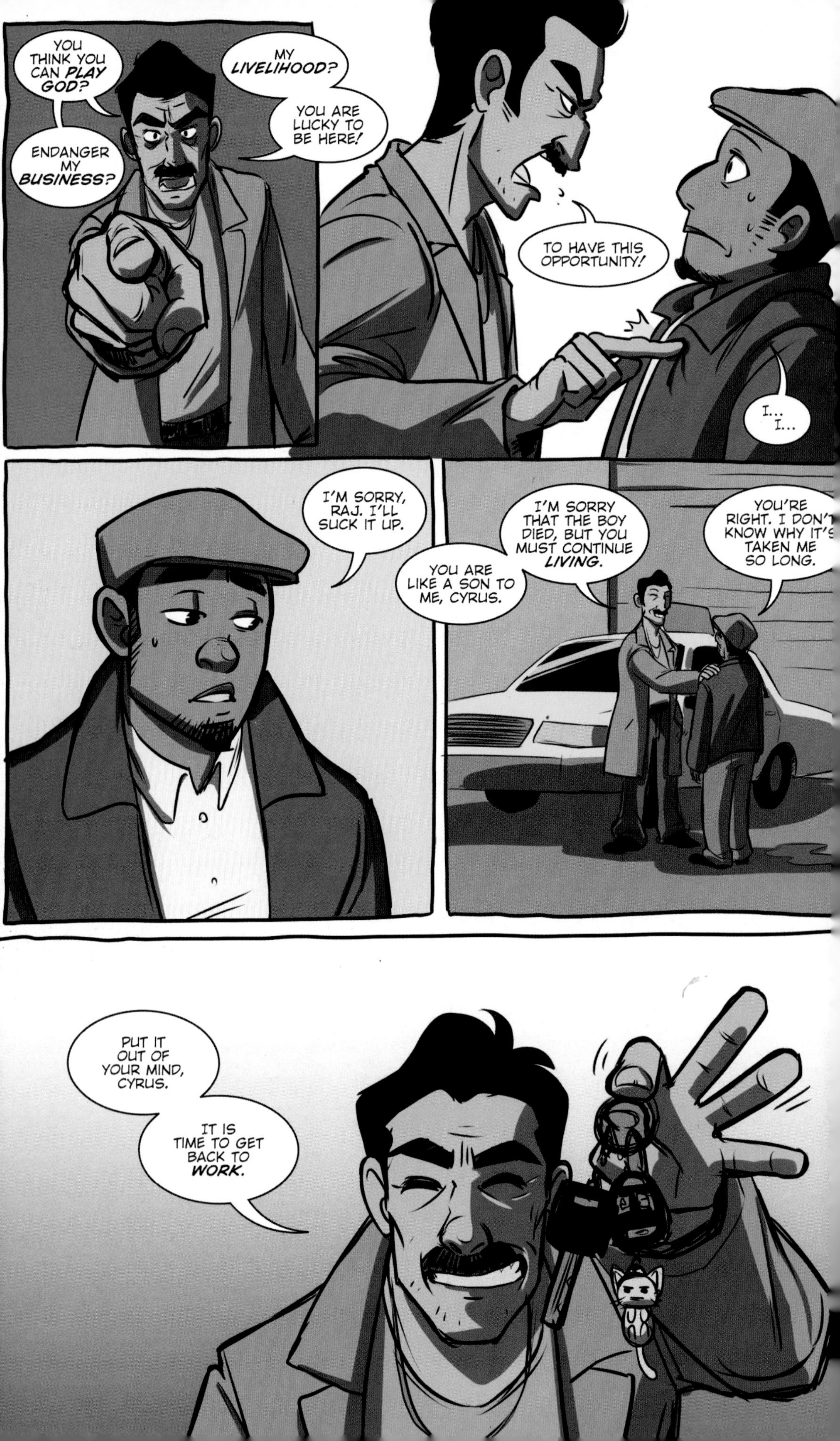
YOU THINK YOU CAN PLAY GOD?
ENDANGER MY BUSINESS?
MY LIVELIHOOD?
YOU ARE LUCKY TO BE HERE!
TO HAVE THIS OPPORTUNITY!
I... I...
I'M SORRY, RAJ. I'LL SUCK IT UP.
YOU ARE LIKE A SON TO ME, CYRUS.
I'M SORRY THAT THE BOY DIED, BUT YOU MUST CONTINUE LIVING.
YOU'RE RIGHT. I DON'T KNOW WHY IT'S TAKEN ME SO LONG.
PUT IT OUT OF YOUR MIND, CYRUS.
IT IS TIME TO GET BACK TO WORK.

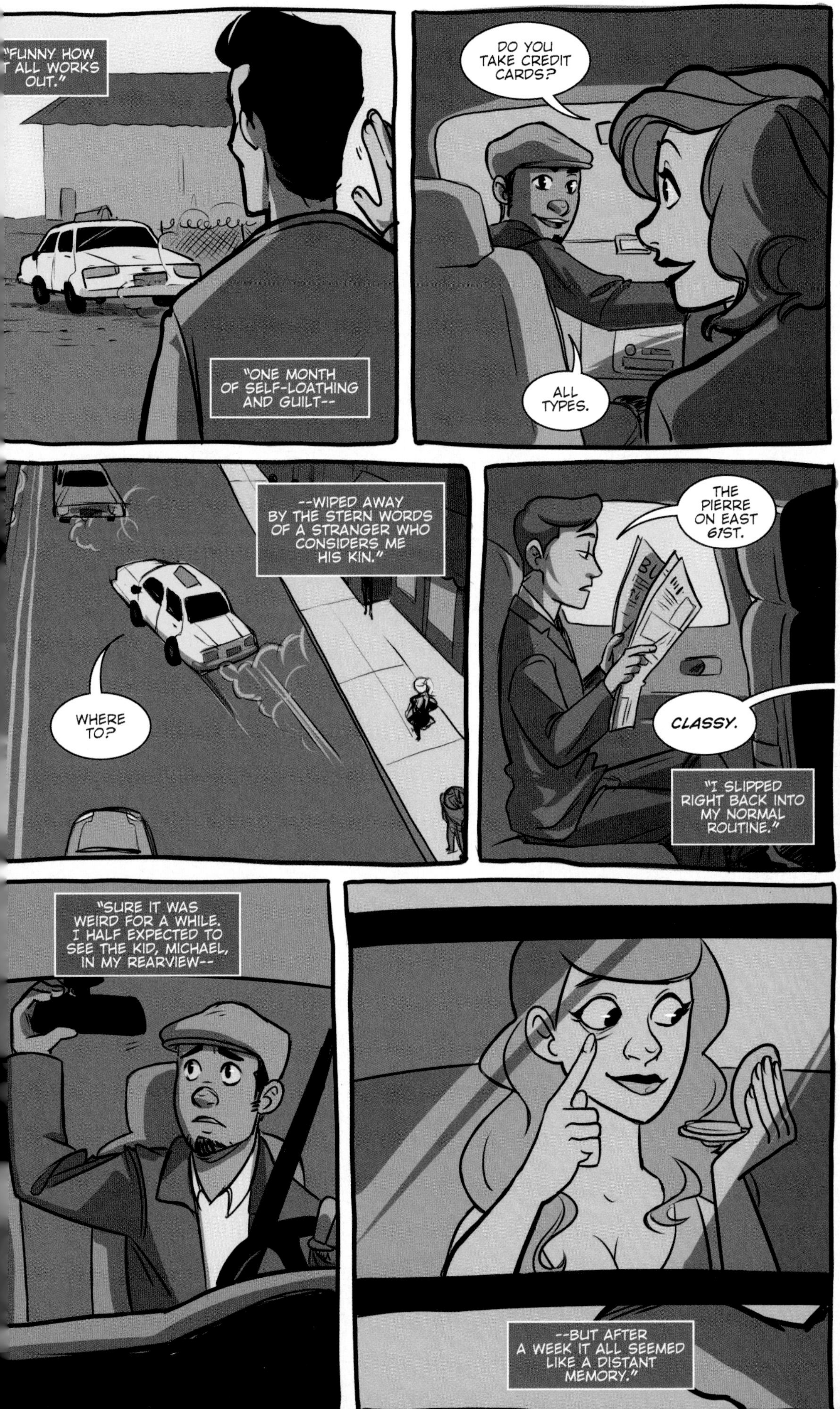
"FUNNY HOW IT ALL WORKS OUT."
"ONE MONTH OF SELF-LOATHING AND GUILT--
DO YOU TAKE CREDIT CARDS?
ALL TYPES.
--WIPED AWAY BY THE STERN WORDS OF A STRANGER WHO CONSIDERS ME HIS KIN."
WHERE TO?
THE PIERRE ON EAST 61ST.
CLASSY.
"I SLIPPED RIGHT BACK INTO MY NORMAL ROUTINE."
"SURE IT WAS WEIRD FOR A WHILE. I HALF EXPECTED TO SEE THE KID, MICHAEL, IN MY REARVIEW--
--BUT AFTER A WEEK IT ALL SEEMED LIKE A DISTANT MEMORY."

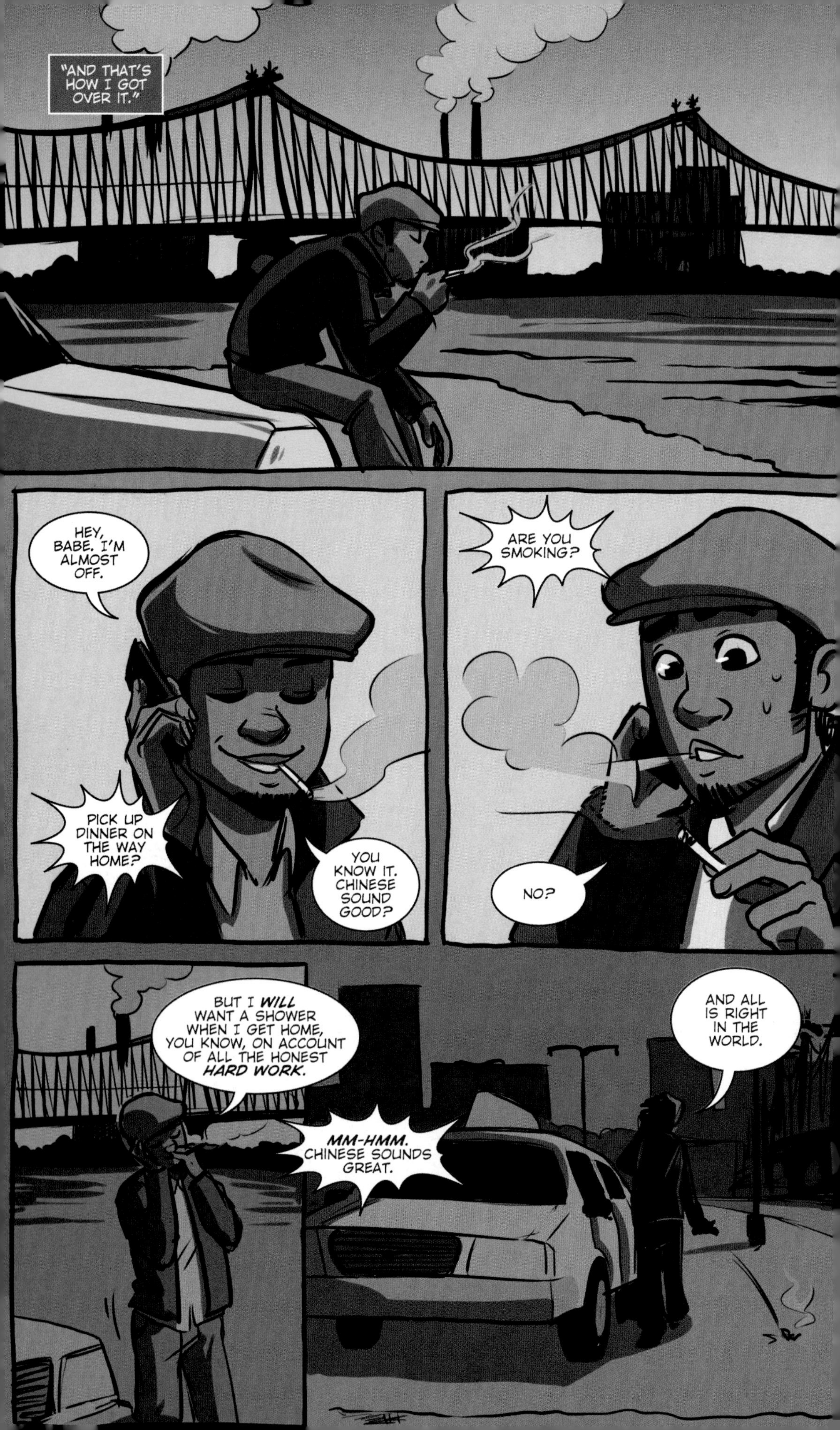
"AND THAT'S HOW I GOT OVER IT."
HEY, BABE. I'M ALMOST OFF.
PICK UP DINNER ON THE WAY HOME?
YOU KNOW IT. CHINESE SOUND GOOD?
ARE YOU SMOKING?
NO?
BUT I *WILL* WANT A SHOWER WHEN I GET HOME, YOU KNOW, ON ACCOUNT OF ALL THE HONEST *HARD WORK.*
MM-HMM. CHINESE SOUNDS GREAT.
AND ALL IS RIGHT IN THE WORLD.

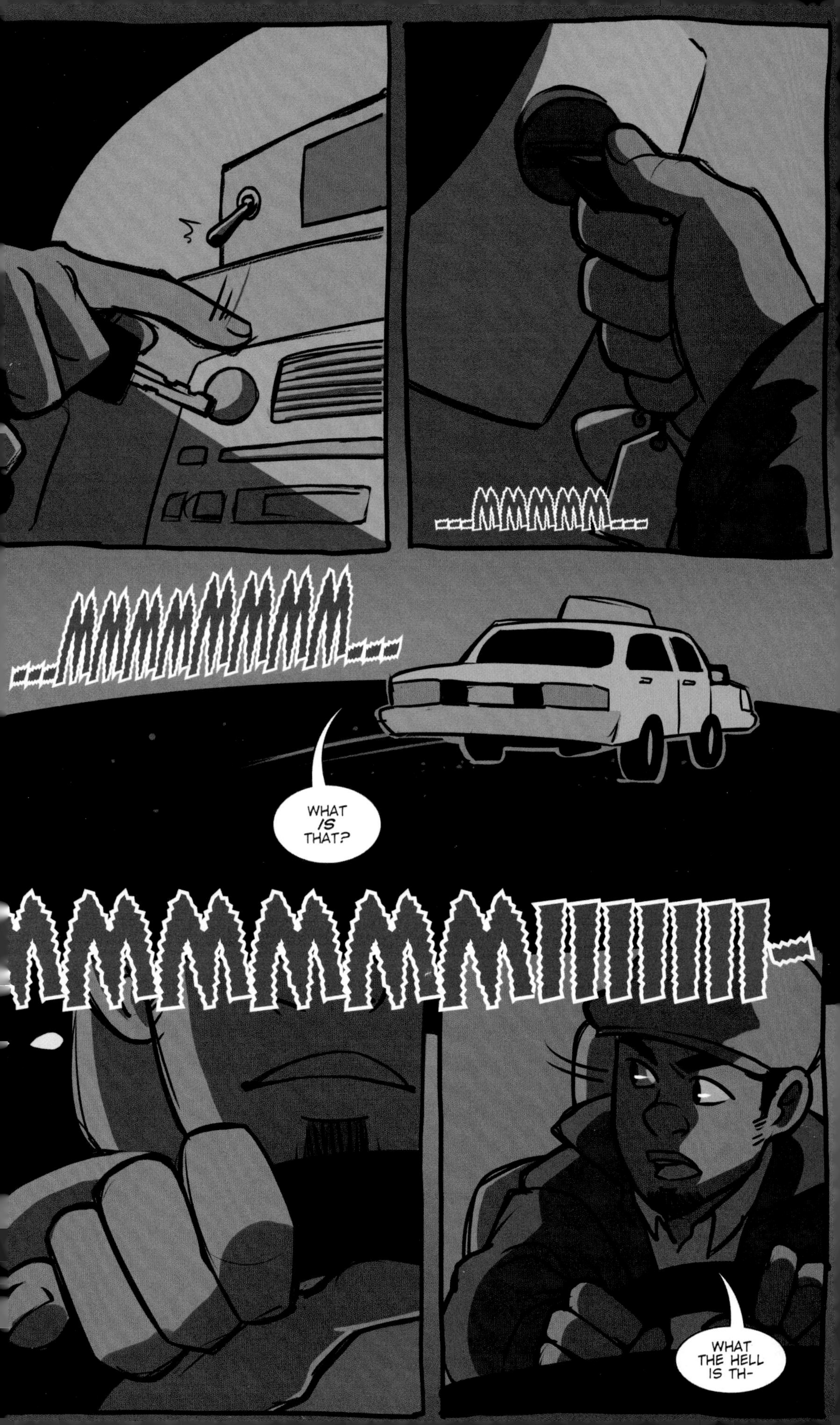

...MMMMM...
...MMMMMMMMM...
WHAT IS THAT?
MMMMMMMMMIIIIIII-
WHAT THE HELL IS TH-

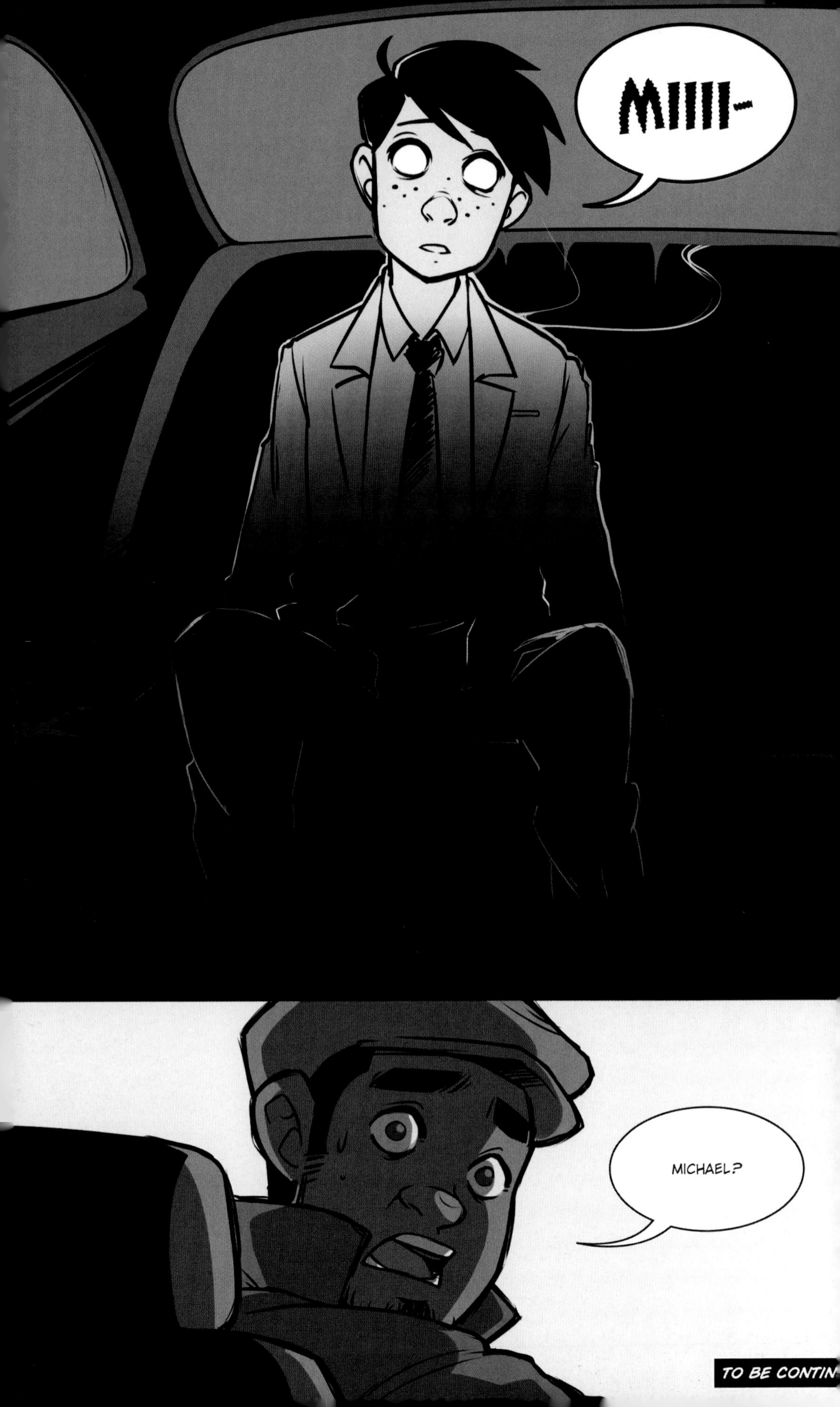
MIIII-
MICHAEL?
TO BE CONTIN

Fall, Part 5: "Pantry Raids" Poppy and Cassia, the teen masterminds behind the addictive Patty Cake brownies, hoping to better understand their product, violate one of the 10 Crime Commandments: they try their own supply.

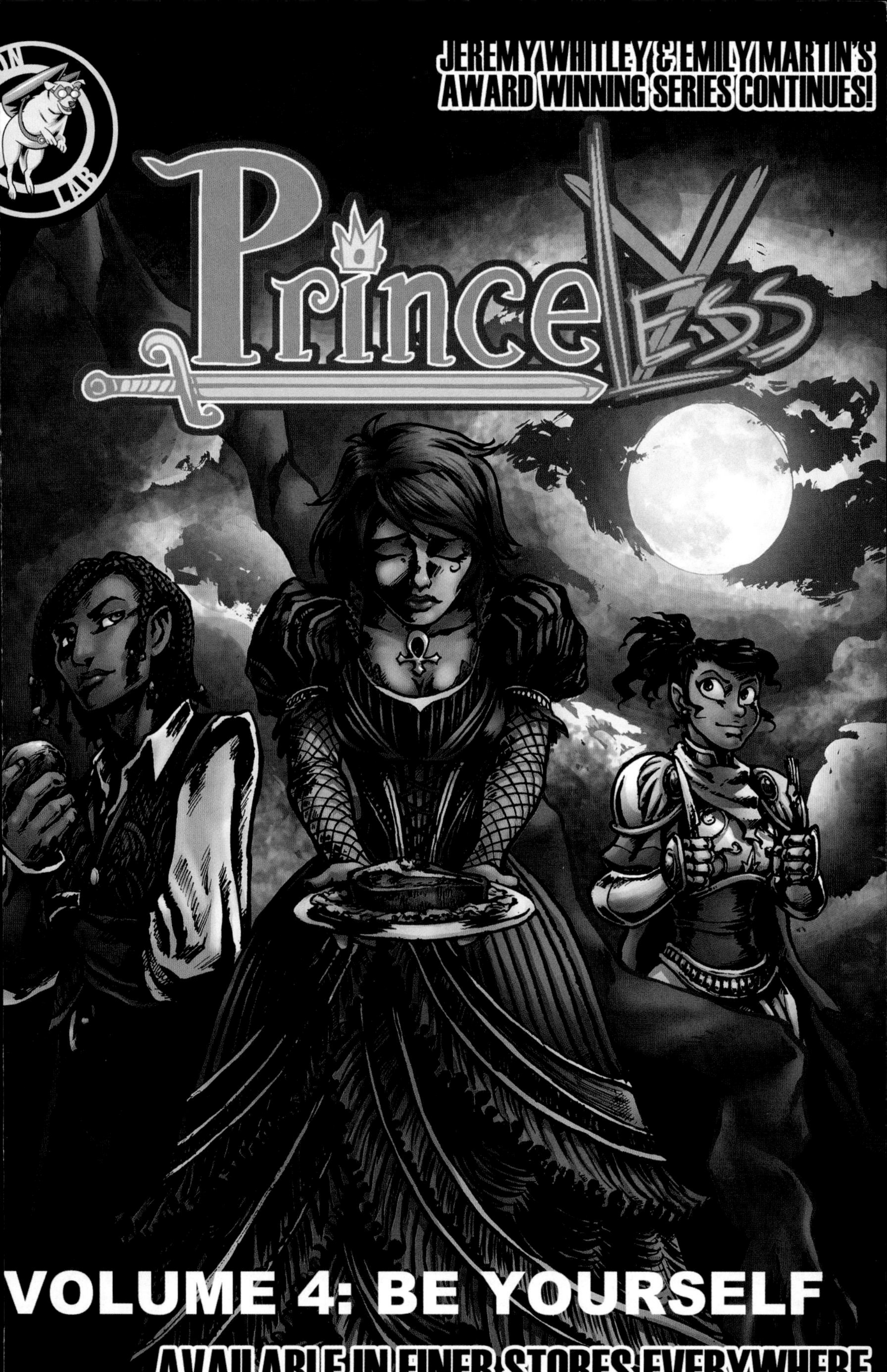
JEREMY WHITLEY & EMILY MARTIN'S
AWARD WINNING SERIES CONTINUES!
LAB
Princeless
VOLUME 4: BE YOURSELF
AVAILABLE IN FINER STORES EVERYWHERE

joisse Ashe, the oft-forgotten middle sister of the Ashe royal family, is locked in a castle eep in the swamp. Not only is her castle guarded by zombies, but the swamp is full of dangerous hazards. Everything from quicksand to goblins to swamp monsters to... AMPIRES! But does that give Adrienne pause? Unfortunately not, as she and Bedelia dive head-first into their most dangerous adventure yet!

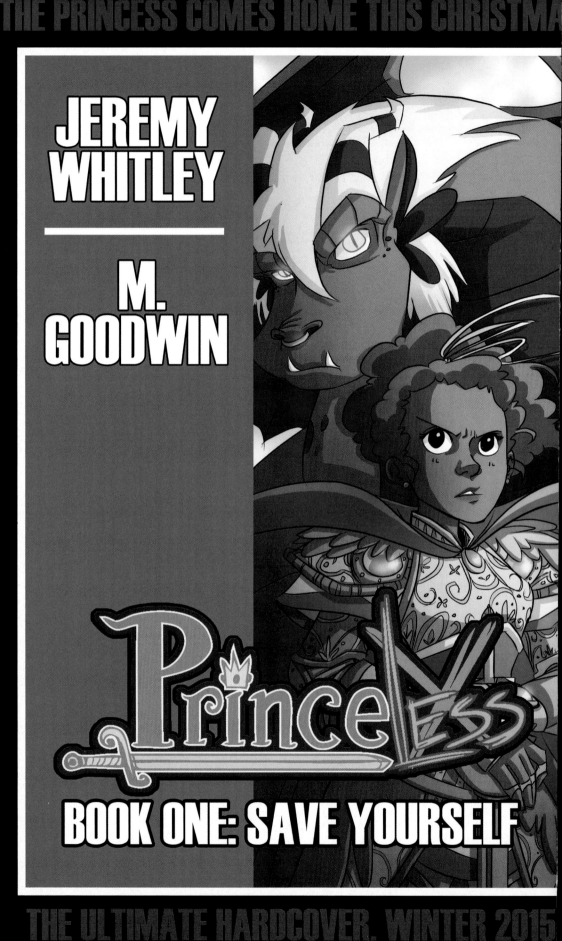

FROM ALL-AGES TO MATURE READERS
ACTION LAB HAS YOU COVERED.

 Appropriate
for everyone.

 Appropriate for age 9 and up.
Absent of profanity or adult content.

 Suggested for 12 and Up. Comics
with this rating are comparable to a
PG-13 movie rating. Recommended
for our teen and young adult readers.

 Appropriate for older teens. Similar
to Teen, but featuring more mature
themes and/or more graphic imagery.

 Contains extreme viloence and some
nudity. Basically the Rated-R of
comics.

ACTION LAB

READ MORE NOW

Cyrus Perkins - Action Lab
www.actionlabcomics.com
00111
7 02382 69111 0

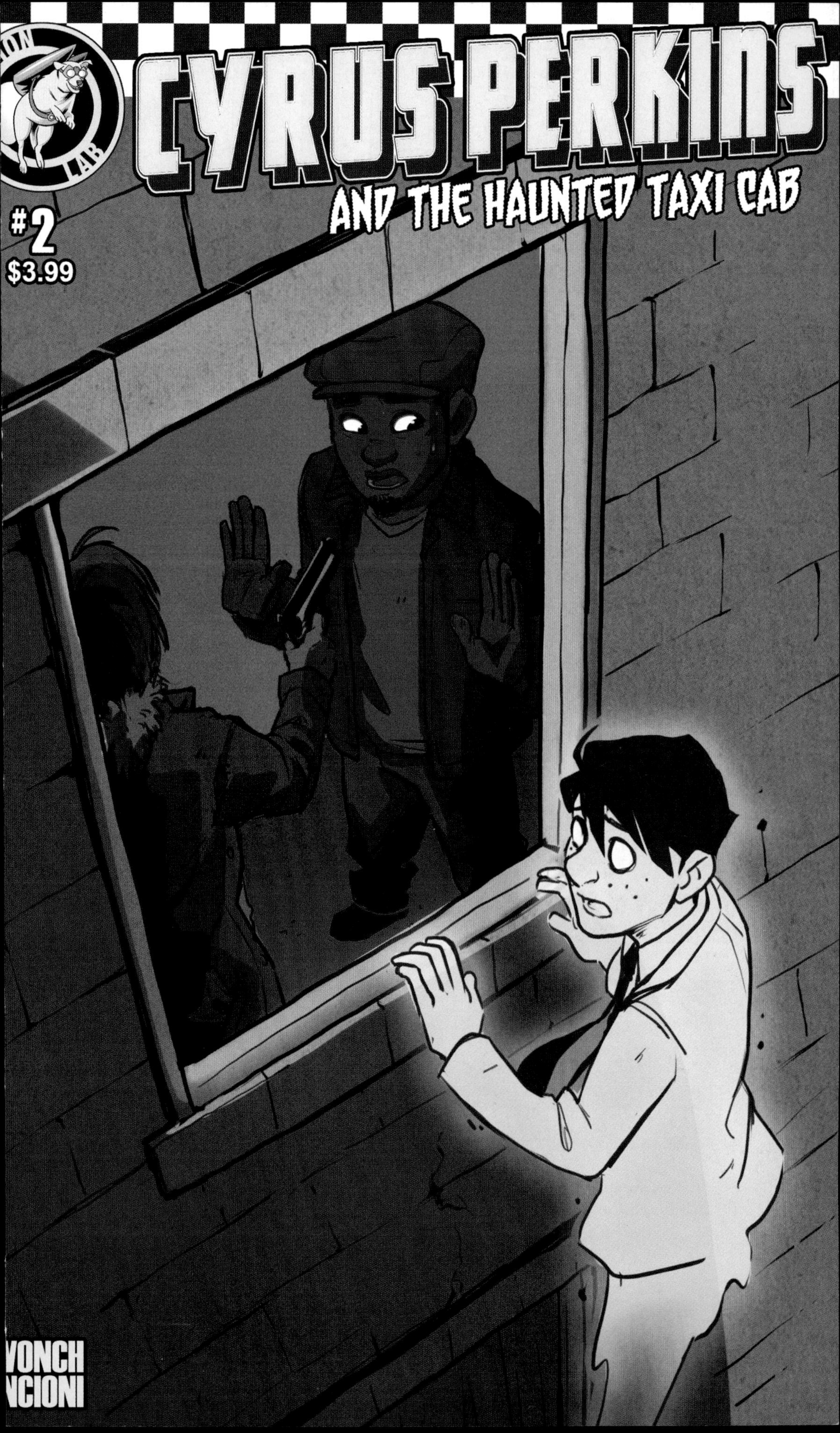
CYRUS PERKINS
AND THE HAUNTED TAXI CAB
#2
$3.99

CYRUS PERKINS
AND THE HAUNTED TAXI CAB!

DAVE DWONCH
STORY/LETTERS/COLORS

ANNA LENCIONI
ART/TONES

BRYAN SEATON= PUBLISHER   KEVIN FREEMAN= PRESIDENT
DAVE DWONCH= CREATIVE DIRECTOR   SHAWN GABBORIN= EDITOR IN CHIEF
JAMAL IGLE= VICE-PRESIDENT OF MARKETING
VITO DELSANTE= DIRECTOR OF MARKETING
JIM DIETZ= SOCIAL MEDIA DIRECTOR
CHAD CICCONI= HAUNTS THE OFFICES

"A BLANK
SLATE."

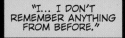
"I... I DON'T
REMEMBER ANYTHING
FROM BEFORE."

"LIVING, I MEAN."

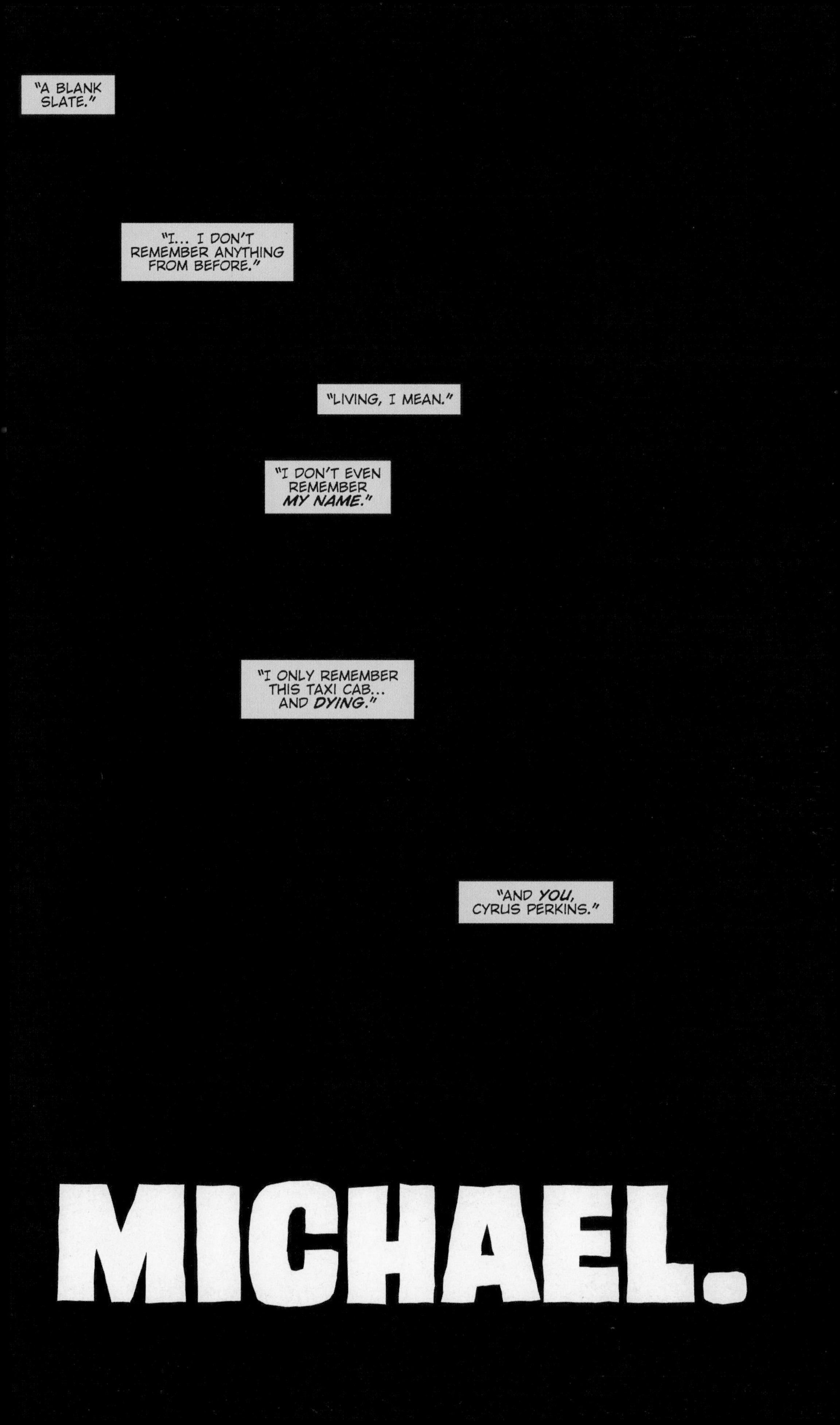

"I DON'T EVEN
REMEMBER
MY NAME."

"I ONLY REMEMBER
THIS TAXI CAB...
AND *DYING.*"

"AND *YOU,*
CYRUS PERKINS."

MICHAEL.

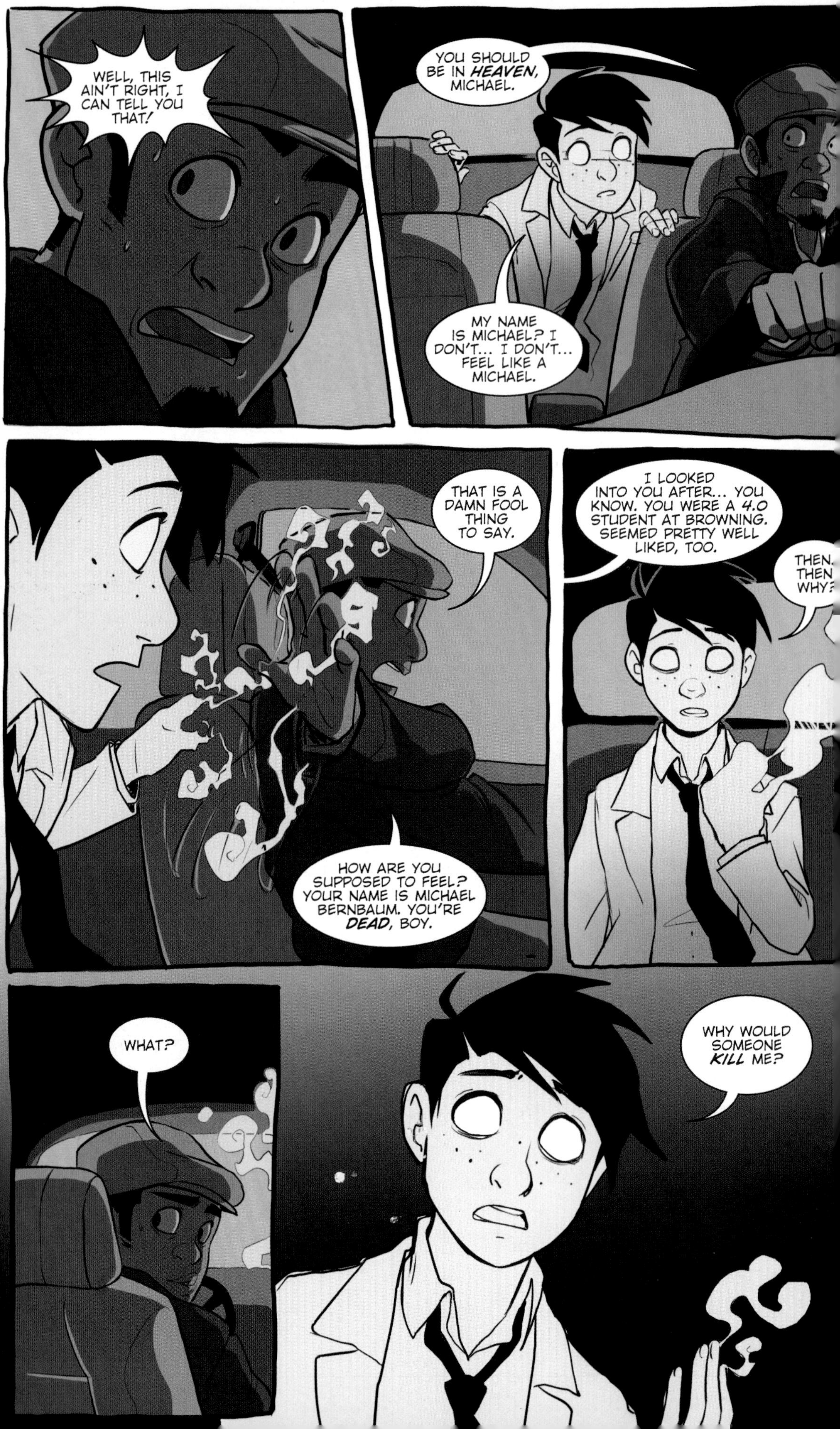
WELL, THIS AIN'T RIGHT, I CAN TELL YOU THAT!
YOU SHOULD BE IN *HEAVEN*, MICHAEL.
MY NAME IS MICHAEL? I DON'T... I DON'T... FEEL LIKE A MICHAEL.
THAT IS A DAMN FOOL THING TO SAY.
HOW ARE YOU SUPPOSED TO FEEL? YOUR NAME IS MICHAEL BERNBAUM. YOU'RE *DEAD*, BOY.
I LOOKED INTO YOU AFTER... YOU KNOW. YOU WERE A 4.0 STUDENT AT BROWNING. SEEMED PRETTY WELL LIKED, TOO.
THEN. THEN WHY?
WHAT?
WHY WOULD SOMEONE *KILL* ME?

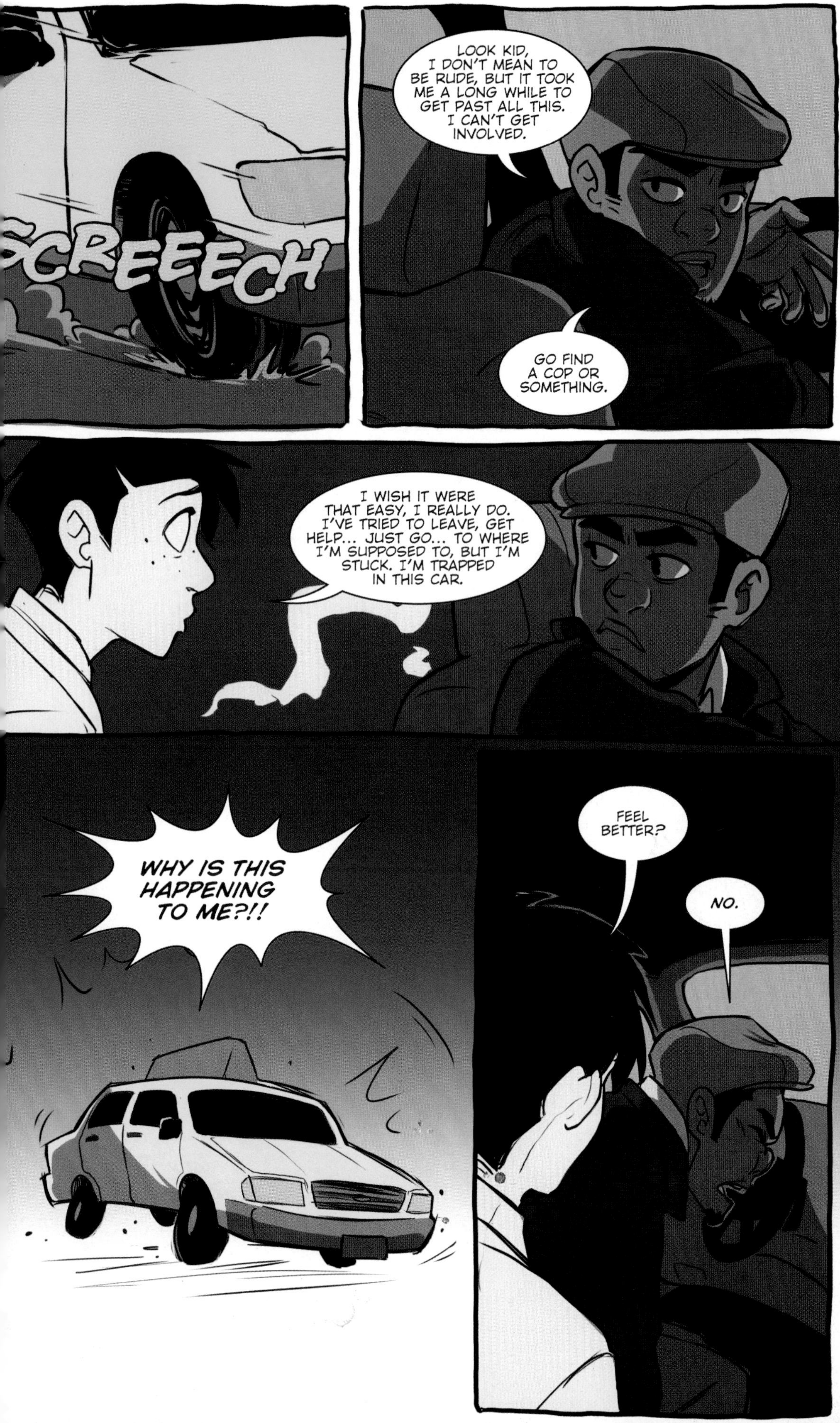
SCREEECH
LOOK KID, I DON'T MEAN TO BE RUDE, BUT IT TOOK ME A LONG WHILE TO GET PAST ALL THIS. I CAN'T GET INVOLVED.
GO FIND A COP OR SOMETHING.
I WISH IT WERE THAT EASY, I REALLY DO. I'VE TRIED TO LEAVE, GET HELP... JUST GO... TO WHERE I'M SUPPOSED TO, BUT I'M STUCK. I'M TRAPPED IN THIS CAR.
WHY IS THIS HAPPENING TO ME?!!
FEEL BETTER?
NO.

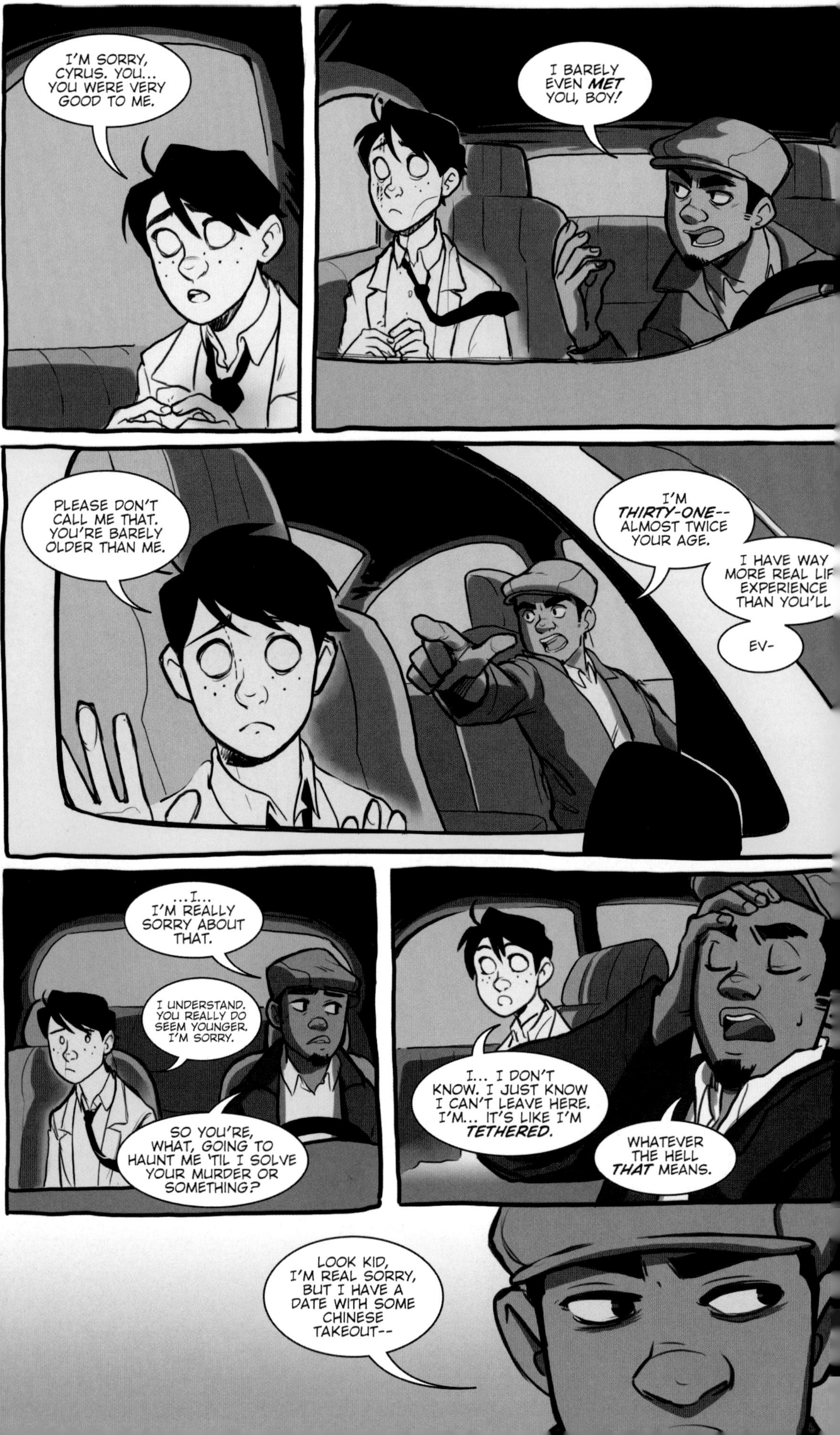
I'M SORRY, CYRUS. YOU... YOU WERE VERY GOOD TO ME.
I BARELY EVEN MET YOU, BOY!
PLEASE DON'T CALL ME THAT. YOU'RE BARELY OLDER THAN ME.
I'M THIRTY-ONE-- ALMOST TWICE YOUR AGE.
I HAVE WAY MORE REAL LIF EXPERIENCE THAN YOU'LL
EV-
...I... I'M REALLY SORRY ABOUT THAT.
I UNDERSTAND. YOU REALLY DO SEEM YOUNGER. I'M SORRY.
SO YOU'RE, WHAT, GOING TO HAUNT ME 'TIL I SOLVE YOUR MURDER OR SOMETHING?
I... I DON'T KNOW. I JUST KNOW I CAN'T LEAVE HERE. I'M... IT'S LIKE I'M TETHERED.
WHATEVER THE HELL THAT MEANS.
LOOK KID, I'M REAL SORRY, BUT I HAVE A DATE WITH SOME CHINESE TAKEOUT--

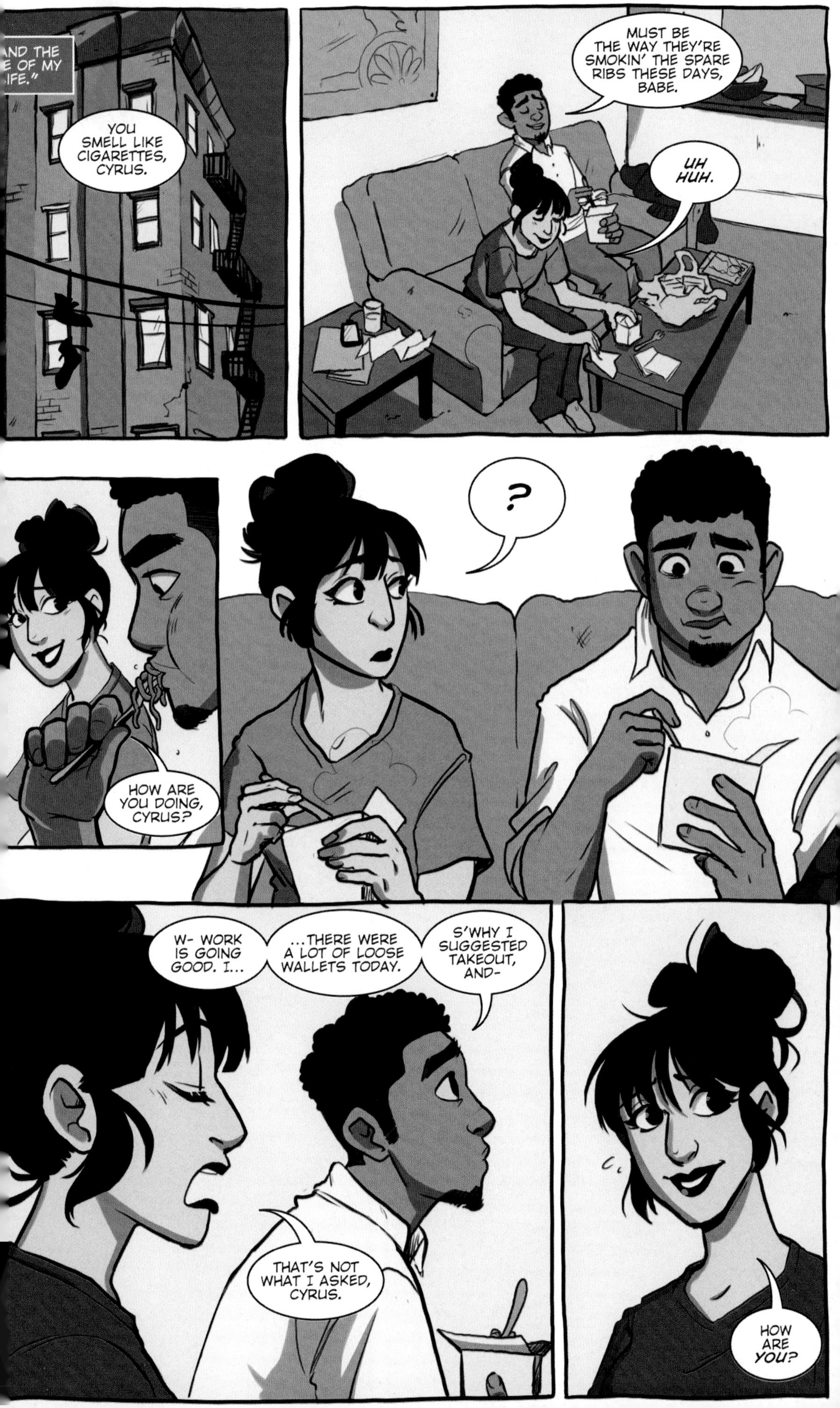
AND THE
E OF MY
IFE."
YOU SMELL LIKE CIGARETTES, CYRUS.
MUST BE THE WAY THEY'RE SMOKIN' THE SPARE RIBS THESE DAYS, BABE.
UH HUH.
HOW ARE YOU DOING, CYRUS?
?
W- WORK IS GOING GOOD. I...
...THERE WERE A LOT OF LOOSE WALLETS TODAY.
S'WHY I SUGGESTED TAKEOUT, AND-
THAT'S NOT WHAT I ASKED, CYRUS.
HOW ARE YOU?

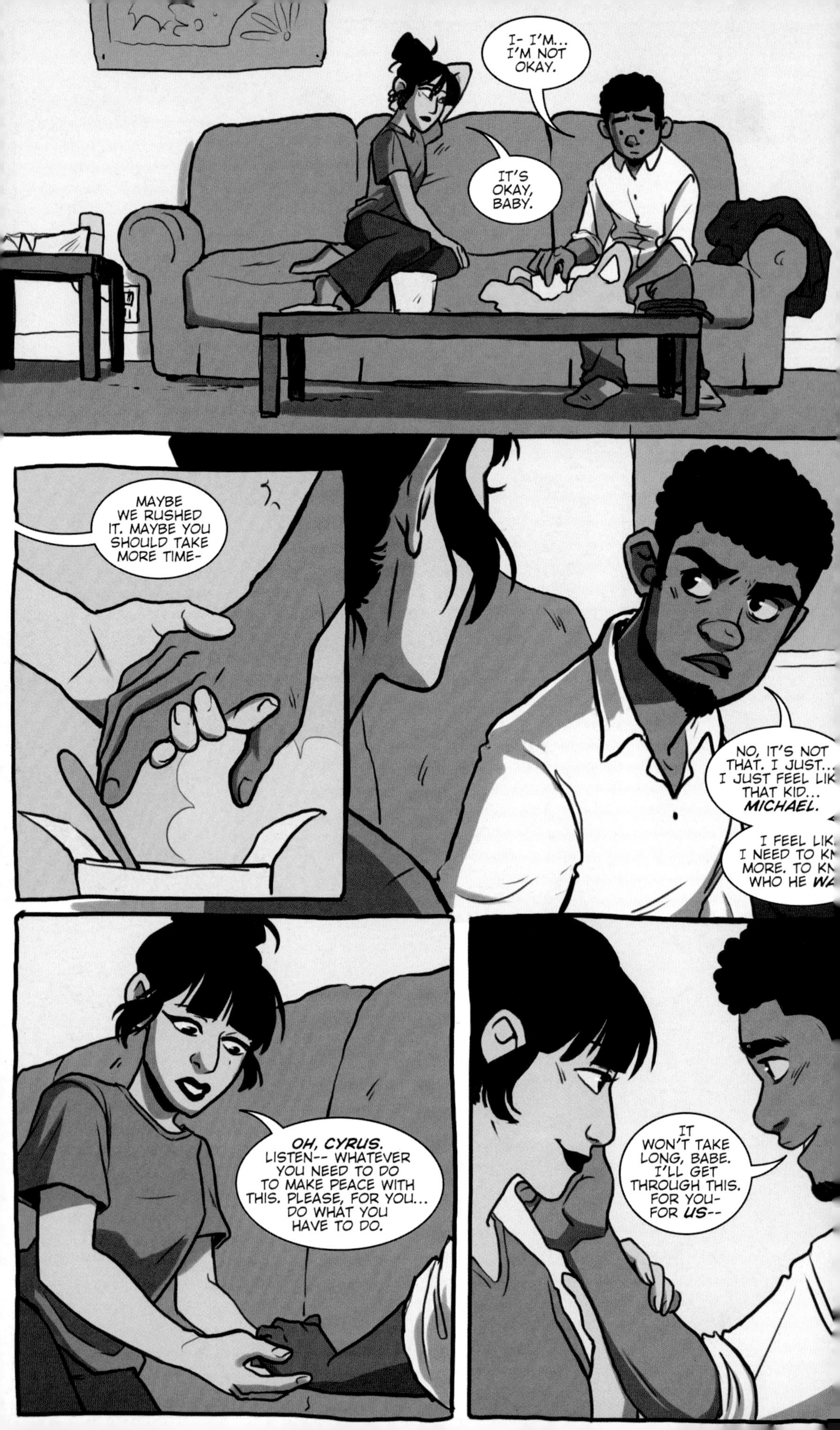

I- I'M... I'M NOT OKAY.
IT'S OKAY, BABY.
MAYBE WE RUSHED IT. MAYBE YOU SHOULD TAKE MORE TIME-
NO, IT'S NOT THAT. I JUST... I JUST FEEL LIK THAT KID... MICHAEL.
I FEEL LIK I NEED TO KN MORE. TO KN WHO HE WA
OH, CYRUS. LISTEN-- WHATEVER YOU NEED TO DO TO MAKE PEACE WITH THIS. PLEASE, FOR YOU... DO WHAT YOU HAVE TO DO.
IT WON'T TAKE LONG, BABE. I'LL GET THROUGH THIS. FOR YOU- FOR US--

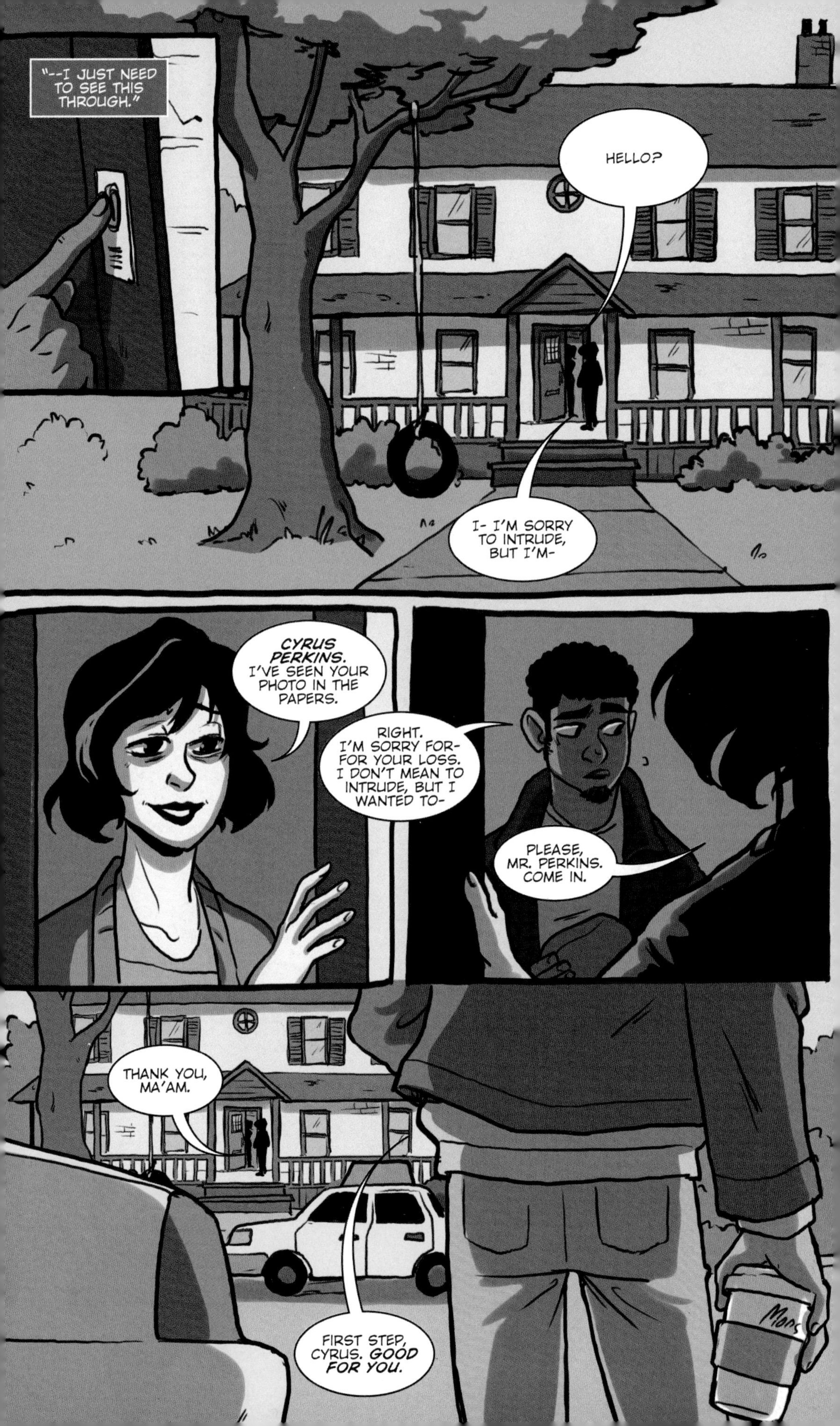
"--I JUST NEED TO SEE THIS THROUGH."
HELLO?
I- I'M SORRY TO INTRUDE, BUT I'M-
CYRUS PERKINS. I'VE SEEN YOUR PHOTO IN THE PAPERS.
RIGHT. I'M SORRY FOR- FOR YOUR LOSS. I DON'T MEAN TO INTRUDE, BUT I WANTED TO-
PLEASE, MR. PERKINS. COME IN.
THANK YOU, MA'AM.
FIRST STEP, CYRUS. GOOD FOR YOU.

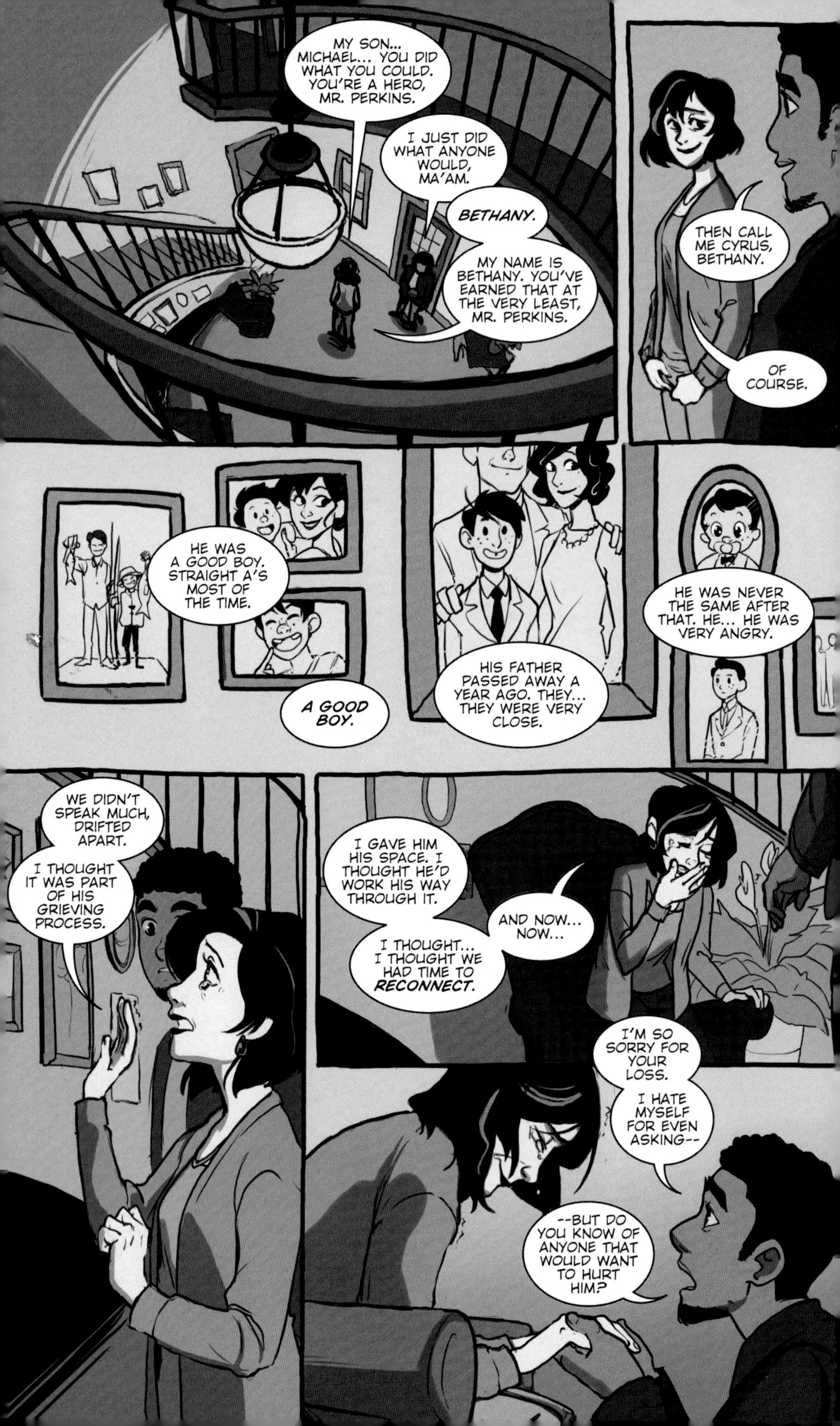

MY SON... MICHAEL... YOU DID WHAT YOU COULD. YOU'RE A HERO, MR. PERKINS.
I JUST DID WHAT ANYONE WOULD, MA'AM.
BETHANY.
MY NAME IS BETHANY. YOU'VE EARNED THAT AT THE VERY LEAST, MR. PERKINS.
THEN CALL ME CYRUS, BETHANY.
OF COURSE.
HE WAS A GOOD BOY. STRAIGHT A'S MOST OF THE TIME.
A GOOD BOY.
HIS FATHER PASSED AWAY A YEAR AGO. THEY... THEY WERE VERY CLOSE.
HE WAS NEVER THE SAME AFTER THAT. HE... HE WAS VERY ANGRY.
WE DIDN'T SPEAK MUCH, DRIFTED APART.
I THOUGHT IT WAS PART OF HIS GRIEVING PROCESS.
I GAVE HIM HIS SPACE. I THOUGHT HE'D WORK HIS WAY THROUGH IT.
I THOUGHT... I THOUGHT WE HAD TIME TO RECONNECT.
AND NOW... NOW...
I'M SO SORRY FOR YOUR LOSS.
I HATE MYSELF FOR EVEN ASKING--
--BUT DO YOU KNOW OF ANYONE THAT WOULD WANT TO HURT HIM?

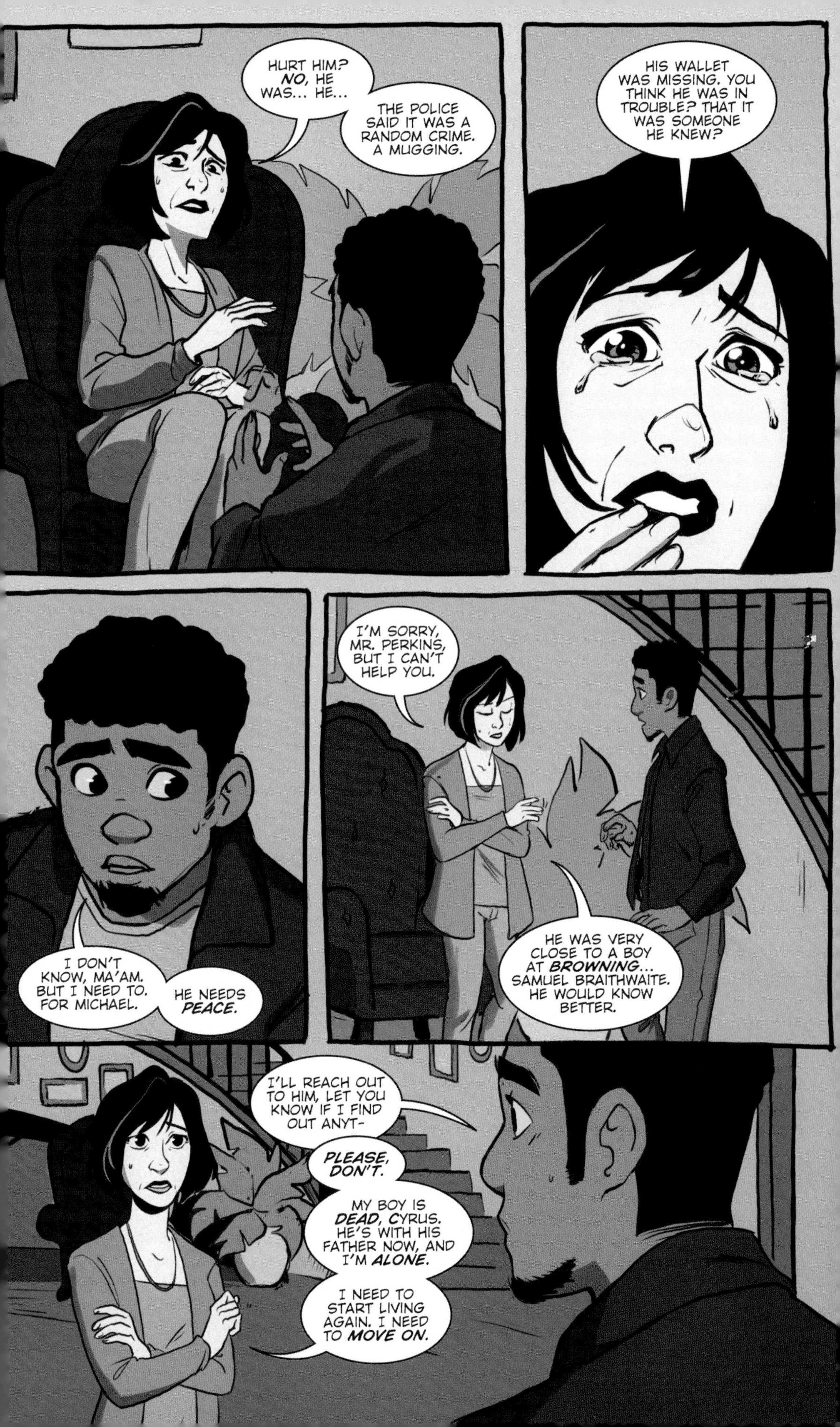
HURT HIM? NO, HE WAS... HE...
THE POLICE SAID IT WAS A RANDOM CRIME. A MUGGING.
HIS WALLET WAS MISSING. YOU THINK HE WAS IN TROUBLE? THAT IT WAS SOMEONE HE KNEW?
I DON'T KNOW, MA'AM. BUT I NEED TO. FOR MICHAEL.
HE NEEDS PEACE.
I'M SORRY, MR. PERKINS, BUT I CAN'T HELP YOU.
HE WAS VERY CLOSE TO A BOY AT BROWNING... SAMUEL BRAITHWAITE. HE WOULD KNOW BETTER.
I'LL REACH OUT TO HIM, LET YOU KNOW IF I FIND OUT ANYT-
PLEASE, DON'T.
MY BOY IS DEAD, CYRUS. HE'S WITH HIS FATHER NOW, AND I'M ALONE.
I NEED TO START LIVING AGAIN. I NEED TO MOVE ON.

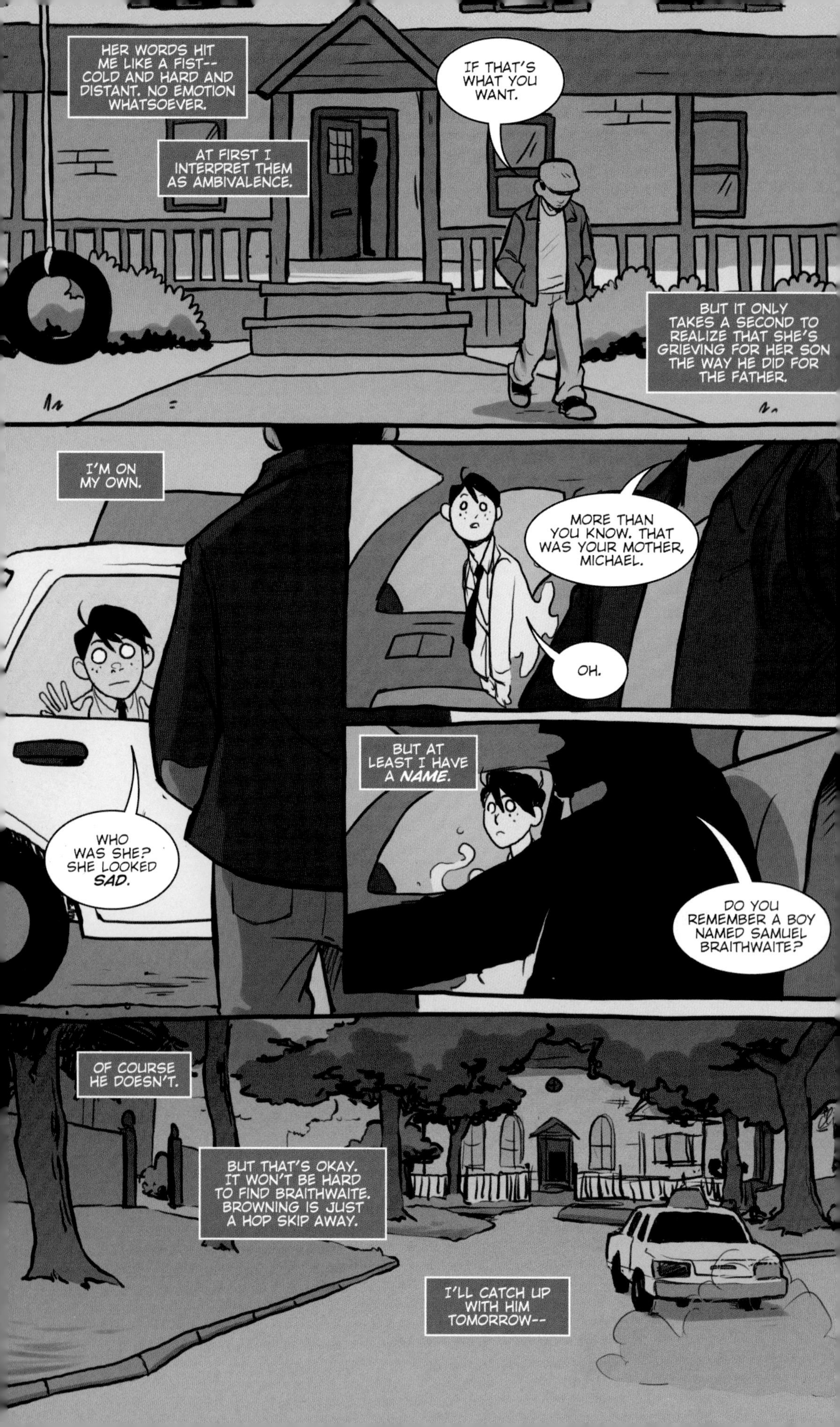
HER WORDS HIT ME LIKE A FIST-- COLD AND HARD AND DISTANT. NO EMOTION WHATSOEVER.
IF THAT'S WHAT YOU WANT.
AT FIRST I INTERPRET THEM AS AMBIVALENCE.
BUT IT ONLY TAKES A SECOND TO REALIZE THAT SHE'S GRIEVING FOR HER SON THE WAY HE DID FOR THE FATHER.
I'M ON MY OWN.
WHO WAS SHE? SHE LOOKED SAD.
MORE THAN YOU KNOW. THAT WAS YOUR MOTHER, MICHAEL.
OH.
BUT AT LEAST I HAVE A NAME.
DO YOU REMEMBER A BOY NAMED SAMUEL BRAITHWAITE?
OF COURSE HE DOESN'T.
BUT THAT'S OKAY. IT WON'T BE HARD TO FIND BRAITHWAITE. BROWNING IS JUST A HOP SKIP AWAY.
I'LL CATCH UP WITH HIM TOMORROW--

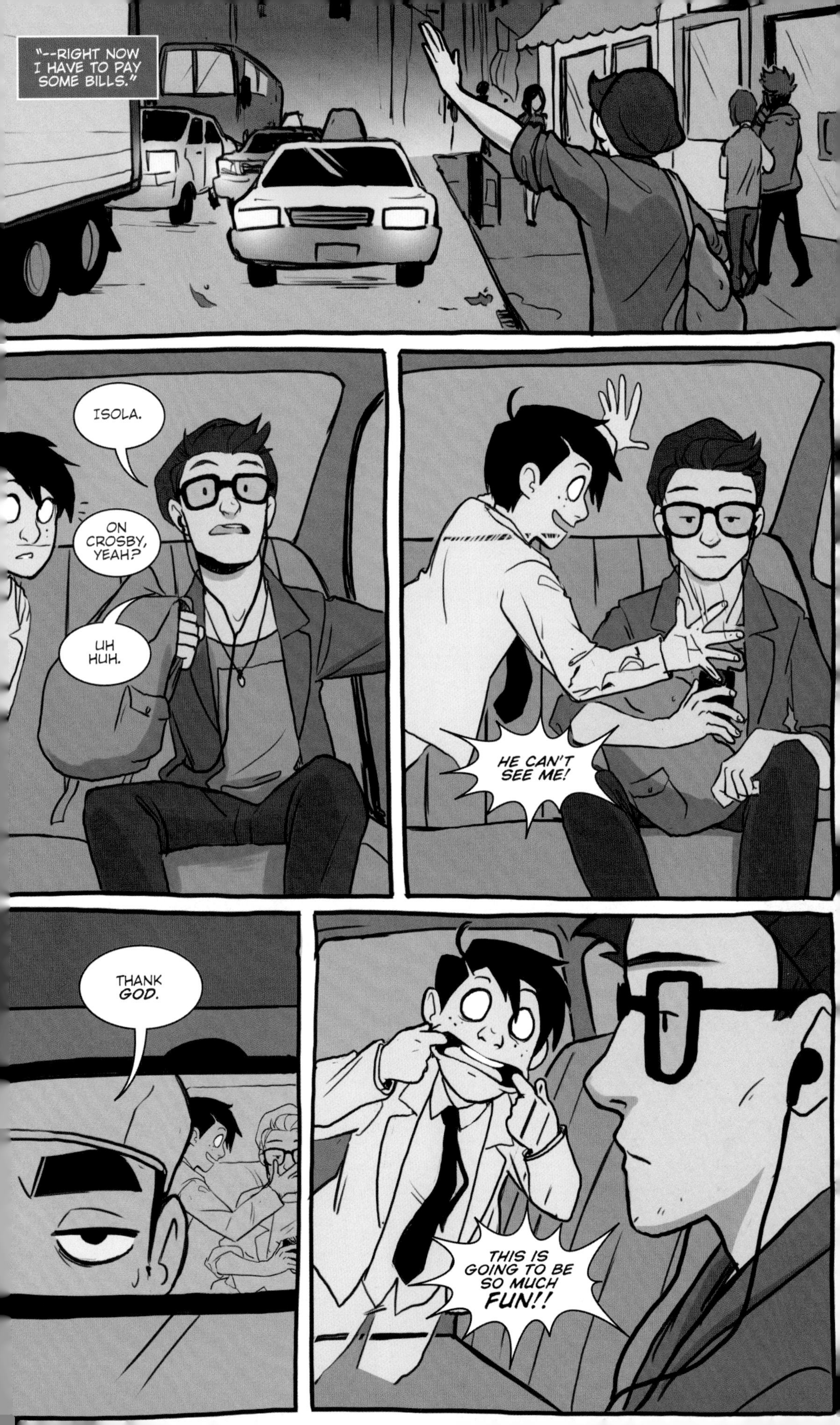
"--RIGHT NOW I HAVE TO PAY SOME BILLS."
ISOLA.
ON CROSBY, YEAH?
UH HUH.
HE CAN'T SEE ME!
THANK GOD.
THIS IS GOING TO BE SO MUCH FUN!!

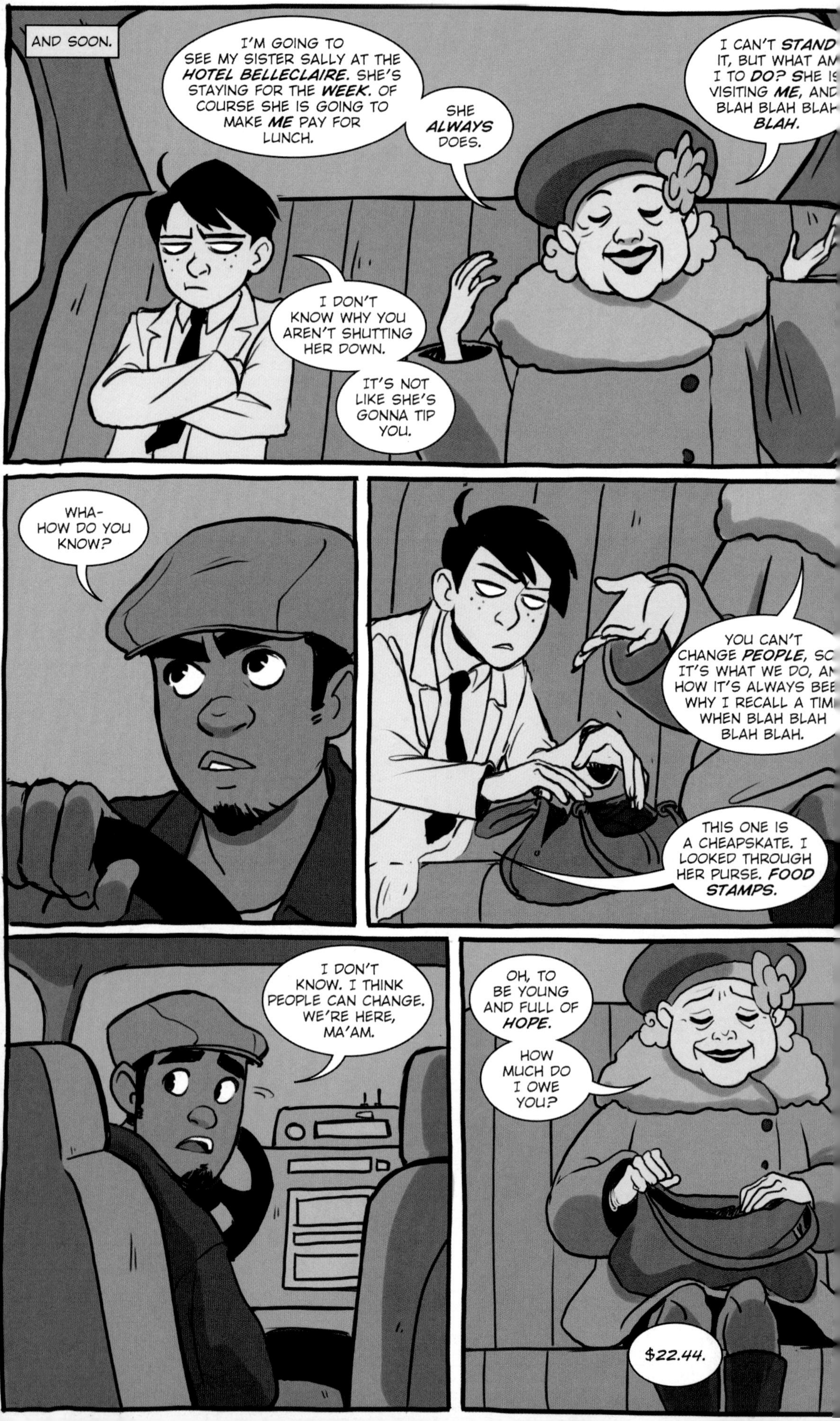
AND SOON.
I'M GOING TO SEE MY SISTER SALLY AT THE HOTEL BELLECLAIRE. SHE'S STAYING FOR THE WEEK. OF COURSE SHE IS GOING TO MAKE ME PAY FOR LUNCH.
SHE ALWAYS DOES.
I CAN'T STAND IT, BUT WHAT AM I TO DO? SHE IS VISITING ME, AND BLAH BLAH BLAH BLAH.
I DON'T KNOW WHY YOU AREN'T SHUTTING HER DOWN.
IT'S NOT LIKE SHE'S GONNA TIP YOU.
WHA- HOW DO YOU KNOW?
YOU CAN'T CHANGE PEOPLE, SO IT'S WHAT WE DO, AN HOW IT'S ALWAYS BEE WHY I RECALL A TIM WHEN BLAH BLAH BLAH BLAH.
THIS ONE IS A CHEAPSKATE. I LOOKED THROUGH HER PURSE. FOOD STAMPS.
I DON'T KNOW. I THINK PEOPLE CAN CHANGE. WE'RE HERE, MA'AM.
OH, TO BE YOUNG AND FULL OF HOPE.
HOW MUCH DO I OWE YOU?
$22.44.

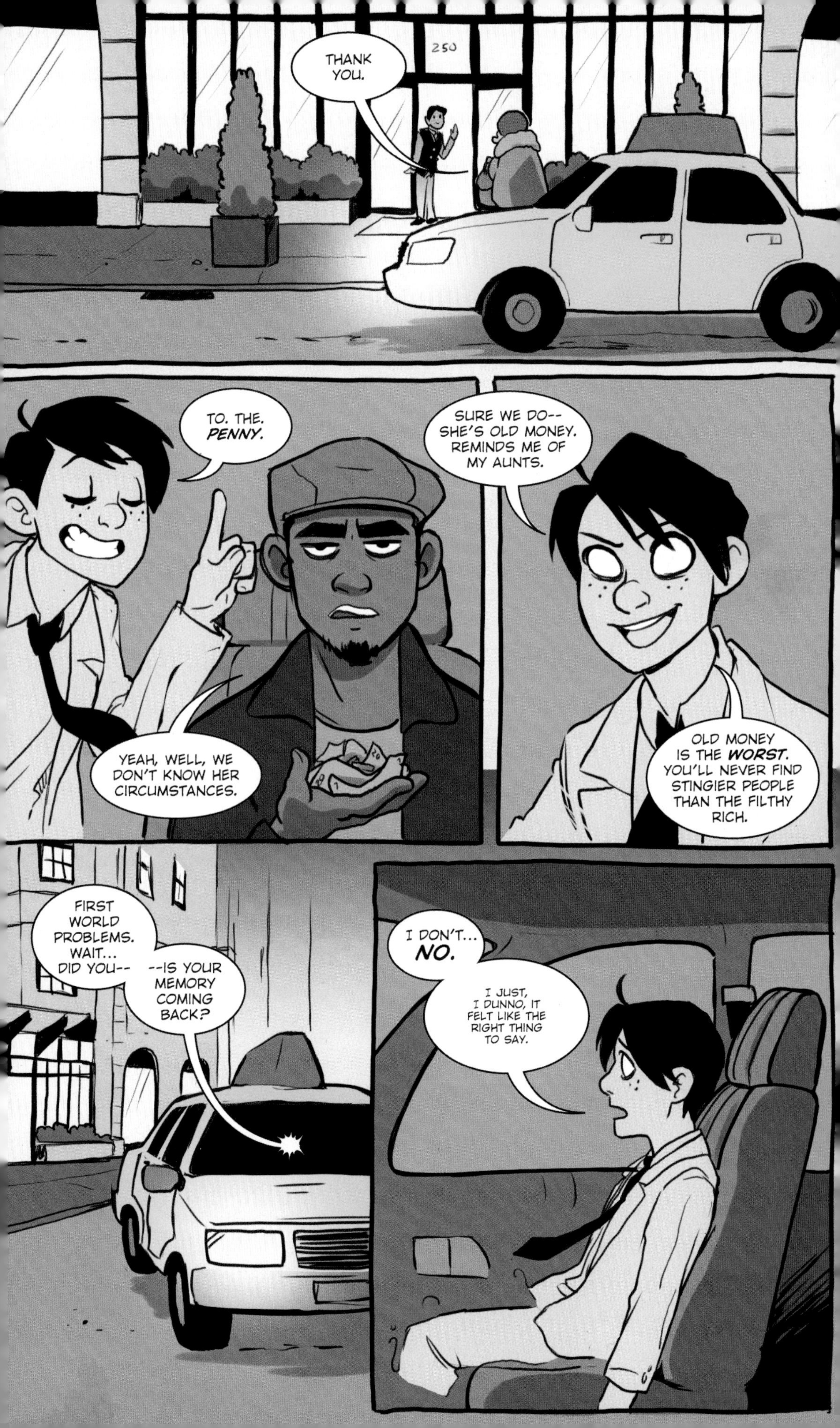
THANK YOU.
250
TO. THE. ***PENNY.***
YEAH, WELL, WE DON'T KNOW HER CIRCUMSTANCES.
SURE WE DO-- SHE'S OLD MONEY. REMINDS ME OF MY AUNTS.
OLD MONEY IS THE ***WORST.*** YOU'LL NEVER FIND STINGIER PEOPLE THAN THE FILTHY RICH.
FIRST WORLD PROBLEMS. WAIT... DID YOU--
--IS YOUR MEMORY COMING BACK?
I DON'T... ***NO.***
I JUST, I DUNNO, IT FELT LIKE THE RIGHT THING TO SAY.

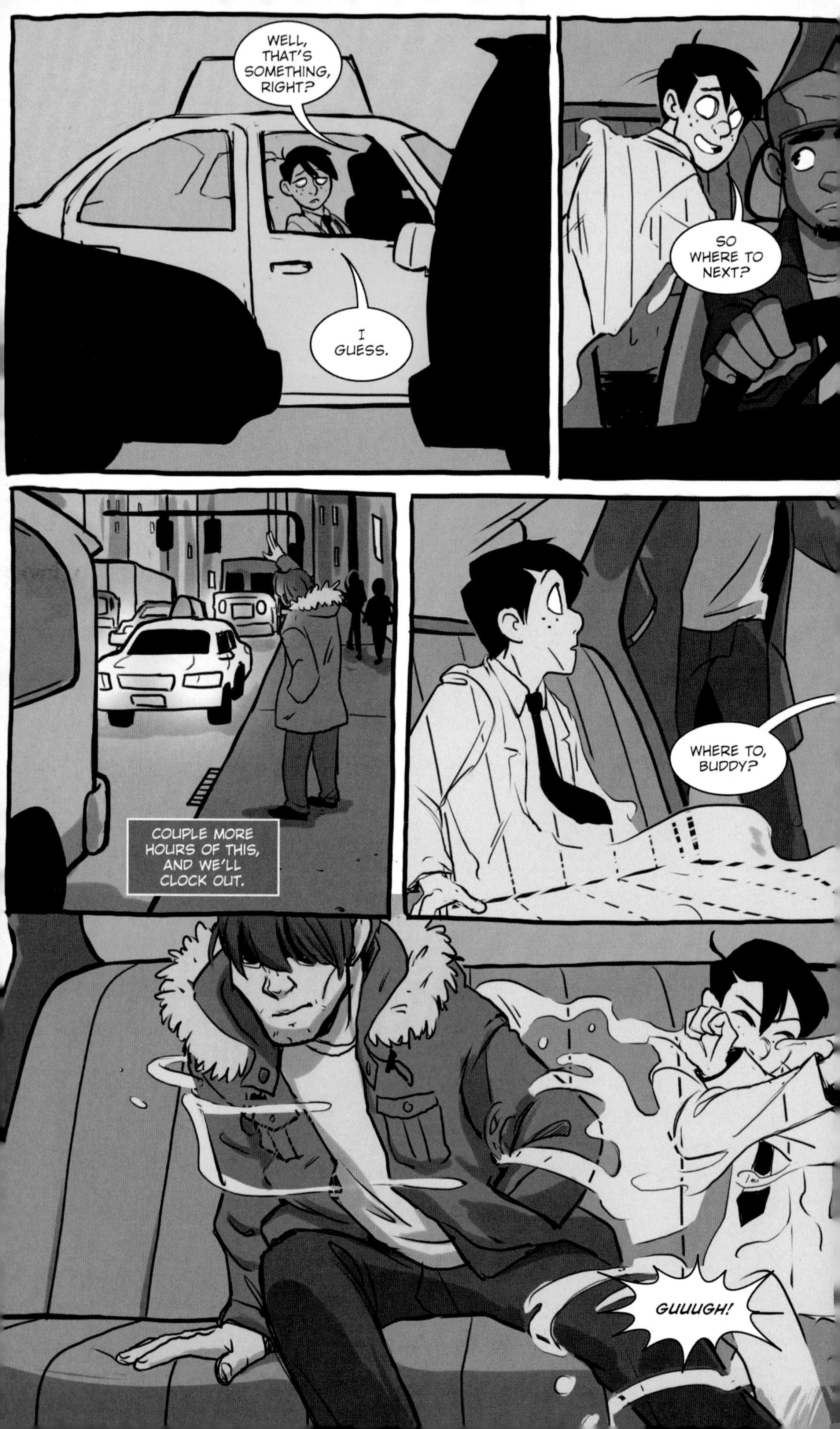
WELL, THAT'S SOMETHING, RIGHT?
I GUESS.
SO WHERE TO NEXT?
COUPLE MORE HOURS OF THIS, AND WE'LL CLOCK OUT.
WHERE TO, BUDDY?
GUUUGH!

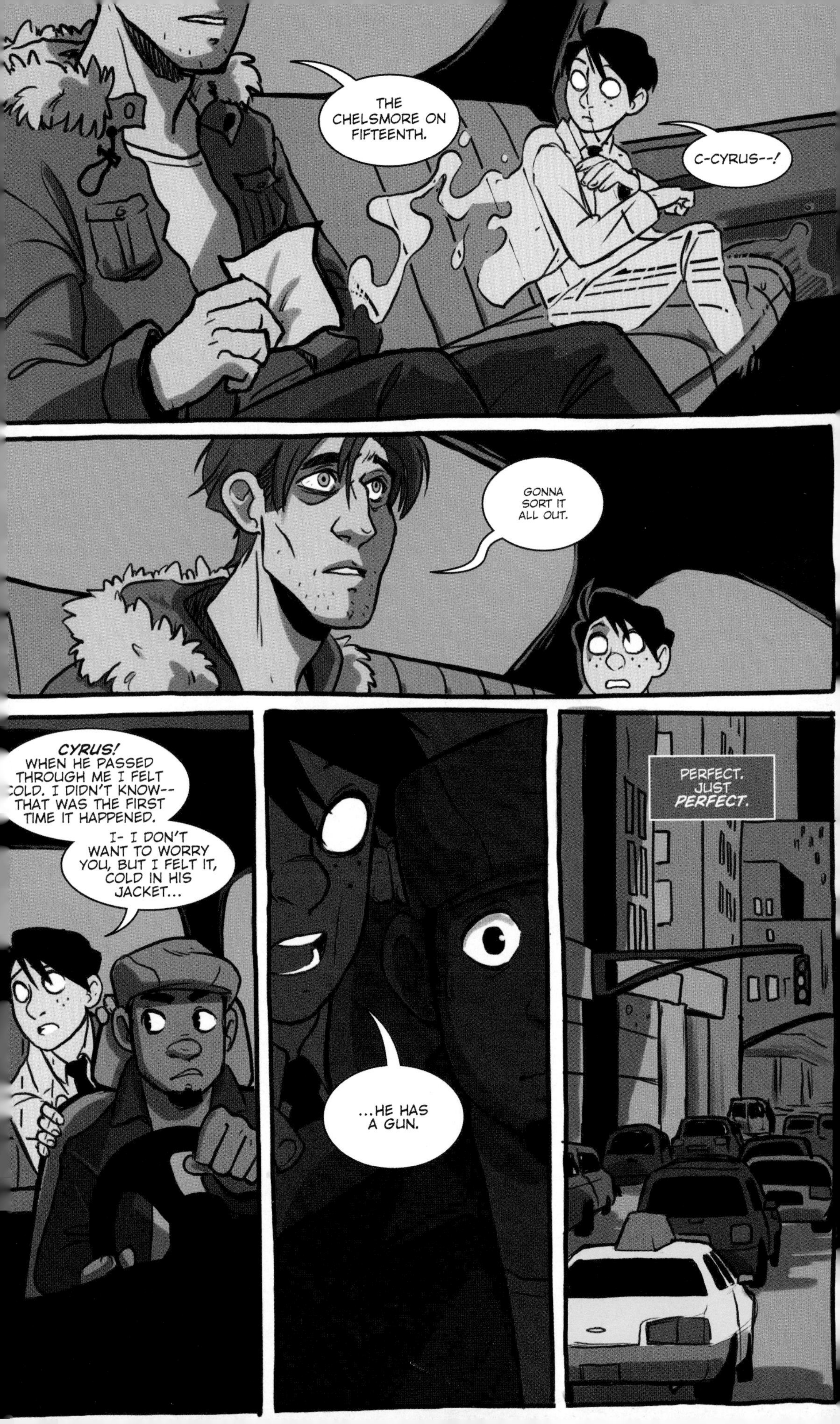
THE CHELSMORE ON FIFTEENTH.
C-CYRUS--!
GONNA SORT IT ALL OUT.
CYRUS! WHEN HE PASSED THROUGH ME I FELT COLD. I DIDN'T KNOW-- THAT WAS THE FIRST TIME IT HAPPENED.
I- I DON'T WANT TO WORRY YOU, BUT I FELT IT, COLD IN HIS JACKET...
...HE HAS A GUN.
PERFECT. JUST PERFECT.

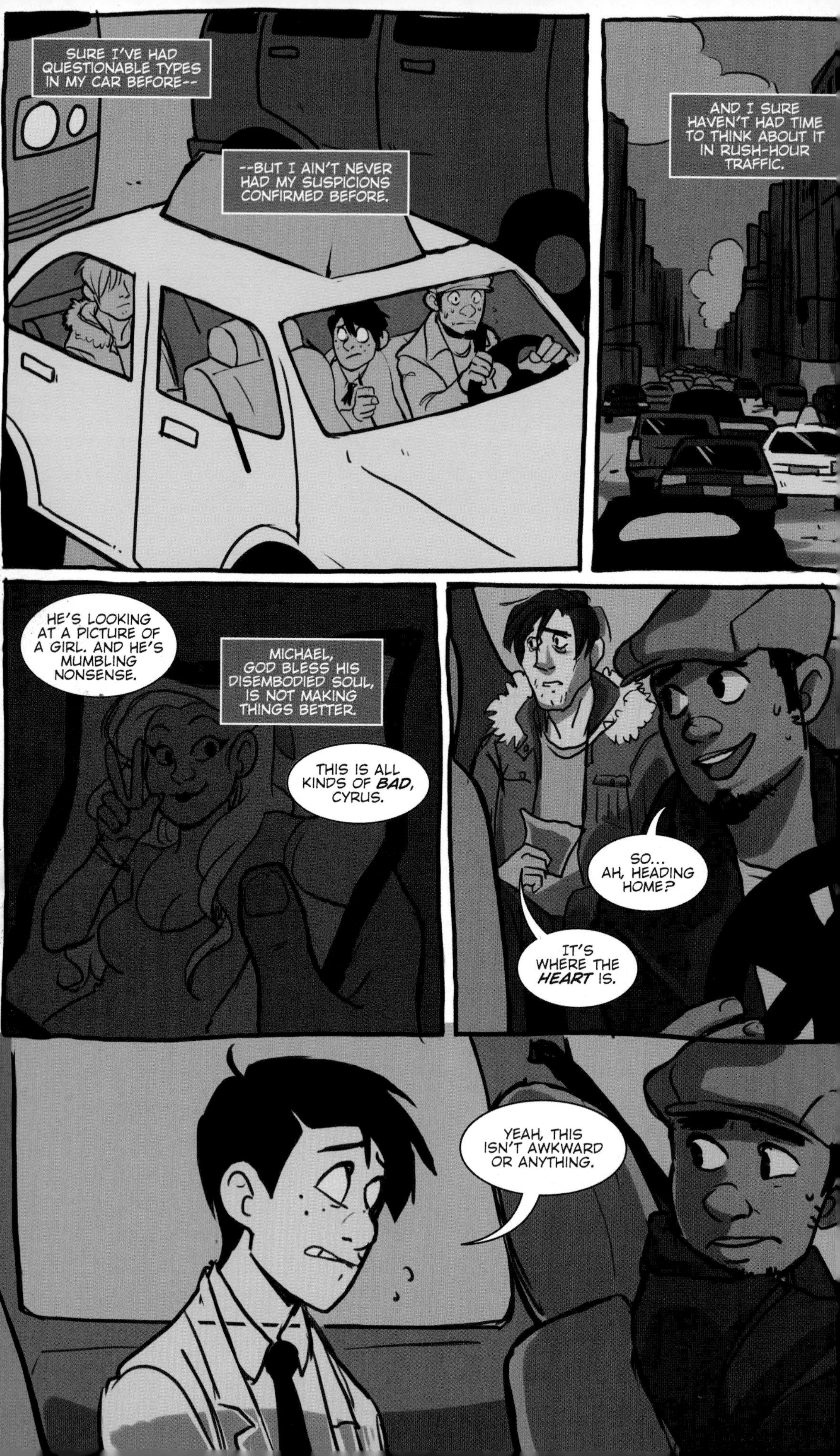
SURE I'VE HAD QUESTIONABLE TYPES IN MY CAR BEFORE--
--BUT I AIN'T NEVER HAD MY SUSPICIONS CONFIRMED BEFORE.
AND I SURE HAVEN'T HAD TIME TO THINK ABOUT IT IN RUSH-HOUR TRAFFIC.
HE'S LOOKING AT A PICTURE OF A GIRL. AND HE'S MUMBLING NONSENSE.
MICHAEL, GOD BLESS HIS DISEMBODIED SOUL, IS NOT MAKING THINGS BETTER.
THIS IS ALL KINDS OF *BAD*, CYRUS.
SO... AH, HEADING HOME?
IT'S WHERE THE *HEART* IS.
YEAH, THIS ISN'T AWKWARD OR ANYTHING.

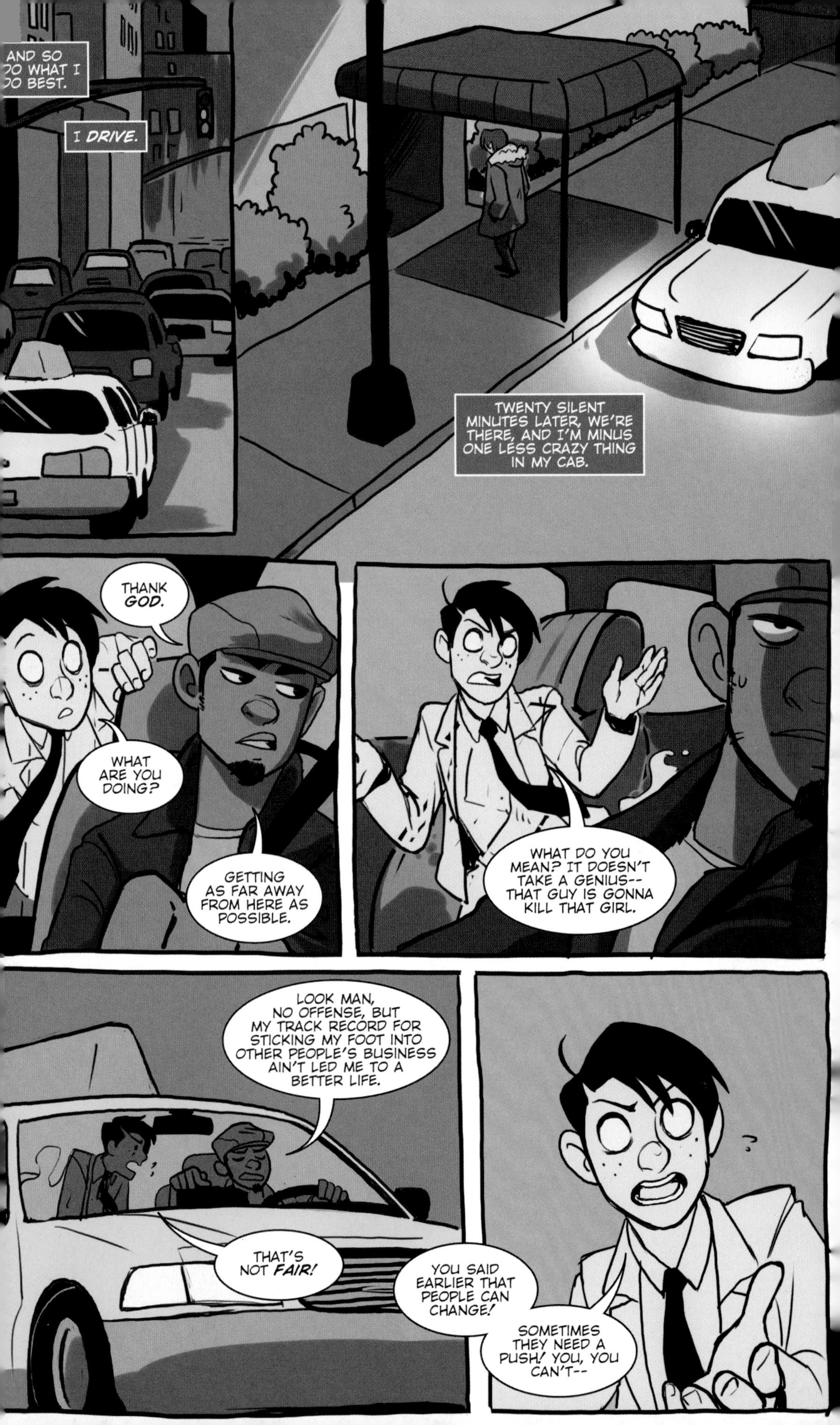
AND SO
DO WHAT I
DO BEST.
I DRIVE.
TWENTY SILENT MINUTES LATER, WE'RE THERE, AND I'M MINUS ONE LESS CRAZY THING IN MY CAB.
THANK GOD.
WHAT ARE YOU DOING?
GETTING AS FAR AWAY FROM HERE AS POSSIBLE.
WHAT DO YOU MEAN? IT DOESN'T TAKE A GENIUS-- THAT GUY IS GONNA KILL THAT GIRL.
LOOK MAN, NO OFFENSE, BUT MY TRACK RECORD FOR STICKING MY FOOT INTO OTHER PEOPLE'S BUSINESS AIN'T LED ME TO A BETTER LIFE.
THAT'S NOT FAIR!
YOU SAID EARLIER THAT PEOPLE CAN CHANGE!
SOMETIMES THEY NEED A PUSH! YOU, YOU CAN'T--

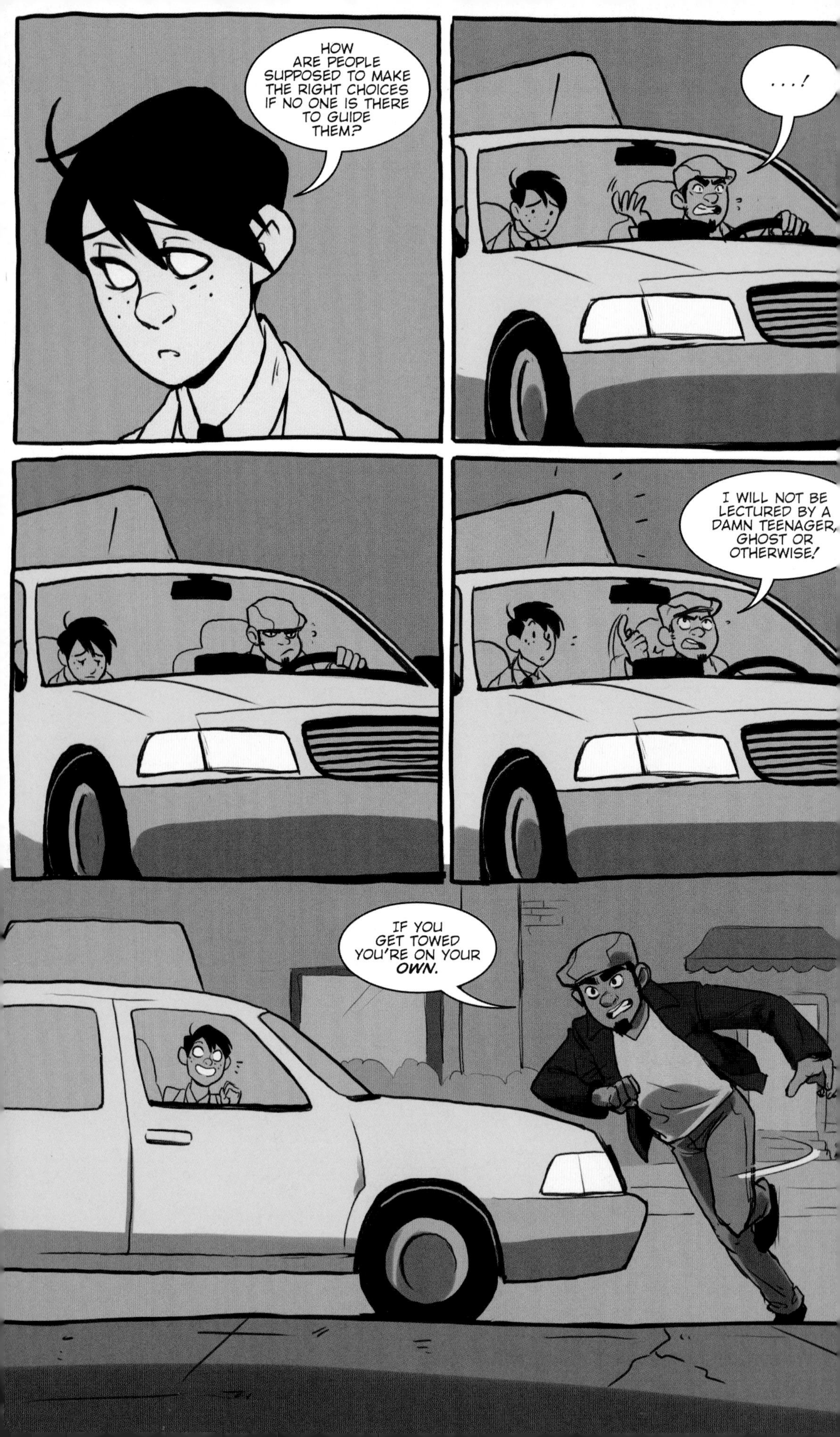
HOW ARE PEOPLE SUPPOSED TO MAKE THE RIGHT CHOICES IF NO ONE IS THERE TO GUIDE THEM?
. . . !
I WILL NOT BE LECTURED BY A DAMN TEENAGER, GHOST OR OTHERWISE!
IF YOU GET TOWED YOU'RE ON YOUR *OWN*.

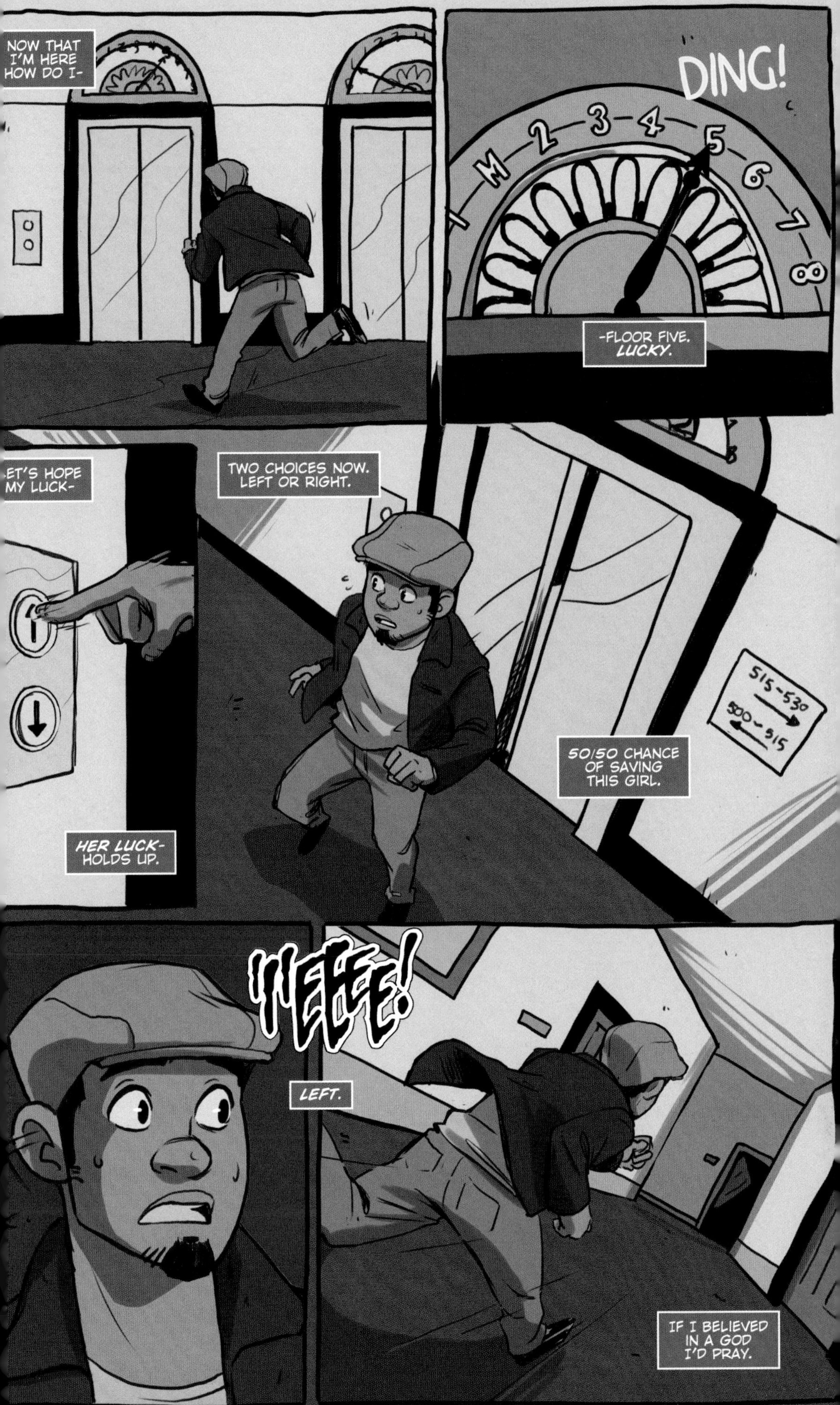
NOW THAT I'M HERE HOW DO I-
DING!
-FLOOR FIVE. LUCKY.
ET'S HOPE MY LUCK-
TWO CHOICES NOW. LEFT OR RIGHT.
515-530
500-515
50/50 CHANCE OF SAVING THIS GIRL.
HER LUCK- HOLDS UP.
IIEEEE!
LEFT.
IF I BELIEVED IN A GOD I'D PRAY.

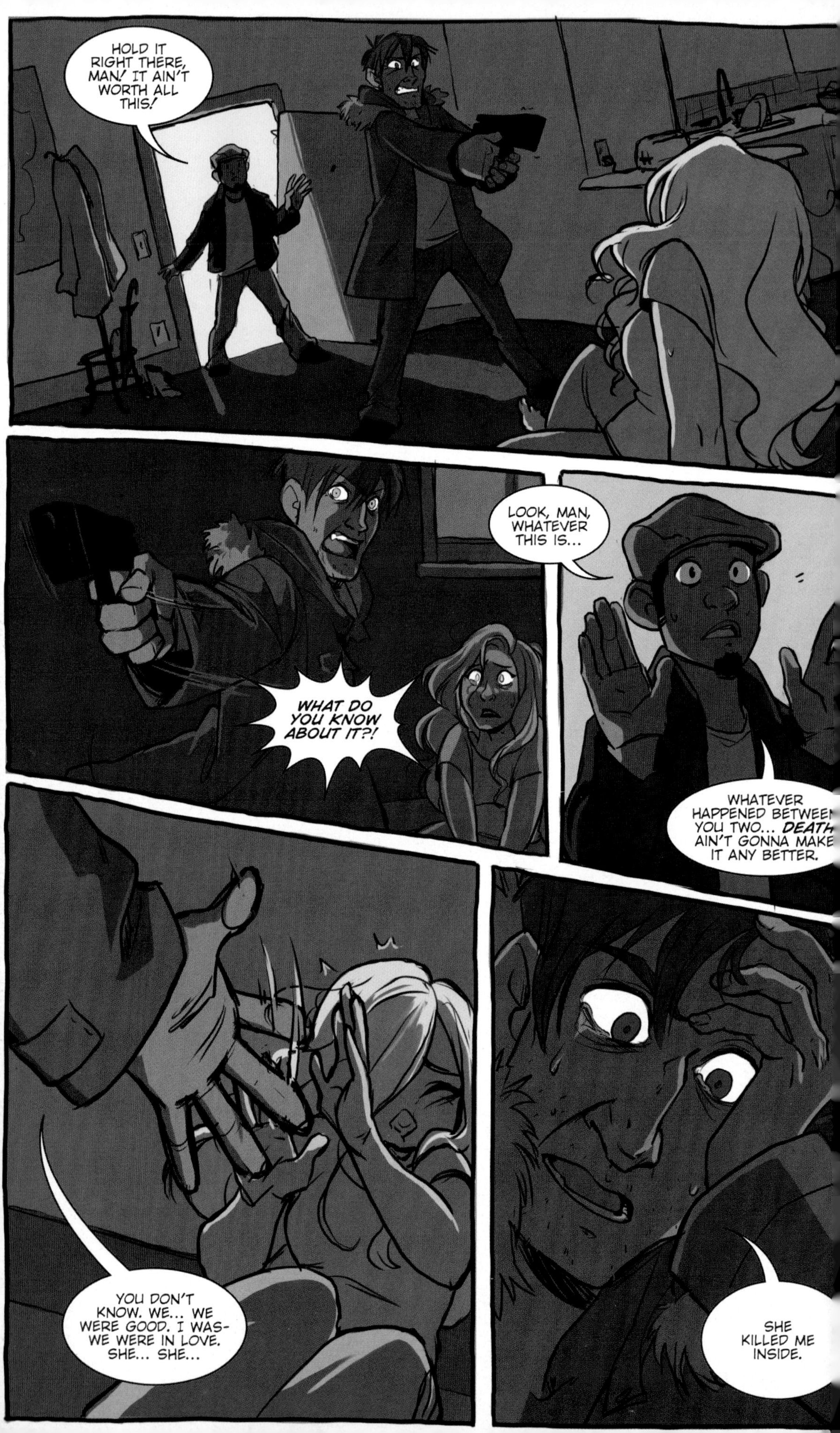
HOLD IT RIGHT THERE, MAN! IT AIN'T WORTH ALL THIS!
WHAT DO YOU KNOW ABOUT IT?!
LOOK, MAN, WHATEVER THIS IS...
WHATEVER HAPPENED BETWEEN YOU TWO... DEATH AIN'T GONNA MAKE IT ANY BETTER.
YOU DON'T KNOW. WE... WE WERE GOOD. I WAS- WE WERE IN LOVE. SHE... SHE...
SHE KILLED ME INSIDE.

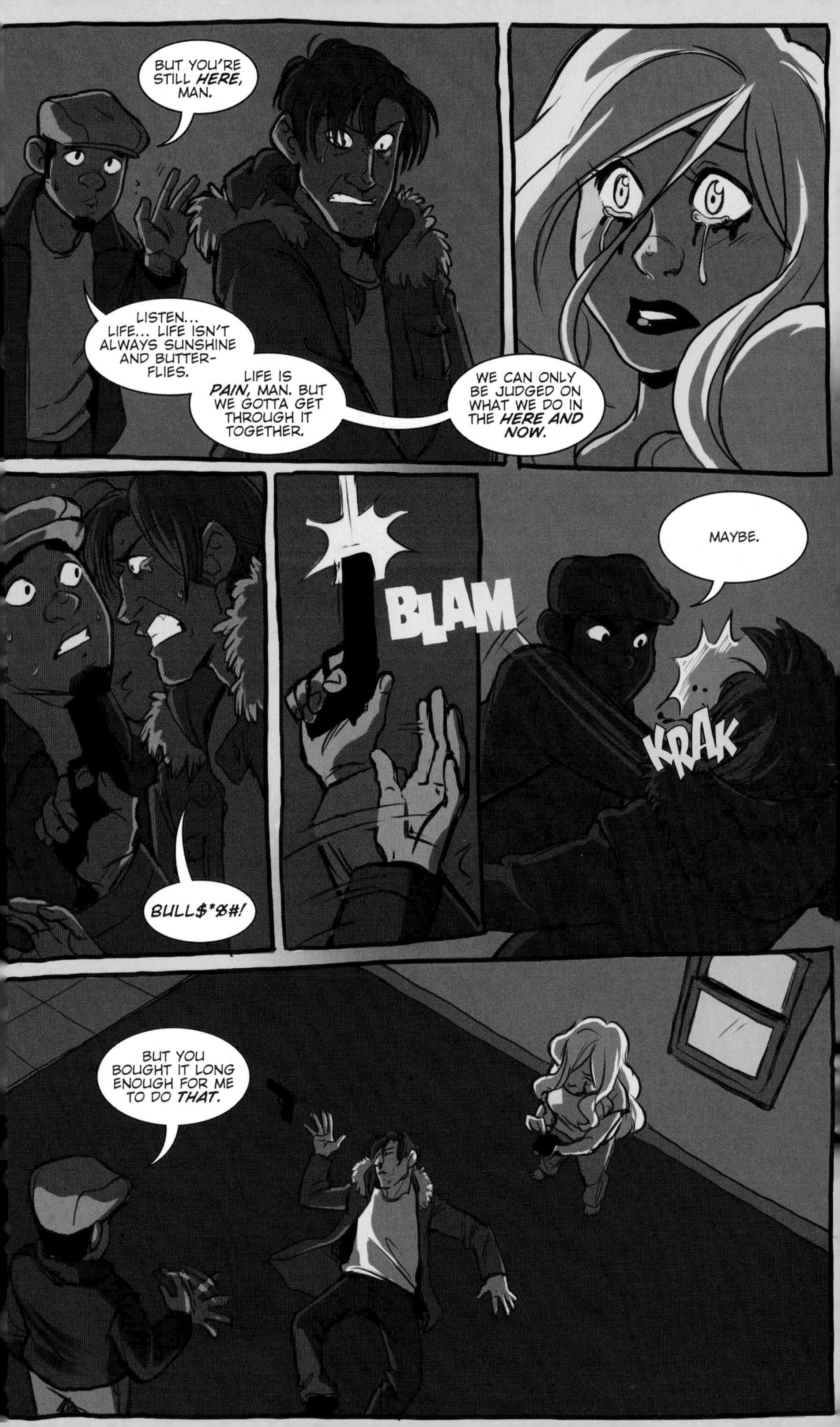
BUT YOU'RE STILL *HERE,* MAN.
LISTEN... LIFE... LIFE ISN'T ALWAYS SUNSHINE AND BUTTER-FLIES.
LIFE IS *PAIN,* MAN. BUT WE GOTTA GET THROUGH IT TOGETHER.
WE CAN ONLY BE JUDGED ON WHAT WE DO IN THE *HERE AND NOW.*
BULL$*%#!
BLAM
MAYBE.
KRAK
BUT YOU BOUGHT IT LONG ENOUGH FOR ME TO DO *THAT.*

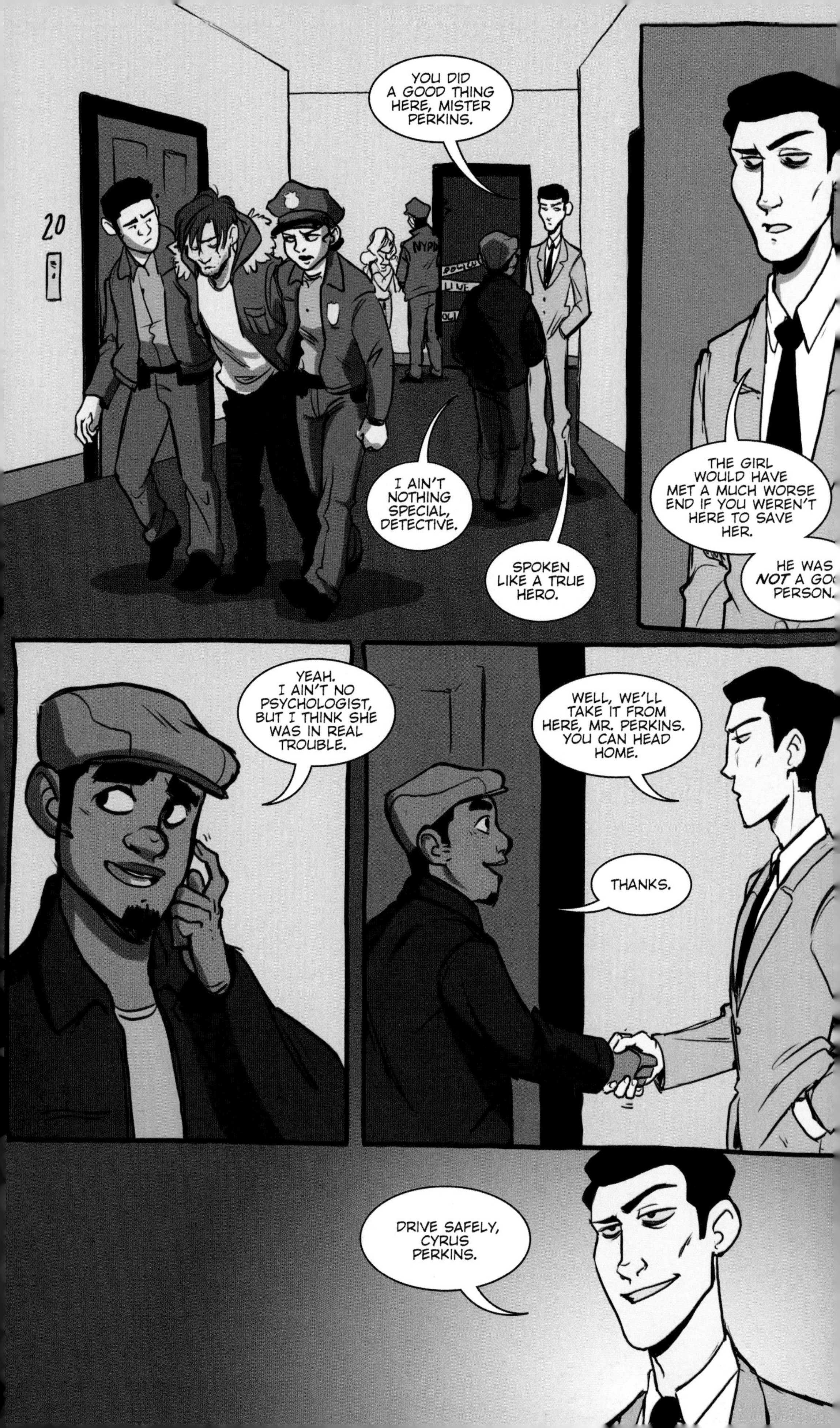
20
YOU DID A GOOD THING HERE, MISTER PERKINS.
I AIN'T NOTHING SPECIAL, DETECTIVE.
SPOKEN LIKE A TRUE HERO.
THE GIRL WOULD HAVE MET A MUCH WORSE END IF YOU WEREN'T HERE TO SAVE HER.
HE WAS ***NOT*** A GO
PERSON.
YEAH. I AIN'T NO PSYCHOLOGIST, BUT I THINK SHE WAS IN REAL TROUBLE.
WELL, WE'LL TAKE IT FROM HERE, MR. PERKINS. YOU CAN HEAD HOME.
THANKS.
DRIVE SAFELY, CYRUS PERKINS.

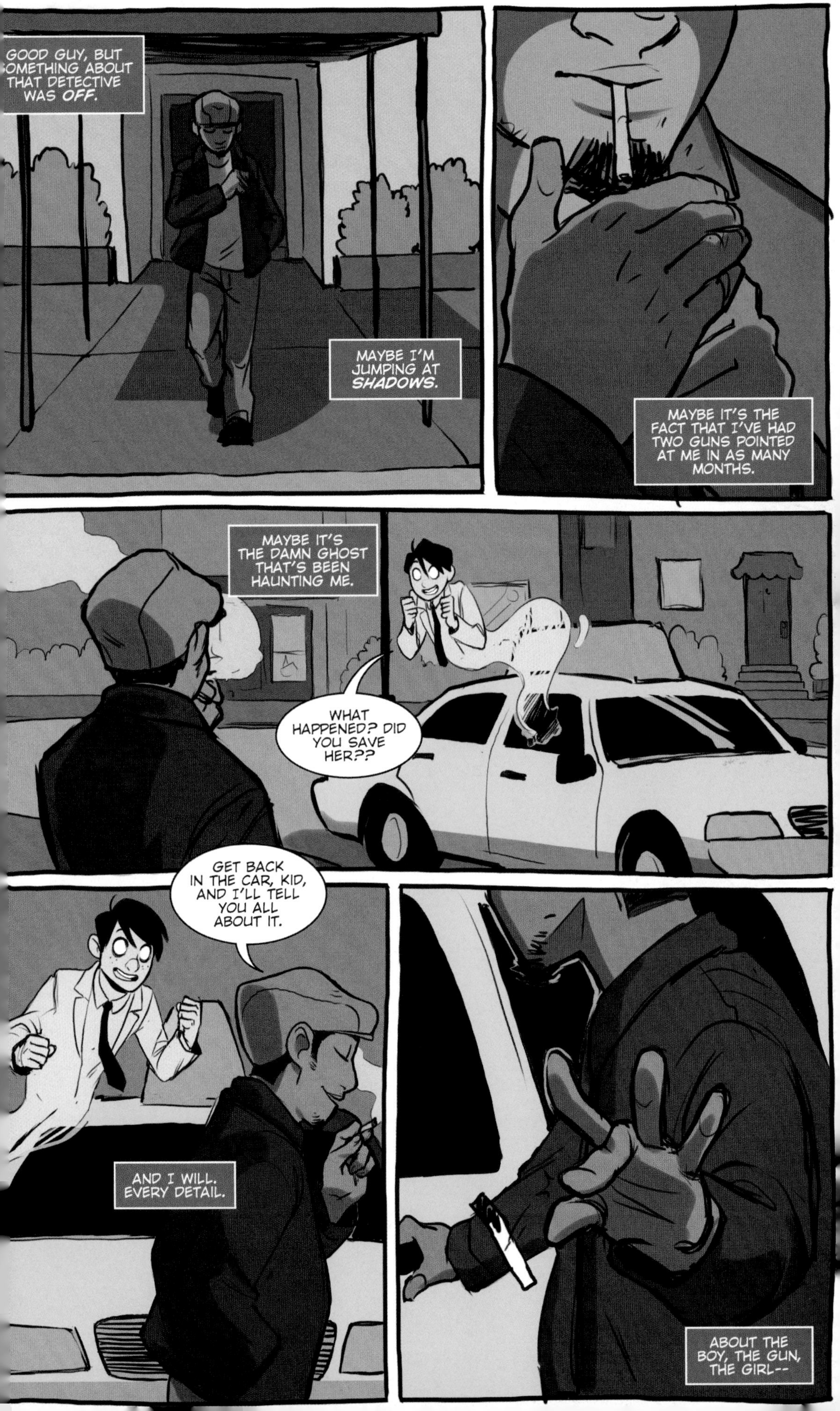
GOOD GUY, BUT SOMETHING ABOUT THAT DETECTIVE WAS OFF.
MAYBE I'M JUMPING AT SHADOWS.
MAYBE IT'S THE FACT THAT I'VE HAD TWO GUNS POINTED AT ME IN AS MANY MONTHS.
MAYBE IT'S THE DAMN GHOST THAT'S BEEN HAUNTING ME.
WHAT HAPPENED? DID YOU SAVE HER??
GET BACK IN THE CAR, KID, AND I'LL TELL YOU ALL ABOUT IT.
AND I WILL. EVERY DETAIL.
ABOUT THE BOY, THE GUN, THE GIRL--

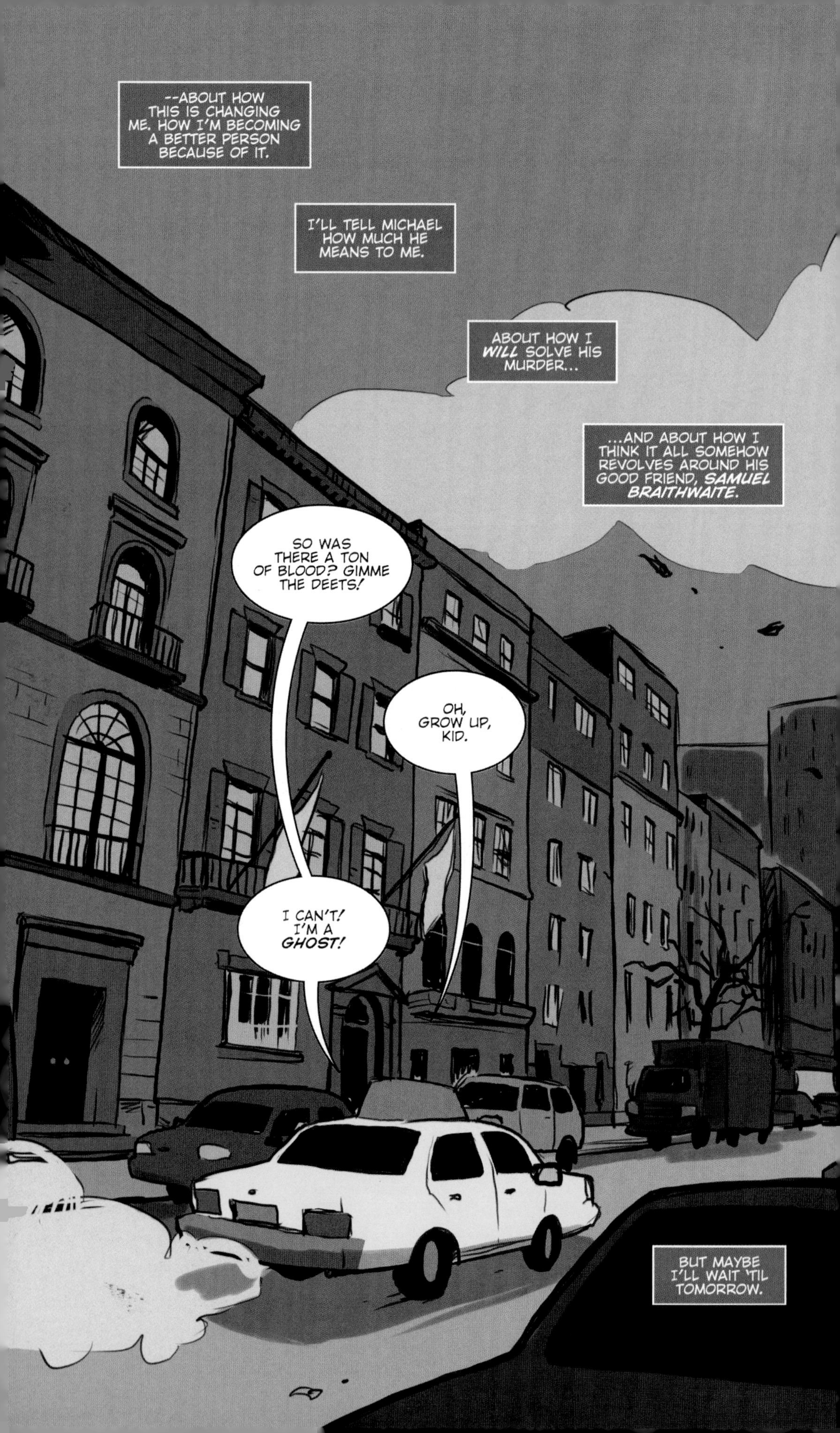
--ABOUT HOW THIS IS CHANGING ME. HOW I'M BECOMING A BETTER PERSON BECAUSE OF IT.
I'LL TELL MICHAEL HOW MUCH HE MEANS TO ME.
ABOUT HOW I *WILL* SOLVE HIS MURDER...
...AND ABOUT HOW I THINK IT ALL SOMEHOW REVOLVES AROUND HIS GOOD FRIEND, *SAMUEL BRAITHWAITE*.
SO WAS THERE A TON OF BLOOD? GIMME THE DEETS!
OH, GROW UP, KID.
I CAN'T! I'M A *GHOST*!
BUT MAYBE I'LL WAIT 'TIL TOMORROW.

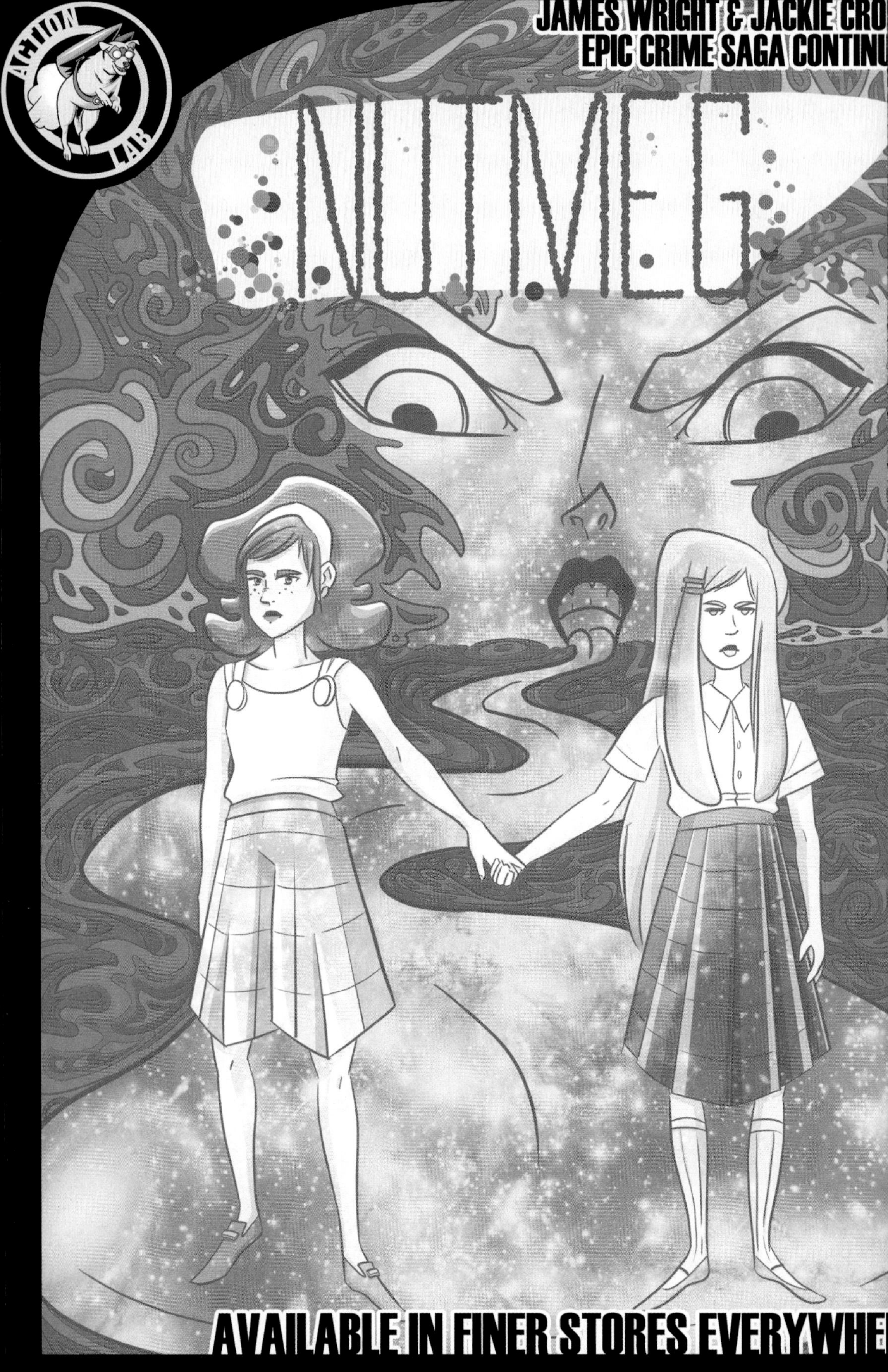

JAMES WRIGHT & JACKIE CRO[...]
EPIC CRIME SAGA CONTINU[...]

NUTMEG

AVAILABLE IN FINER STORES EVERYWHE[...]

Fall, Part 5: "Pantry Raids" Poppy and Cassia, the teen masterminds behind the addictive Patty Cake brownies, hoping to better understand their product, violate one o[...] the 10 Crime Commandments: they try their own supply.

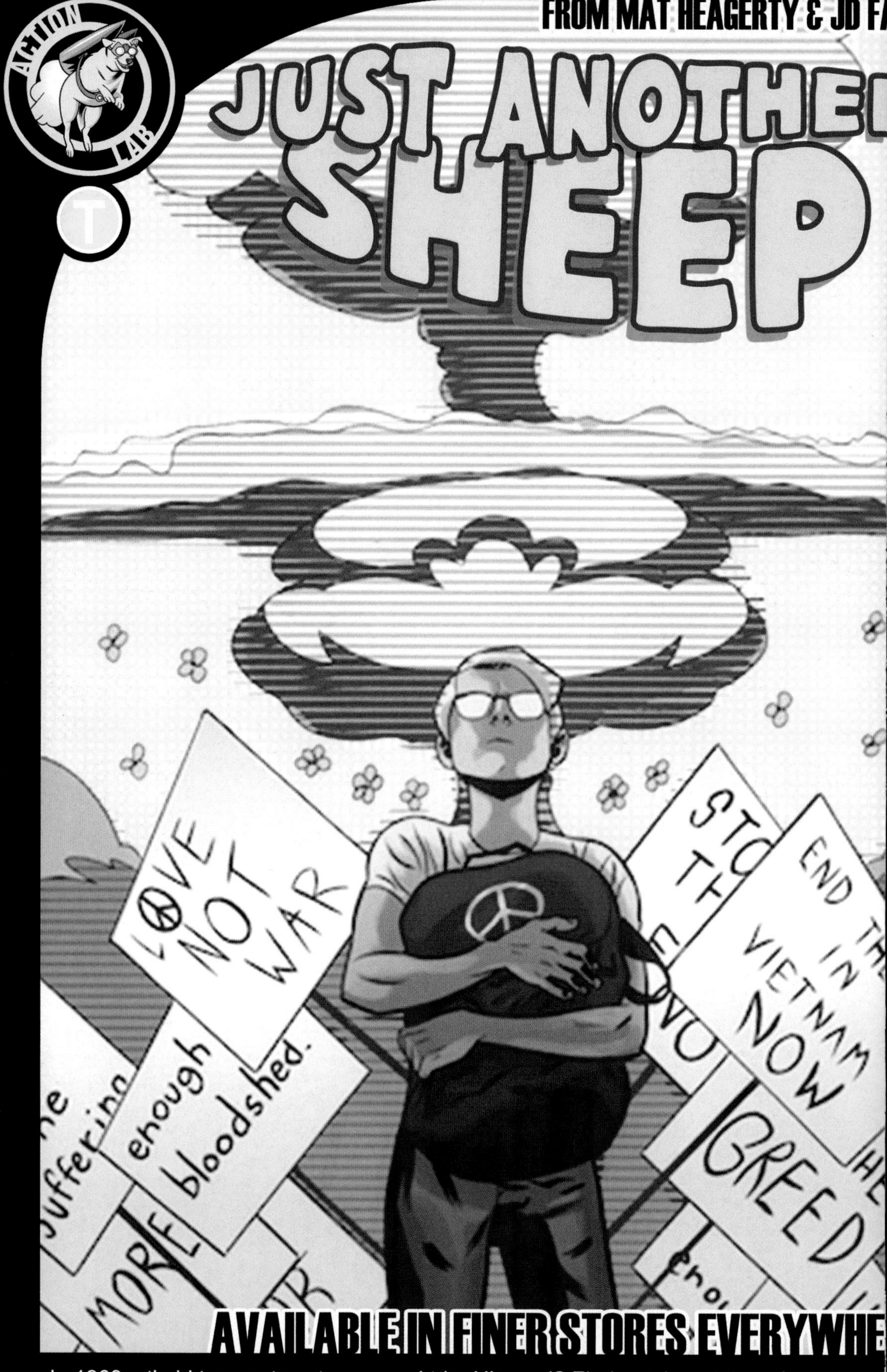
FROM MAT HEAGERTY & JD FA
JUST ANOTHE
SHEEP
LOVE NOT WAR
enough bloodshed.
END IN VIETNAM NOW
GREED
AVAILABLE IN FINER STORES EVERYWHE

FROM ALL-AGES TO MATURE READERS
ACTION LAB HAS YOU COVERED.

E Appropriate for everyone.

A Appropriate for age 9 and up. Absent of profanity or adult content.

T Suggested for 12 and Up. Comics with this rating are comparable to a PG-13 movie rating. Recommended for our teen and young adult readers.

T+ Appropriate for older teens. Similar to Teen, but featuring more mature themes and/or more graphic imagery.

M Contains extreme viloence and some nudity. Basically the Rated-R of comics.

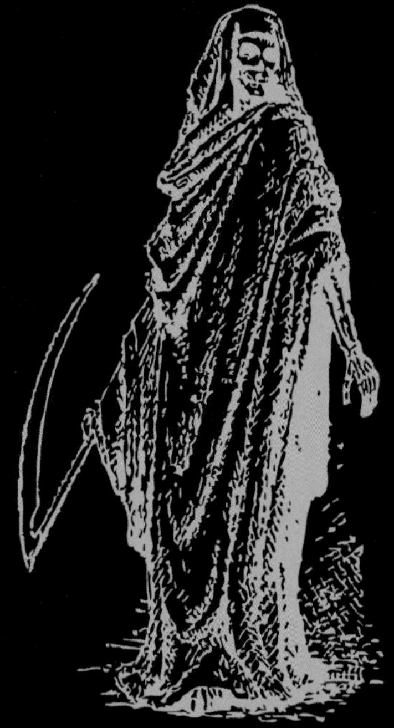

Cyrus Perkins - Action Lab
www.actionlabcomics.com
00211
7 02382 69111 0

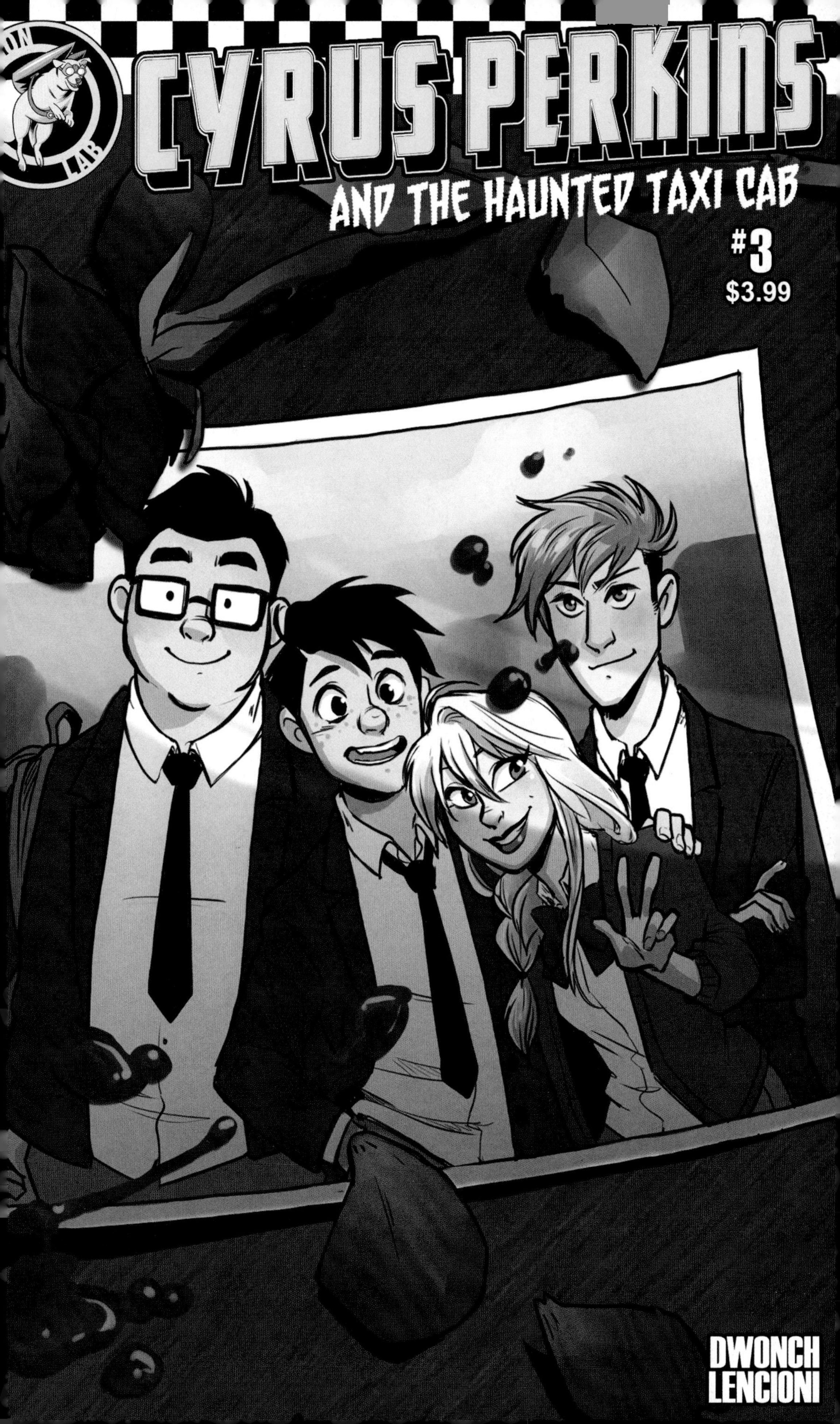

ON LAB
CYRUS PERKINS
AND THE HAUNTED TAXI CAB
#3
$3.99
DWONCH
LENCIONI

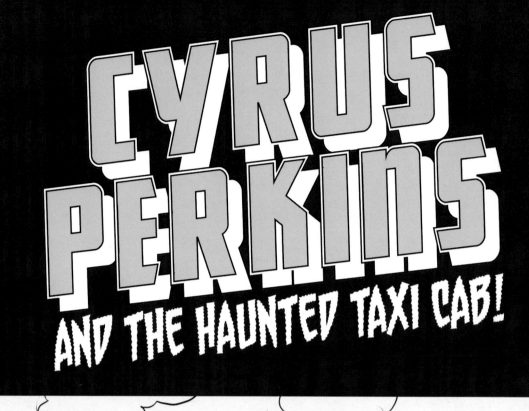

CYRUS PERKINS

AND THE HAUNTED TAXI CAB!

DAVE DWONCH
STORY/LETTERS/COLORS

ANNA LENCIONI
ART/TONES

BRYAN SEATON: PUBLISHER   KEVIN FREEMAN: PRESIDENT
DAVE DWONCH: CREATIVE DIRECTOR   SHAWN GABBORIN: EDITOR IN CHIEF
JAMAL IGLE: VICE-PRESIDENT OF MARKETING
VITO DELSANTE: DIRECTOR OF MARKETING
JIM DIETZ: SOCIAL MEDIA DIRECTOR
CHAD CICCONI: WAS A PREP SCHOOL DROPOUT

"HE WAS ALWAYS PLAYING PRANKS ON PEOPLE. A REAL TRICKSTER."

"HE FELL INTO SOME BAD HABITS AFTER HIS DAD DIED. STARTED SMOKING A LITTLE, MISSING CLASSES, BUT IT NEVER EFFECTED WHO HE WAS ON THE *INSIDE*."

"HE WAS A GOOD FRIEND."

SAMUEL.

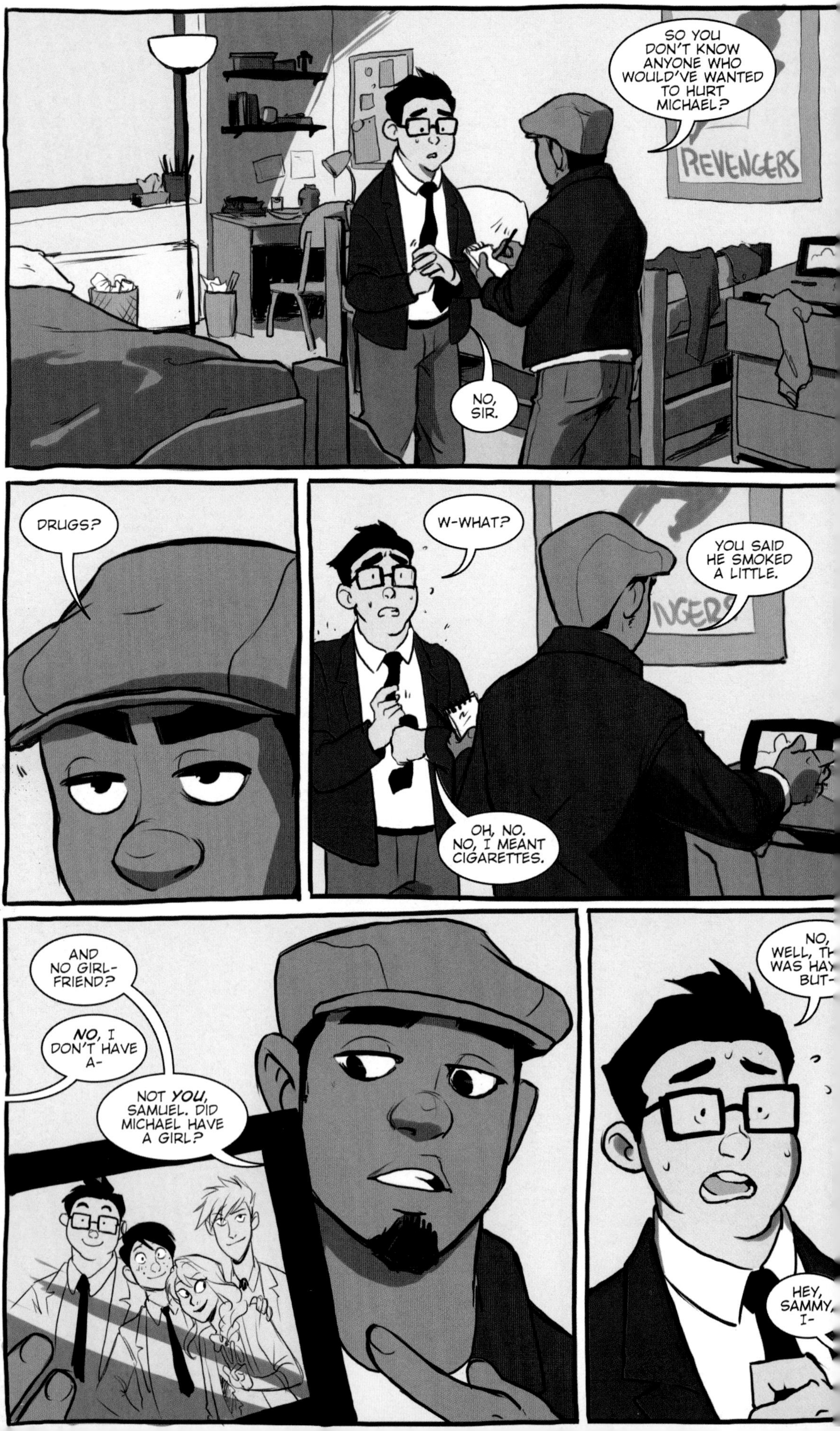

REVENGERS
SO YOU DON'T KNOW ANYONE WHO WOULD'VE WANTED TO HURT MICHAEL?
NO, SIR.
DRUGS?
W-WHAT?
YOU SAID HE SMOKED A LITTLE.
OH, NO. NO, I MEANT CIGARETTES.
AND NO GIRL-FRIEND?
NO, I DON'T HAVE A-
NOT YOU, SAMUEL. DID MICHAEL HAVE A GIRL?
NO, WELL, TH WAS HAY BUT-
HEY, SAMMY, I-

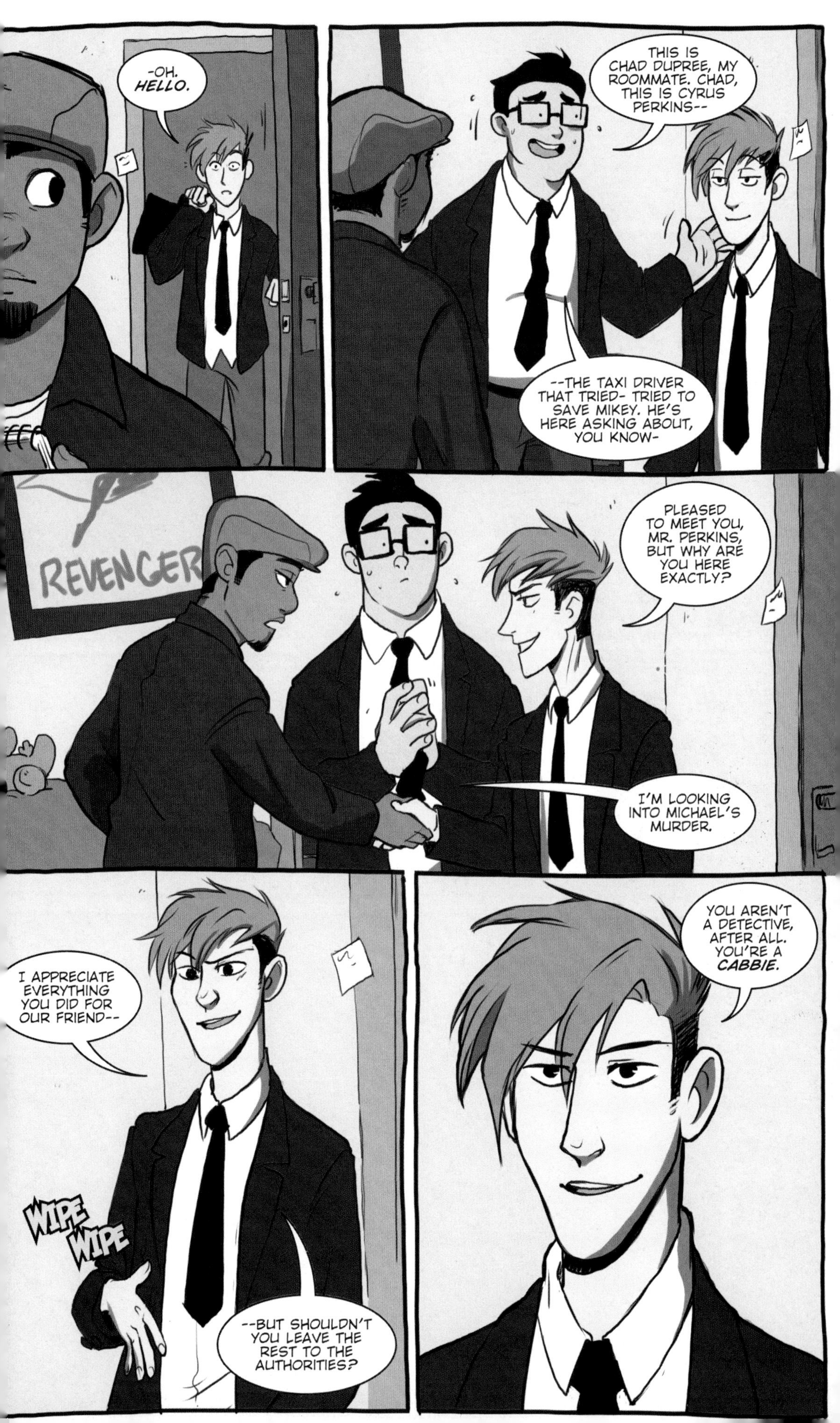

-OH. *HELLO.*
THIS IS CHAD DUPREE, MY ROOMMATE. CHAD, THIS IS CYRUS PERKINS--
--THE TAXI DRIVER THAT TRIED- TRIED TO SAVE MIKEY. HE'S HERE ASKING ABOUT, YOU KNOW-
REVENGER
PLEASED TO MEET YOU, MR. PERKINS, BUT WHY ARE YOU HERE EXACTLY?
I'M LOOKING INTO MICHAEL'S MURDER.
I APPRECIATE EVERYTHING YOU DID FOR OUR FRIEND--
WIPE WIPE
--BUT SHOULDN'T YOU LEAVE THE REST TO THE AUTHORITIES?
YOU AREN'T A DETECTIVE, AFTER ALL. YOU'RE A *CABBIE*.

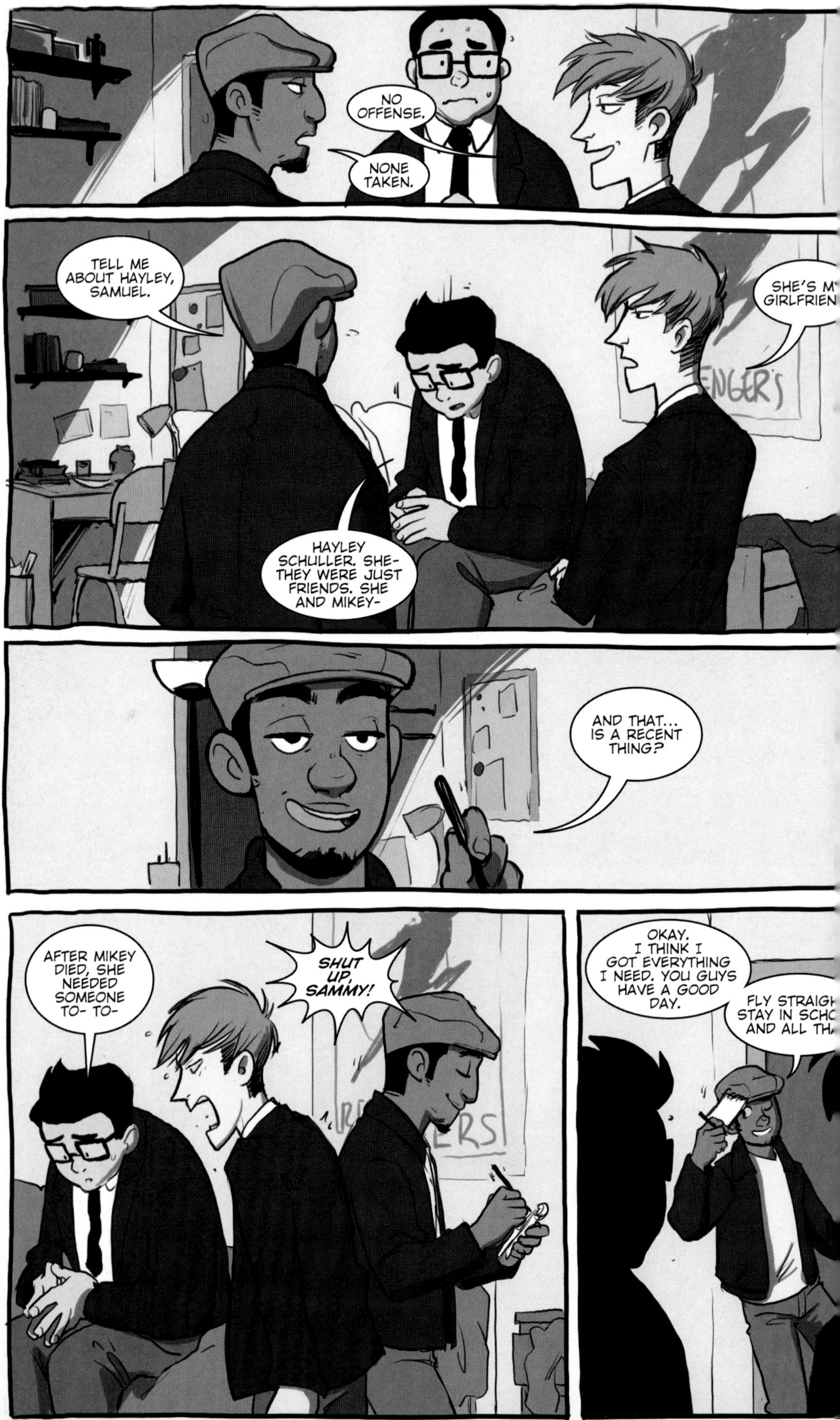
NO OFFENSE.
NONE TAKEN.
TELL ME ABOUT HAYLEY, SAMUEL.
SHE'S M GIRLFRIEN
HAYLEY SCHULLER. SHE- THEY WERE JUST FRIENDS. SHE AND MIKEY-
AND THAT... IS A RECENT THING?
AFTER MIKEY DIED, SHE NEEDED SOMEONE TO- TO-
SHUT UP, SAMMY!
OKAY. I THINK I GOT EVERYTHING I NEED. YOU GUYS HAVE A GOOD DAY.
FLY STRAIG STAY IN SCH AND ALL TH

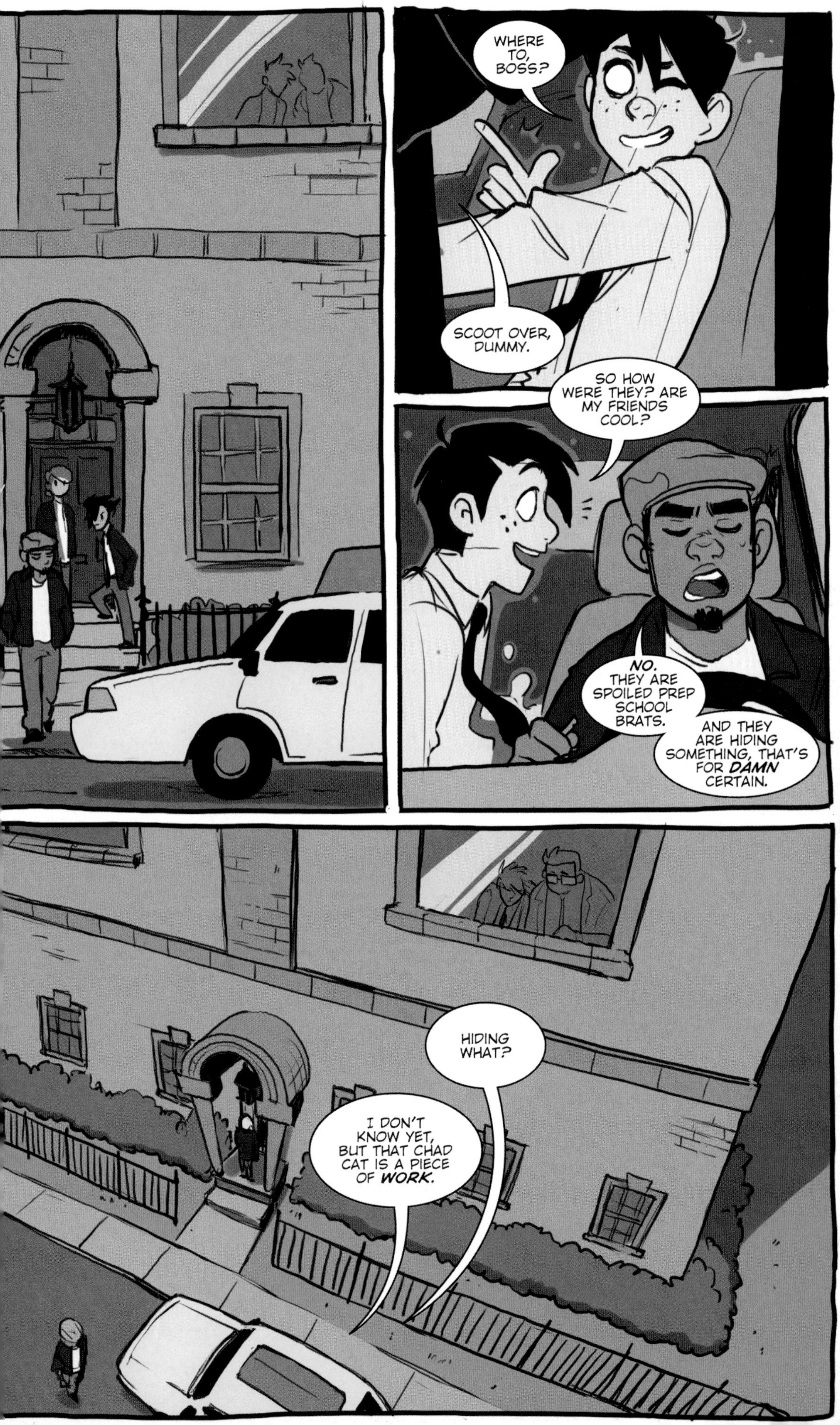

WHERE TO, BOSS?
SCOOT OVER, DUMMY.
SO HOW WERE THEY? ARE MY FRIENDS COOL?
NO. THEY ARE SPOILED PREP SCHOOL BRATS.
AND THEY ARE HIDING SOMETHING, THAT'S FOR DAMN CERTAIN.
HIDING WHAT?
I DON'T KNOW YET, BUT THAT CHAD CAT IS A PIECE OF WORK.

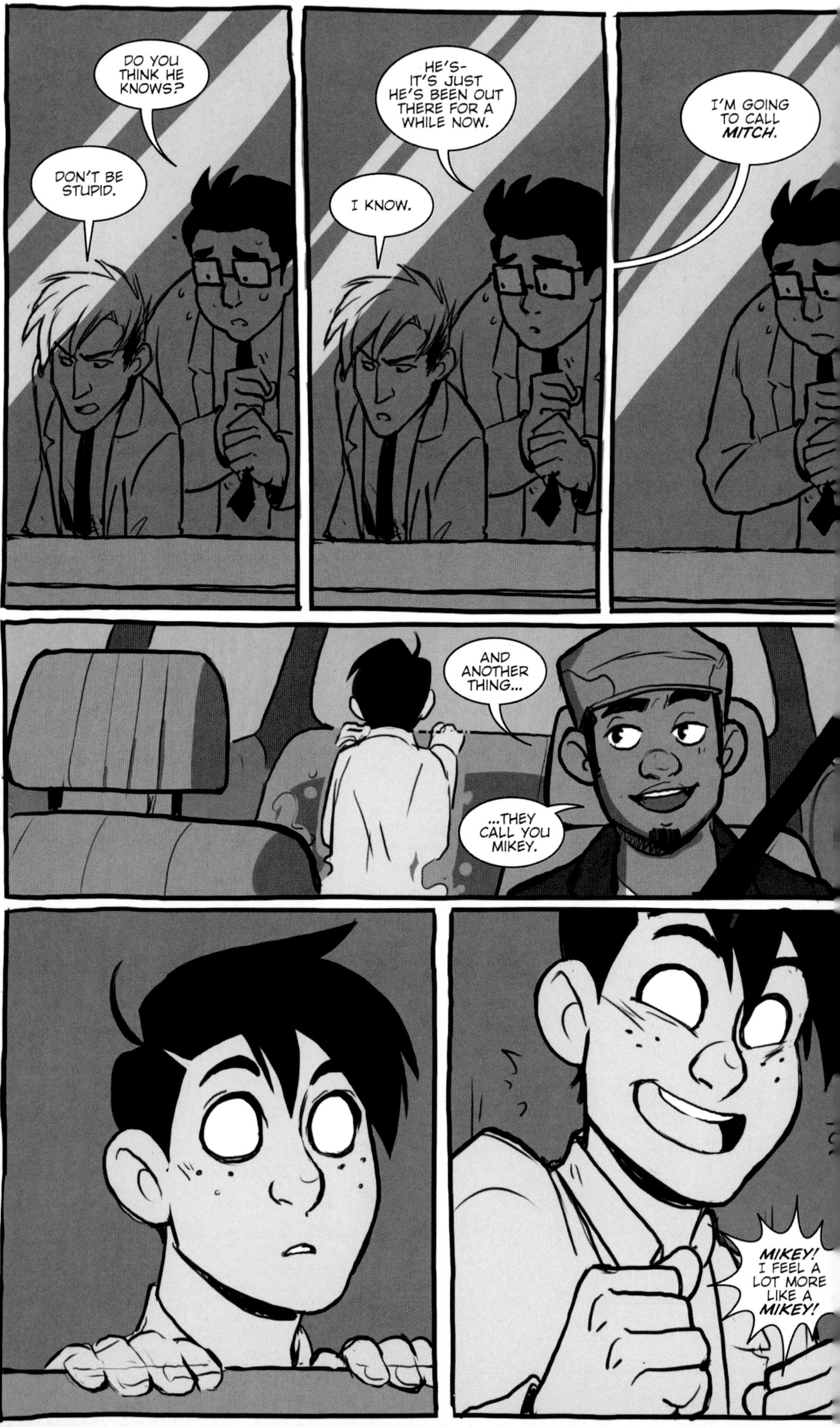
DO YOU THINK HE KNOWS?
DON'T BE STUPID.
HE'S- IT'S JUST HE'S BEEN OUT THERE FOR A WHILE NOW.
I KNOW.
I'M GOING TO CALL MITCH.
AND ANOTHER THING...
...THEY CALL YOU MIKEY.
MIKEY! I FEEL A LOT MORE LIKE A MIKEY!

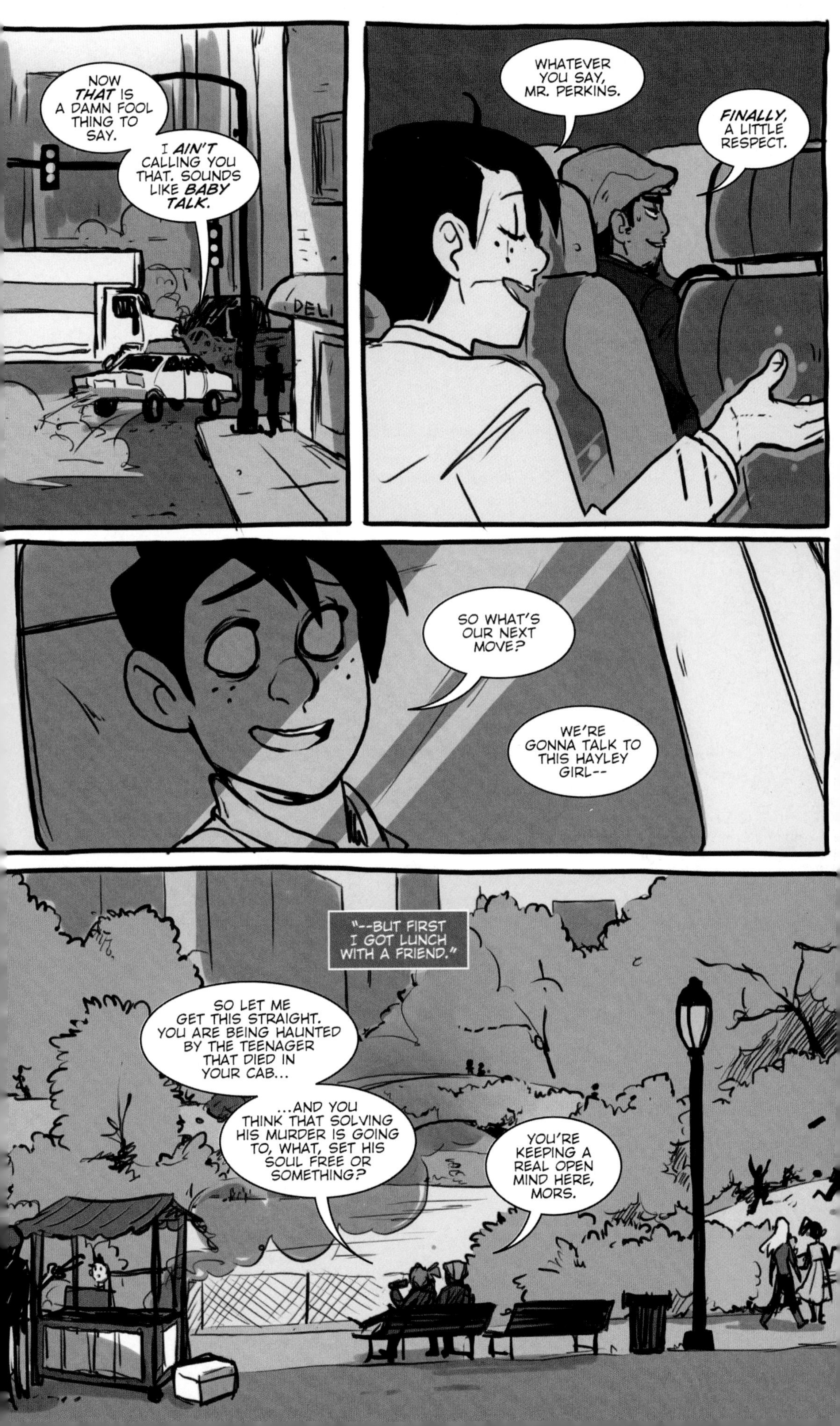
NOW THAT IS A DAMN FOOL THING TO SAY.
I AIN'T CALLING YOU THAT. SOUNDS LIKE BABY TALK.
DELI
WHATEVER YOU SAY, MR. PERKINS.
FINALLY, A LITTLE RESPECT.
SO WHAT'S OUR NEXT MOVE?
WE'RE GONNA TALK TO THIS HAYLEY GIRL--
"--BUT FIRST I GOT LUNCH WITH A FRIEND."
SO LET ME GET THIS STRAIGHT. YOU ARE BEING HAUNTED BY THE TEENAGER THAT DIED IN YOUR CAB...
...AND YOU THINK THAT SOLVING HIS MURDER IS GOING TO, WHAT, SET HIS SOUL FREE OR SOMETHING?
YOU'RE KEEPING A REAL OPEN MIND HERE, MORS.

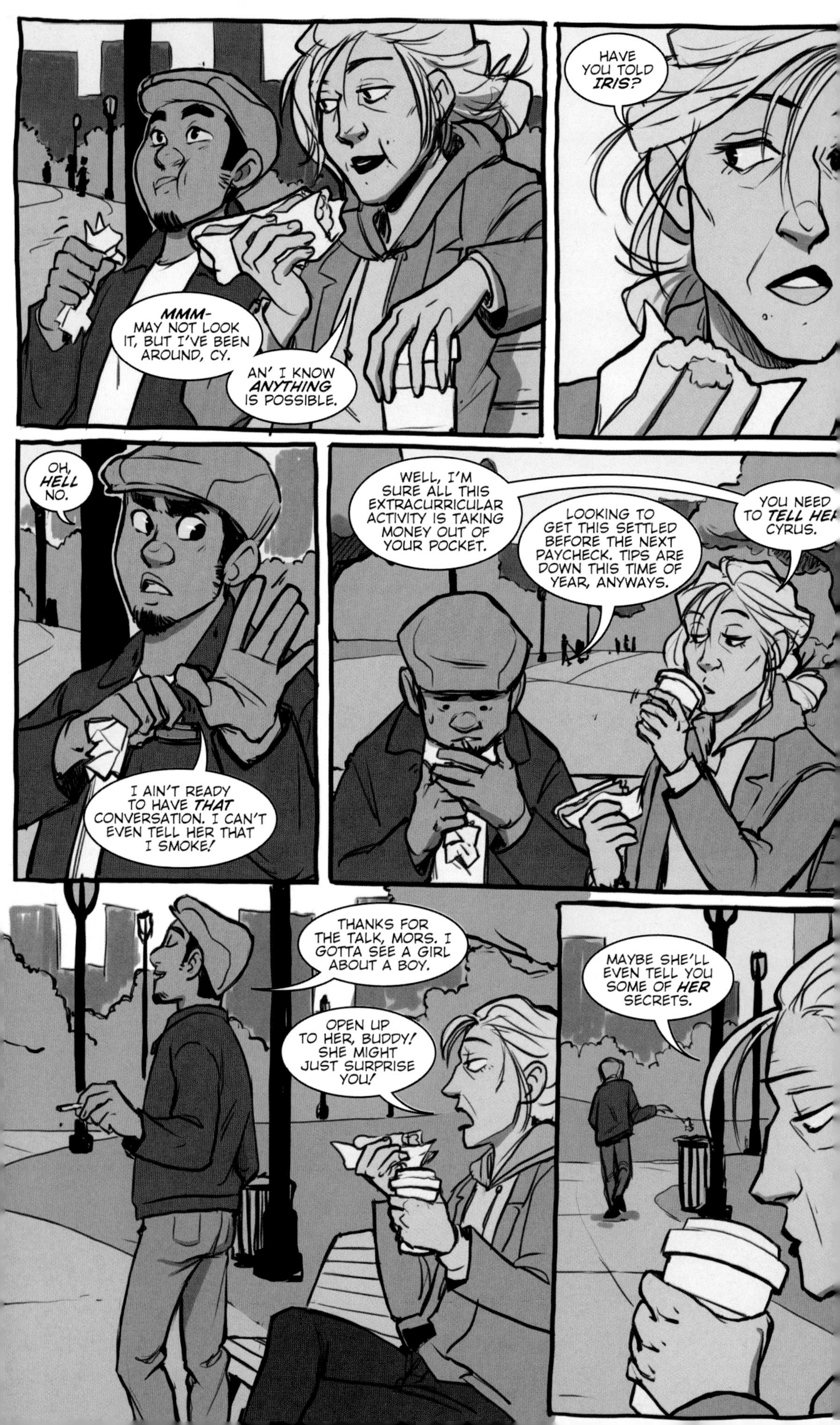
MMM-
MAY NOT LOOK IT, BUT I'VE BEEN AROUND, CY.
AN' I KNOW ANYTHING IS POSSIBLE.
HAVE YOU TOLD IRIS?
OH, HELL NO.
I AIN'T READY TO HAVE THAT CONVERSATION. I CAN'T EVEN TELL HER THAT I SMOKE!
WELL, I'M SURE ALL THIS EXTRACURRICULAR ACTIVITY IS TAKING MONEY OUT OF YOUR POCKET.
LOOKING TO GET THIS SETTLED BEFORE THE NEXT PAYCHECK. TIPS ARE DOWN THIS TIME OF YEAR, ANYWAYS.
YOU NEED TO TELL HE
CYRUS.
THANKS FOR THE TALK, MORS. I GOTTA SEE A GIRL ABOUT A BOY.
OPEN UP TO HER, BUDDY! SHE MIGHT JUST SURPRISE YOU!
MAYBE SHE'LL EVEN TELL YOU SOME OF HER SECRETS.

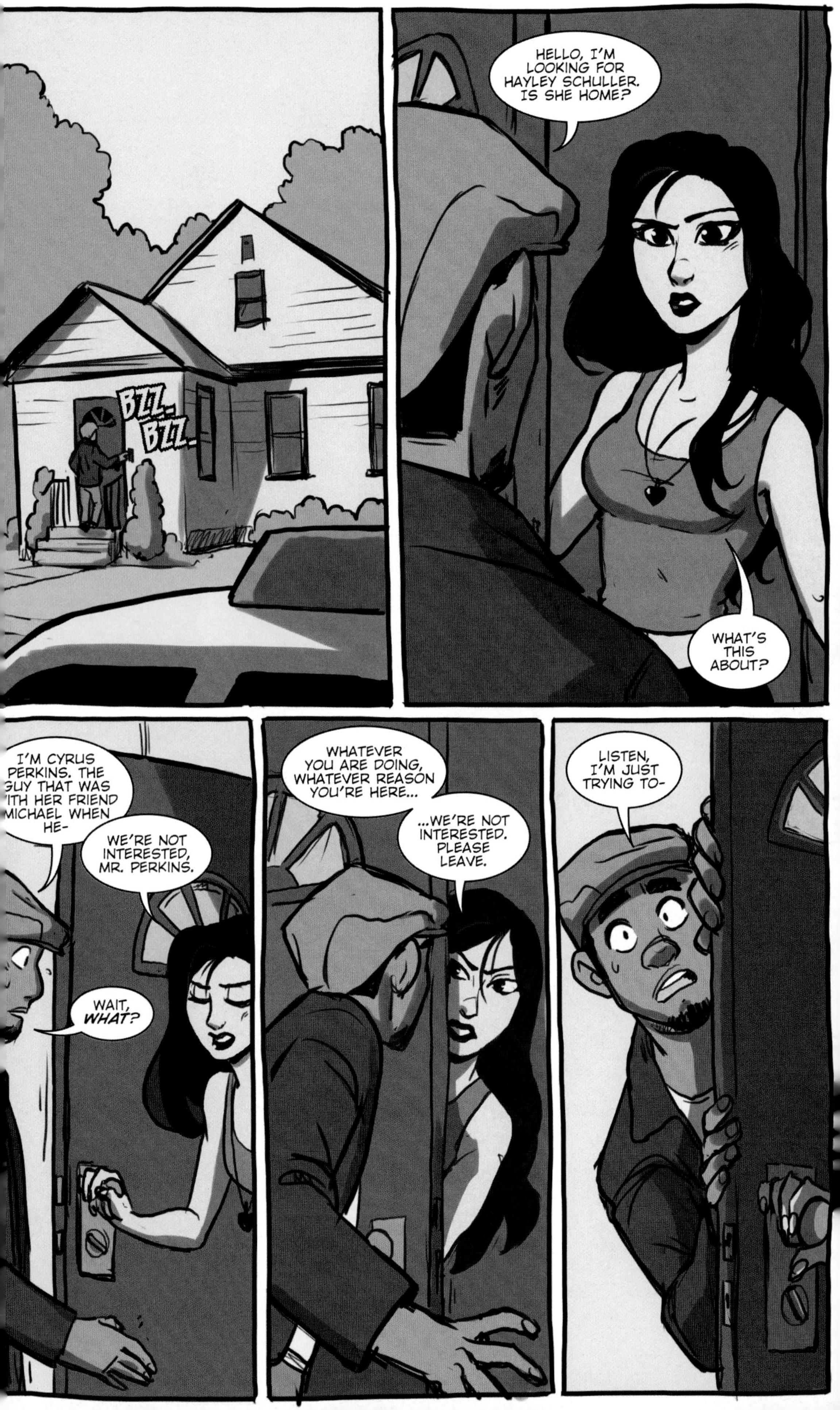
BZZ-BZZ-
HELLO, I'M LOOKING FOR HAYLEY SCHULLER. IS SHE HOME?
WHAT'S THIS ABOUT?
I'M CYRUS PERKINS. THE GUY THAT WAS WITH HER FRIEND MICHAEL WHEN HE-
WE'RE NOT INTERESTED, MR. PERKINS.
WAIT, *WHAT*?
WHATEVER YOU ARE DOING, WHATEVER REASON YOU'RE HERE...
...WE'RE NOT INTERESTED. PLEASE LEAVE.
LISTEN, I'M JUST TRYING TO-

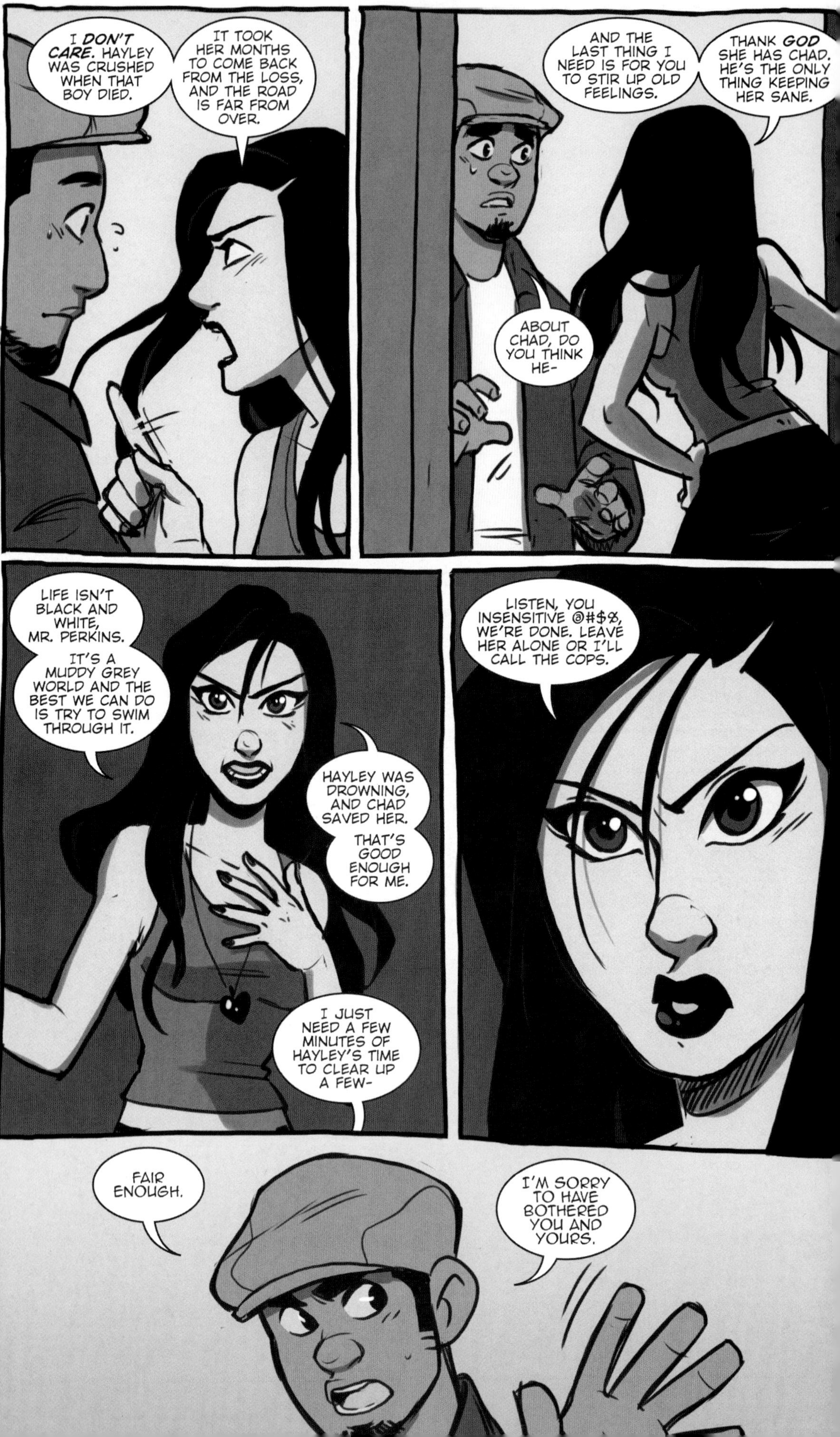
I DON'T CARE. HAYLEY WAS CRUSHED WHEN THAT BOY DIED.
IT TOOK HER MONTHS TO COME BACK FROM THE LOSS, AND THE ROAD IS FAR FROM OVER.
AND THE LAST THING I NEED IS FOR YOU TO STIR UP OLD FEELINGS.
THANK GOD SHE HAS CHAD. HE'S THE ONLY THING KEEPING HER SANE.
ABOUT CHAD, DO YOU THINK HE-
LIFE ISN'T BLACK AND WHITE, MR. PERKINS.
IT'S A MUDDY GREY WORLD AND THE BEST WE CAN DO IS TRY TO SWIM THROUGH IT.
HAYLEY WAS DROWNING, AND CHAD SAVED HER.
THAT'S GOOD ENOUGH FOR ME.
I JUST NEED A FEW MINUTES OF HAYLEY'S TIME TO CLEAR UP A FEW-
LISTEN, YOU INSENSITIVE @#$%, WE'RE DONE. LEAVE HER ALONE OR I'LL CALL THE COPS.
FAIR ENOUGH.
I'M SORRY TO HAVE BOTHERED YOU AND YOURS.

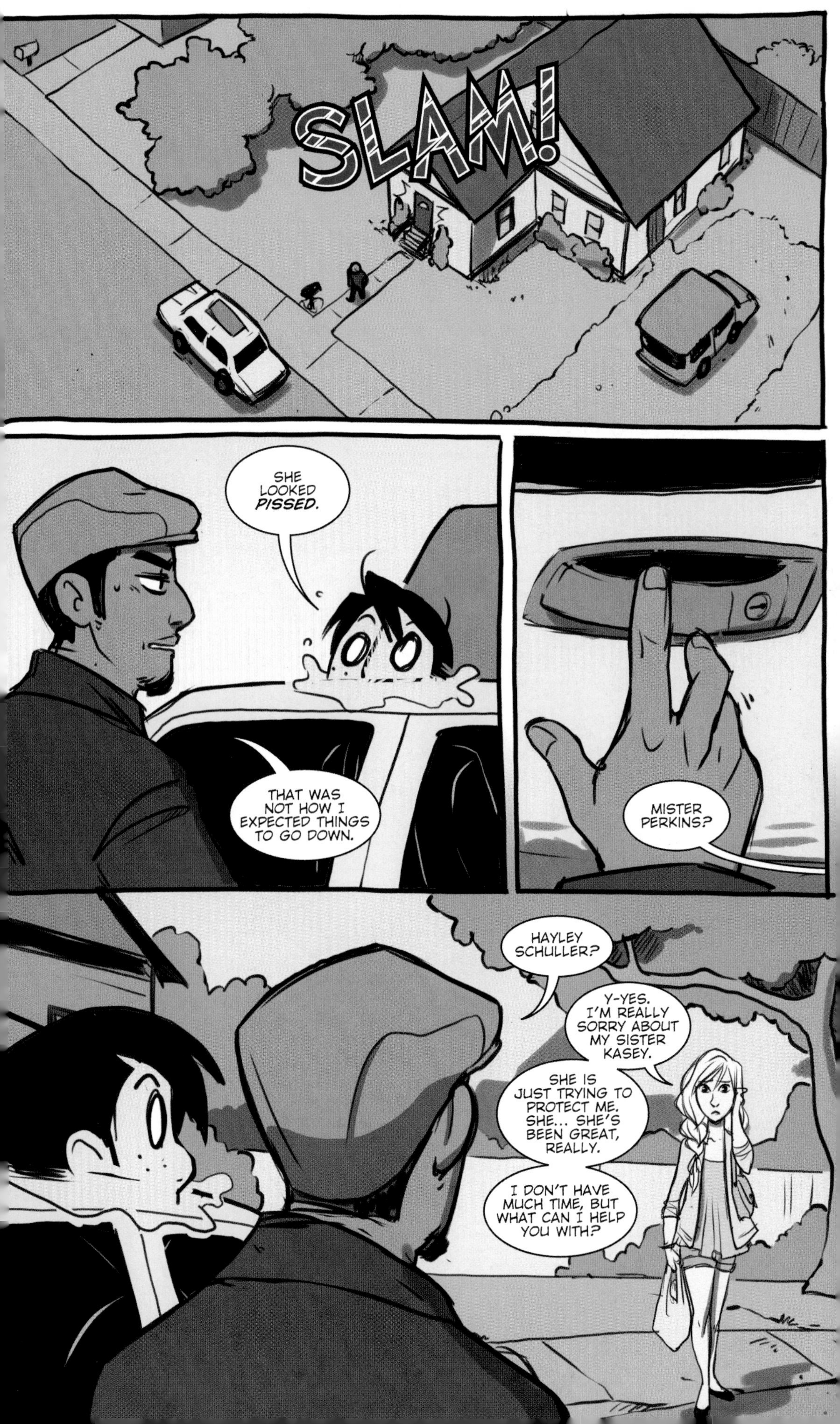
SLAM!
SHE LOOKED PISSED.
THAT WAS NOT HOW I EXPECTED THINGS TO GO DOWN.
MISTER PERKINS?
HAYLEY SCHULLER?
Y-YES. I'M REALLY SORRY ABOUT MY SISTER KASEY.
SHE IS JUST TRYING TO PROTECT ME. SHE... SHE'S BEEN GREAT, REALLY.
I DON'T HAVE MUCH TIME, BUT WHAT CAN I HELP YOU WITH?

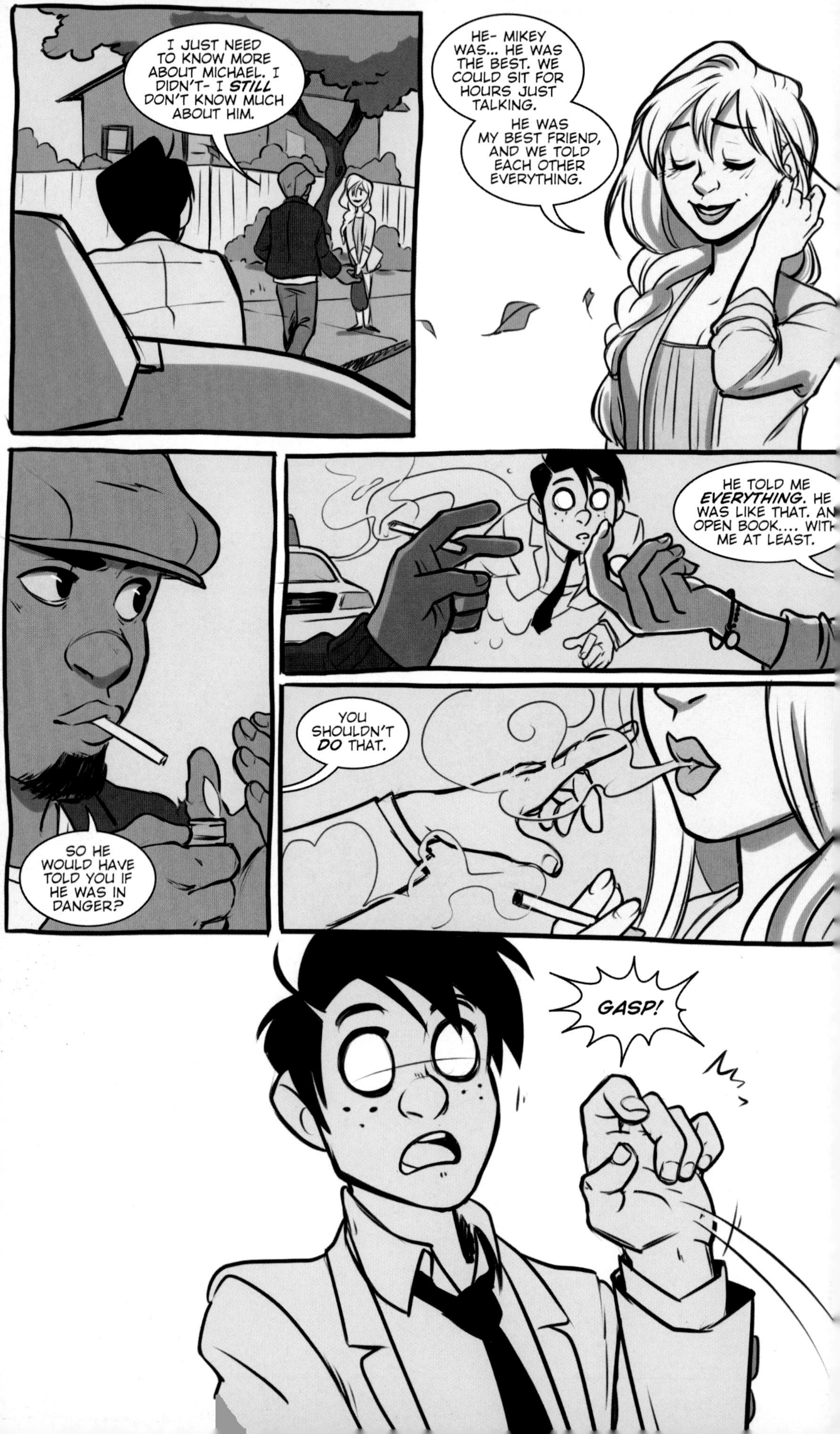
I JUST NEED TO KNOW MORE ABOUT MICHAEL. I DIDN'T- I *STILL* DON'T KNOW MUCH ABOUT HIM.
HE- MIKEY WAS... HE WAS THE BEST. WE COULD SIT FOR HOURS JUST TALKING.
HE WAS MY BEST FRIEND, AND WE TOLD EACH OTHER EVERYTHING.
HE TOLD ME *EVERYTHING*. HE WAS LIKE THAT. AN OPEN BOOK.... WITH ME AT LEAST.
SO HE WOULD HAVE TOLD YOU IF HE WAS IN DANGER?
YOU SHOULDN'T *DO* THAT.
GASP!

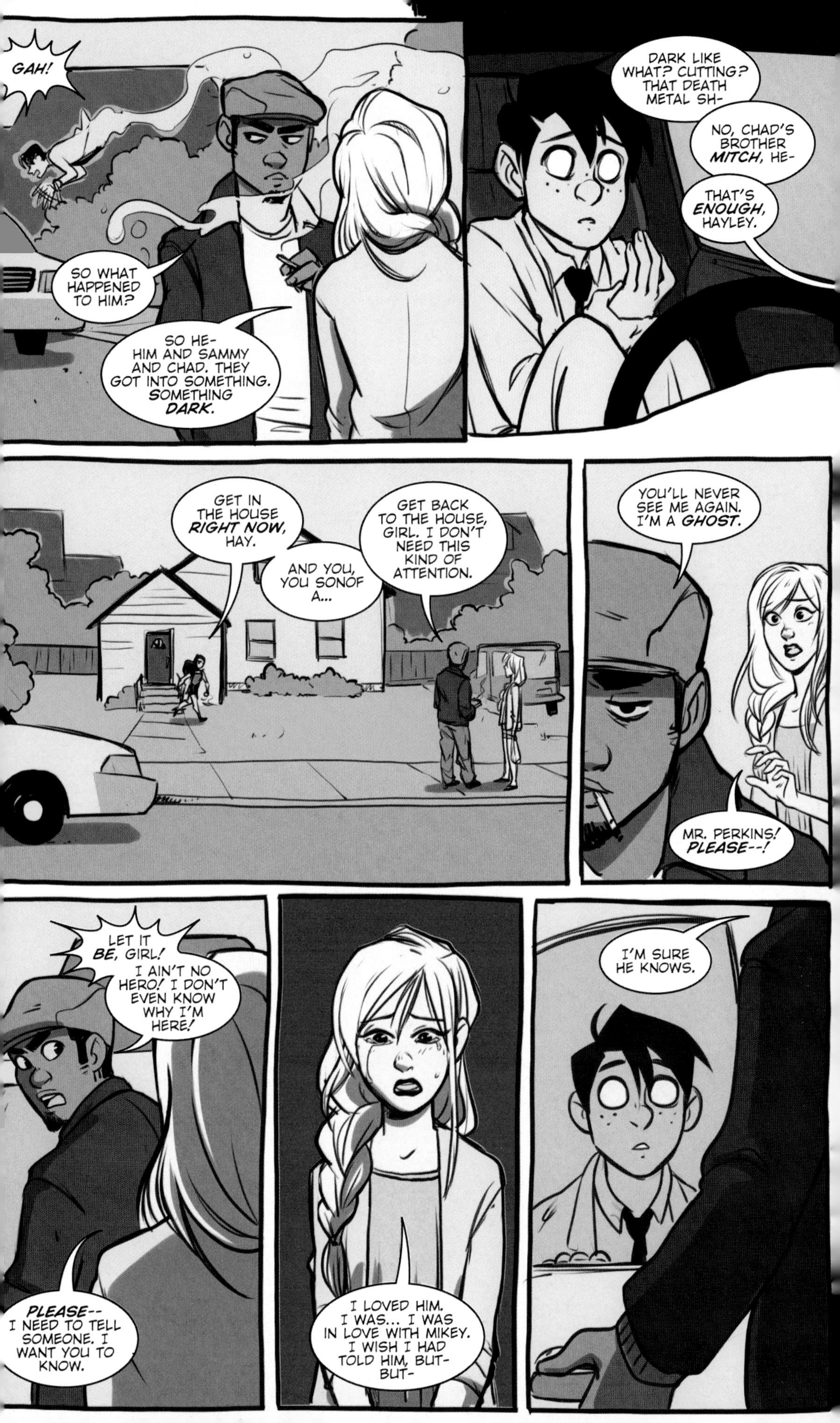
GAH!
SO WHAT HAPPENED TO HIM?
SO HE- HIM AND SAMMY AND CHAD. THEY GOT INTO SOMETHING. SOMETHING DARK.
DARK LIKE WHAT? CUTTING? THAT DEATH METAL SH-
NO, CHAD'S BROTHER MITCH, HE-
THAT'S ENOUGH, HAYLEY.
GET IN THE HOUSE RIGHT NOW, HAY.
AND YOU, YOU SONOF A...
GET BACK TO THE HOUSE, GIRL. I DON'T NEED THIS KIND OF ATTENTION.
YOU'LL NEVER SEE ME AGAIN. I'M A GHOST.
MR. PERKINS! PLEASE--!
LET IT BE, GIRL!
I AIN'T NO HERO! I DON'T EVEN KNOW WHY I'M HERE!
PLEASE-- I NEED TO TELL SOMEONE. I WANT YOU TO KNOW.
I LOVED HIM. I WAS... I WAS IN LOVE WITH MIKEY. I WISH I HAD TOLD HIM, BUT- BUT-
I'M SURE HE KNOWS.

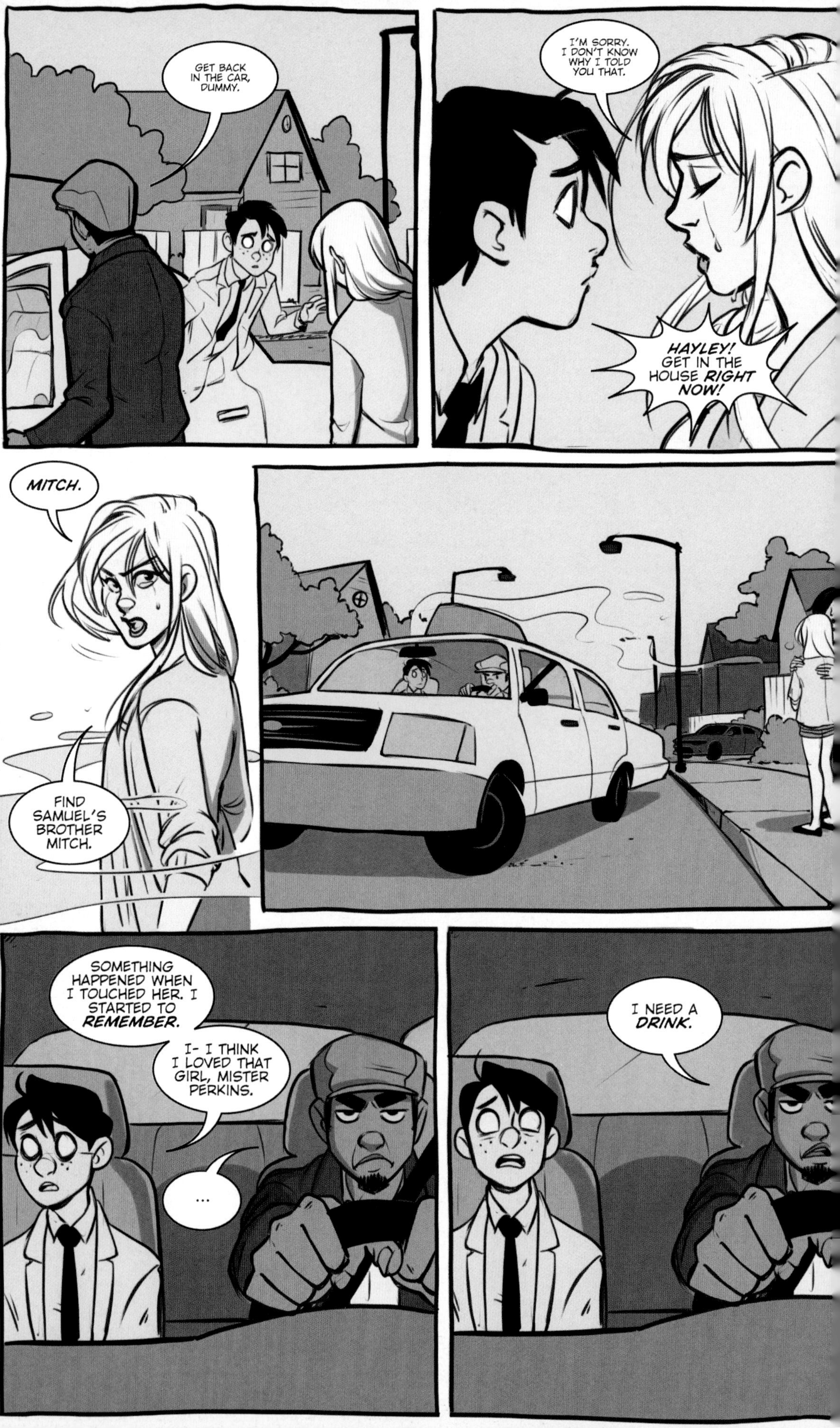
GET BACK IN THE CAR, DUMMY.
I'M SORRY. I DON'T KNOW WHY I TOLD YOU THAT.
HAYLEY! GET IN THE HOUSE RIGHT NOW!
MITCH.
FIND SAMUEL'S BROTHER MITCH.
SOMETHING HAPPENED WHEN I TOUCHED HER. I STARTED TO REMEMBER.
I- I THINK I LOVED THAT GIRL, MISTER PERKINS.
...
I NEED A DRINK.

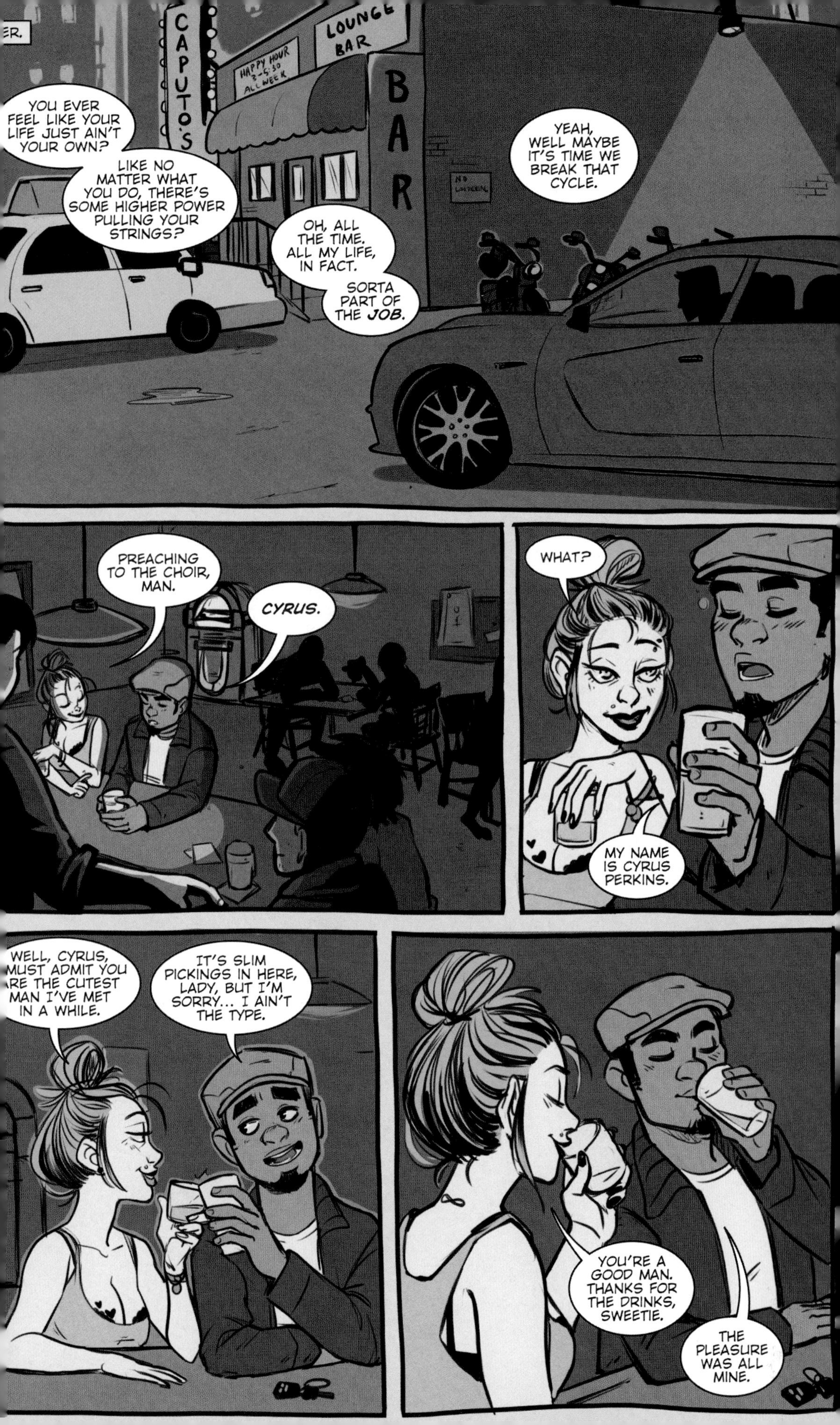
ER.
CAPUTO'S
LOUNGE BAR
HAPPY HOUR 3-5:30 ALL WEEK
BAR
YOU EVER FEEL LIKE YOUR LIFE JUST AIN'T YOUR OWN?
LIKE NO MATTER WHAT YOU DO, THERE'S SOME HIGHER POWER PULLING YOUR STRINGS?
OH, ALL THE TIME. ALL MY LIFE, IN FACT.
SORTA PART OF THE *JOB*.
YEAH, WELL MAYBE IT'S TIME WE BREAK THAT CYCLE.
PREACHING TO THE CHOIR, MAN.
CYRUS.
WHAT?
MY NAME IS CYRUS PERKINS.
WELL, CYRUS, MUST ADMIT YOU ARE THE CUTEST MAN I'VE MET IN A WHILE.
IT'S SLIM PICKINGS IN HERE, LADY, BUT I'M SORRY... I AIN'T THE TYPE.
YOU'RE A GOOD MAN. THANKS FOR THE DRINKS, SWEETIE.
THE PLEASURE WAS ALL MINE.

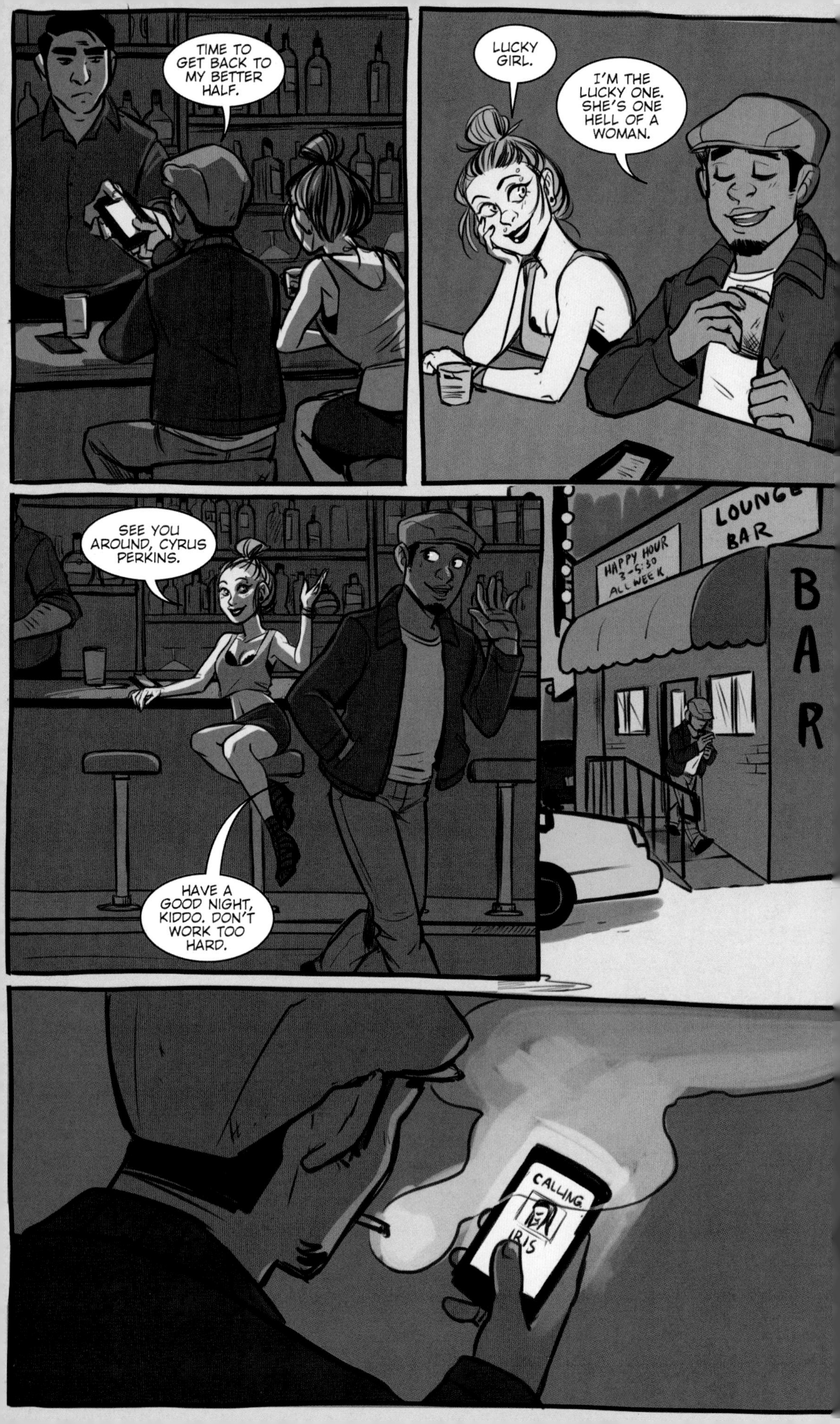
TIME TO GET BACK TO MY BETTER HALF.
LUCKY GIRL.
I'M THE LUCKY ONE. SHE'S ONE HELL OF A WOMAN.
SEE YOU AROUND, CYRUS PERKINS.
HAVE A GOOD NIGHT, KIDDO. DON'T WORK TOO HARD.
LOUNGE BAR
HAPPY HOUR 3-5:30 ALL WEEK
BAR
CALLING
IRIS

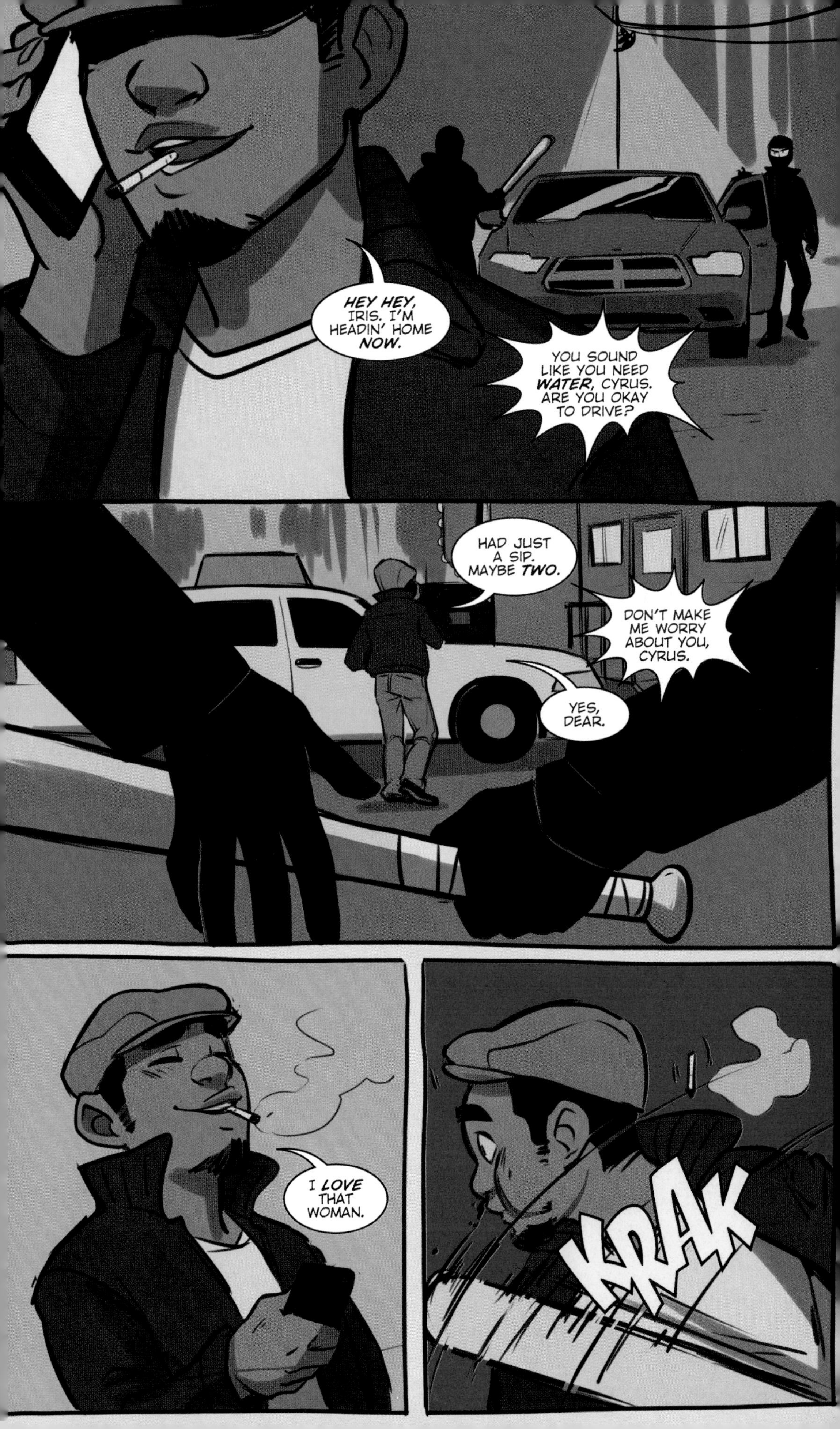
HEY HEY, IRIS. I'M HEADIN' HOME NOW.
YOU SOUND LIKE YOU NEED WATER, CYRUS. ARE YOU OKAY TO DRIVE?
HAD JUST A SIP. MAYBE TWO.
DON'T MAKE ME WORRY ABOUT YOU, CYRUS.
YES, DEAR.
I LOVE THAT WOMAN.
KRAK

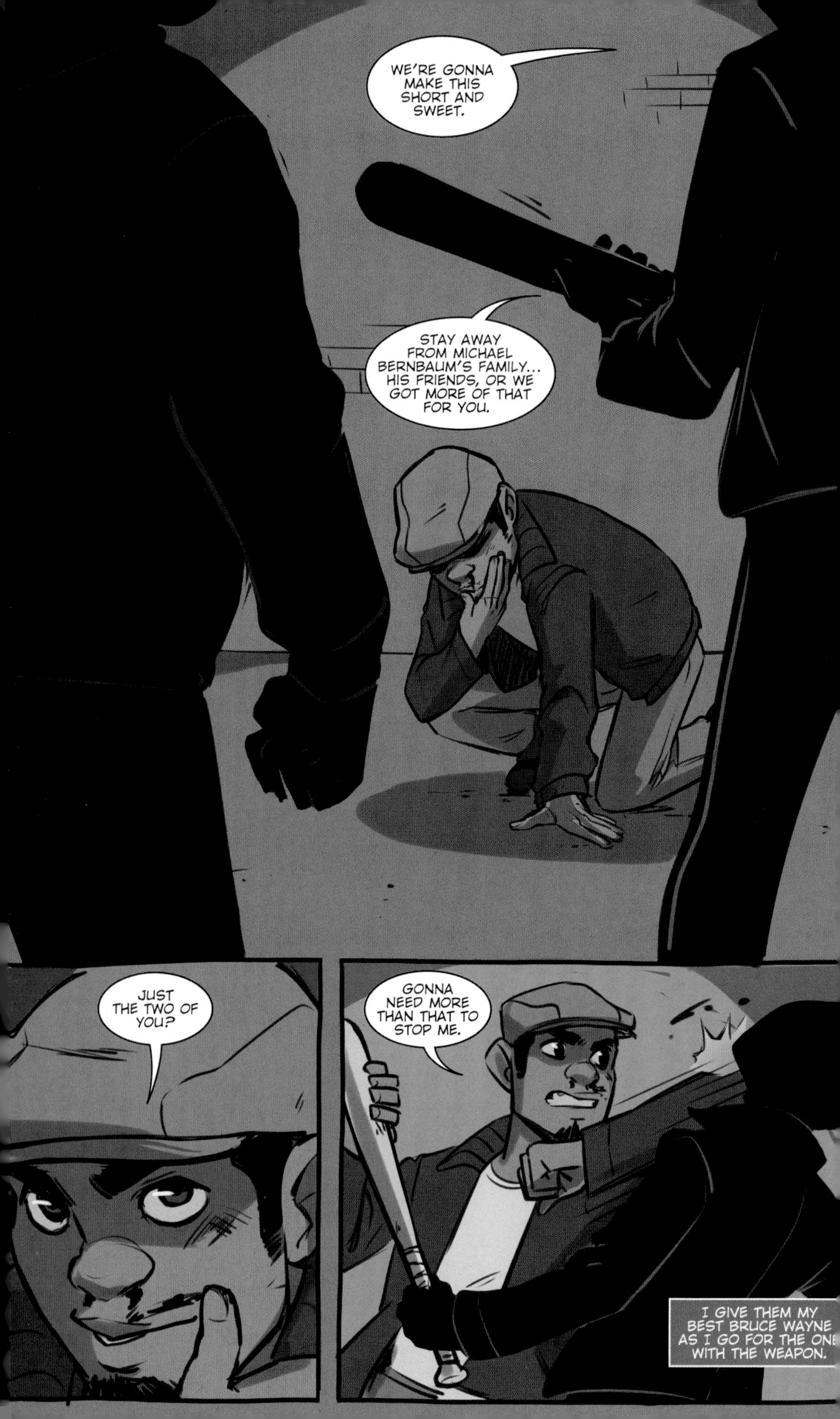
WE'RE GONNA MAKE THIS SHORT AND SWEET.
STAY AWAY FROM MICHAEL BERNBAUM'S FAMILY... HIS FRIENDS, OR WE GOT MORE OF THAT FOR YOU.
JUST THE TWO OF YOU?
GONNA NEED MORE THAN THAT TO STOP ME.
I GIVE THEM MY BEST BRUCE WAYNE AS I GO FOR THE ONE WITH THE WEAPON.

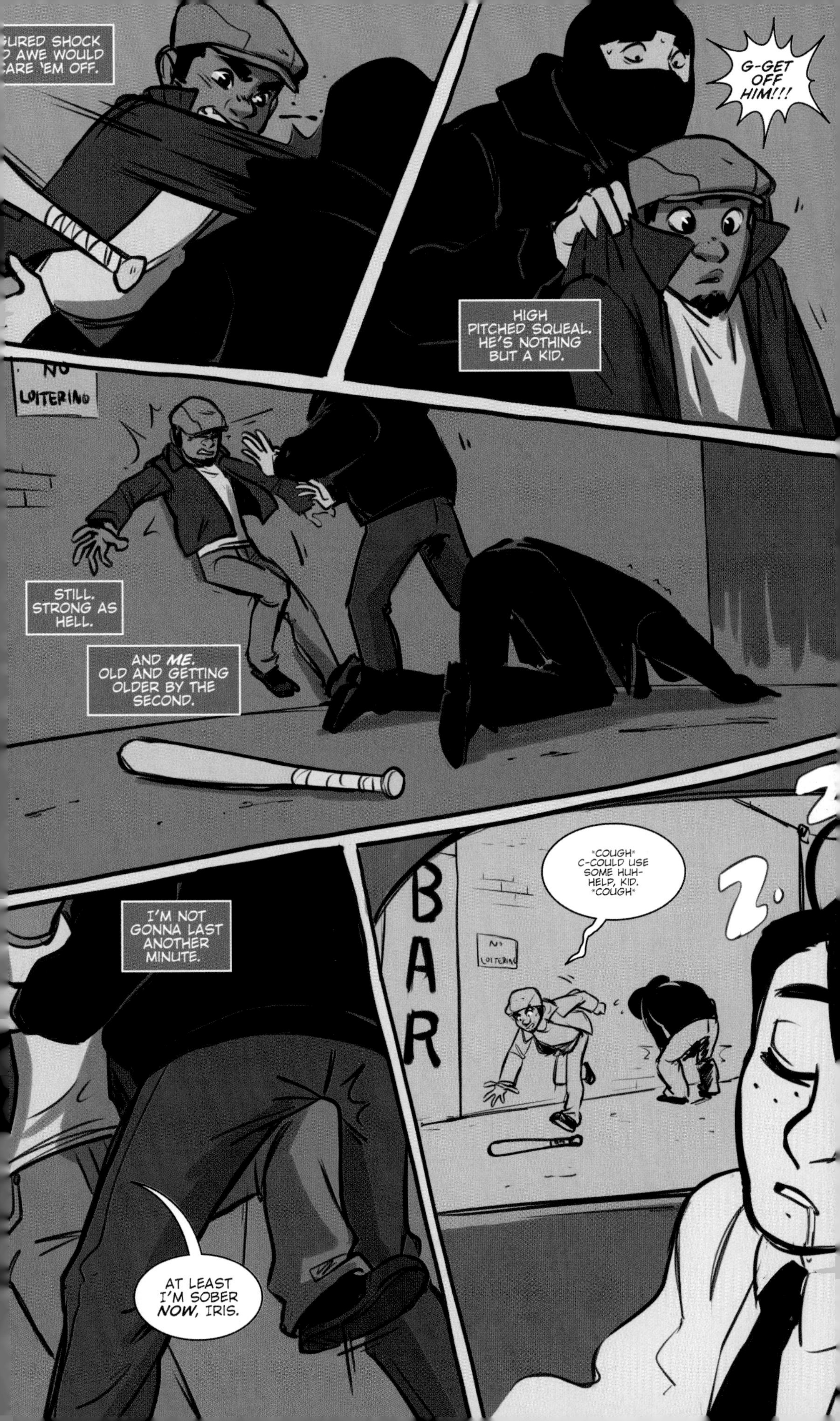

...GURED SHOCK
...D AWE WOULD
...CARE 'EM OFF.
G-GET OFF HIM!!!
HIGH PITCHED SQUEAL. HE'S NOTHING BUT A KID.
NO LOITERING
STILL. STRONG AS HELL.
AND *ME.* OLD AND GETTING OLDER BY THE SECOND.
I'M NOT GONNA LAST ANOTHER MINUTE.
BAR
NO LOITERING
COUGH C-COULD USE SOME HUH-HELP, KID. *COUGH*
AT LEAST I'M SOBER *NOW,* IRIS.

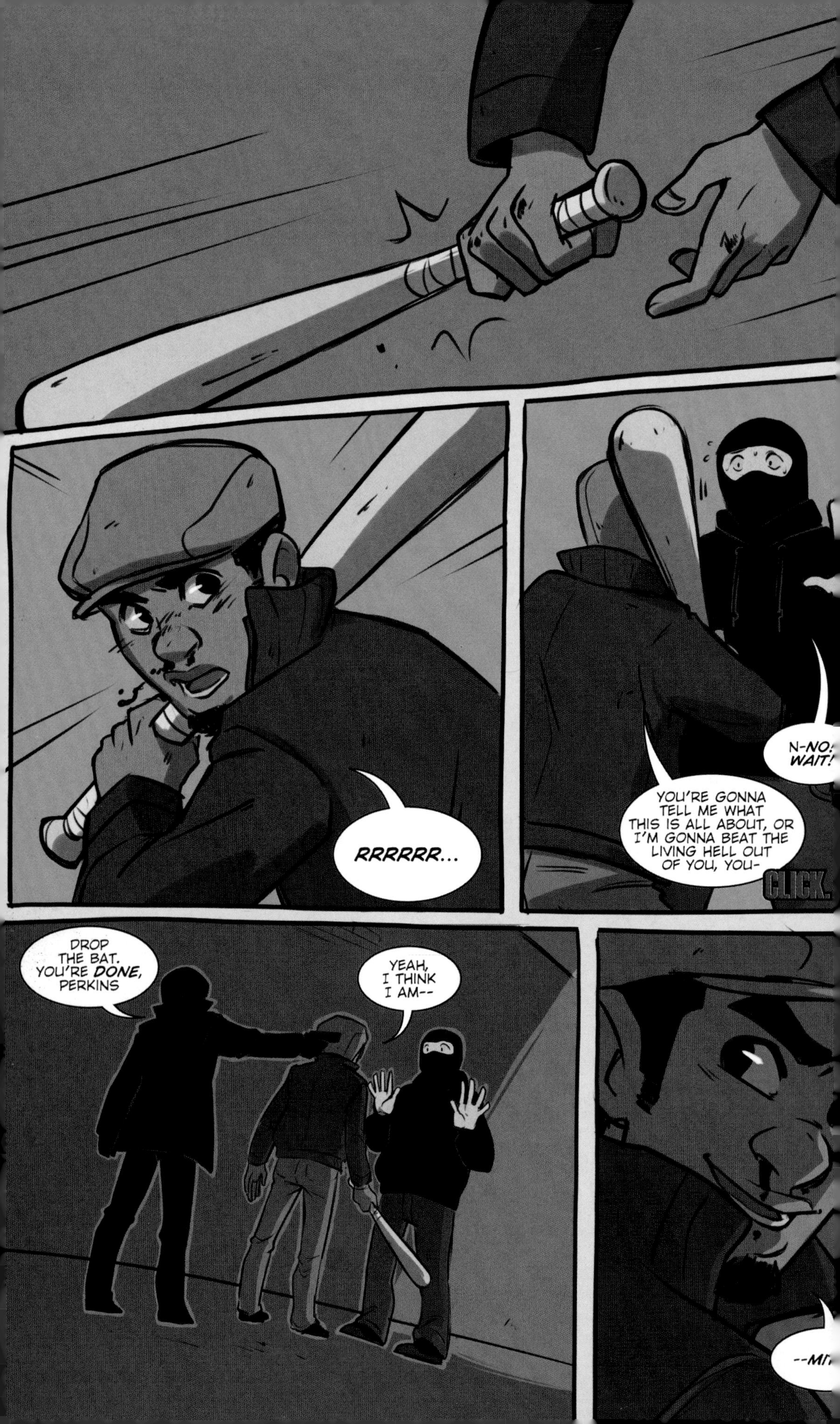

RRRRRR...
YOU'RE GONNA TELL ME WHAT THIS IS ALL ABOUT, OR I'M GONNA BEAT THE LIVING HELL OUT OF YOU, YOU-
N-NO! WAIT!
CLICK.
DROP THE BAT. YOU'RE DONE, PERKINS
YEAH, I THINK I AM--

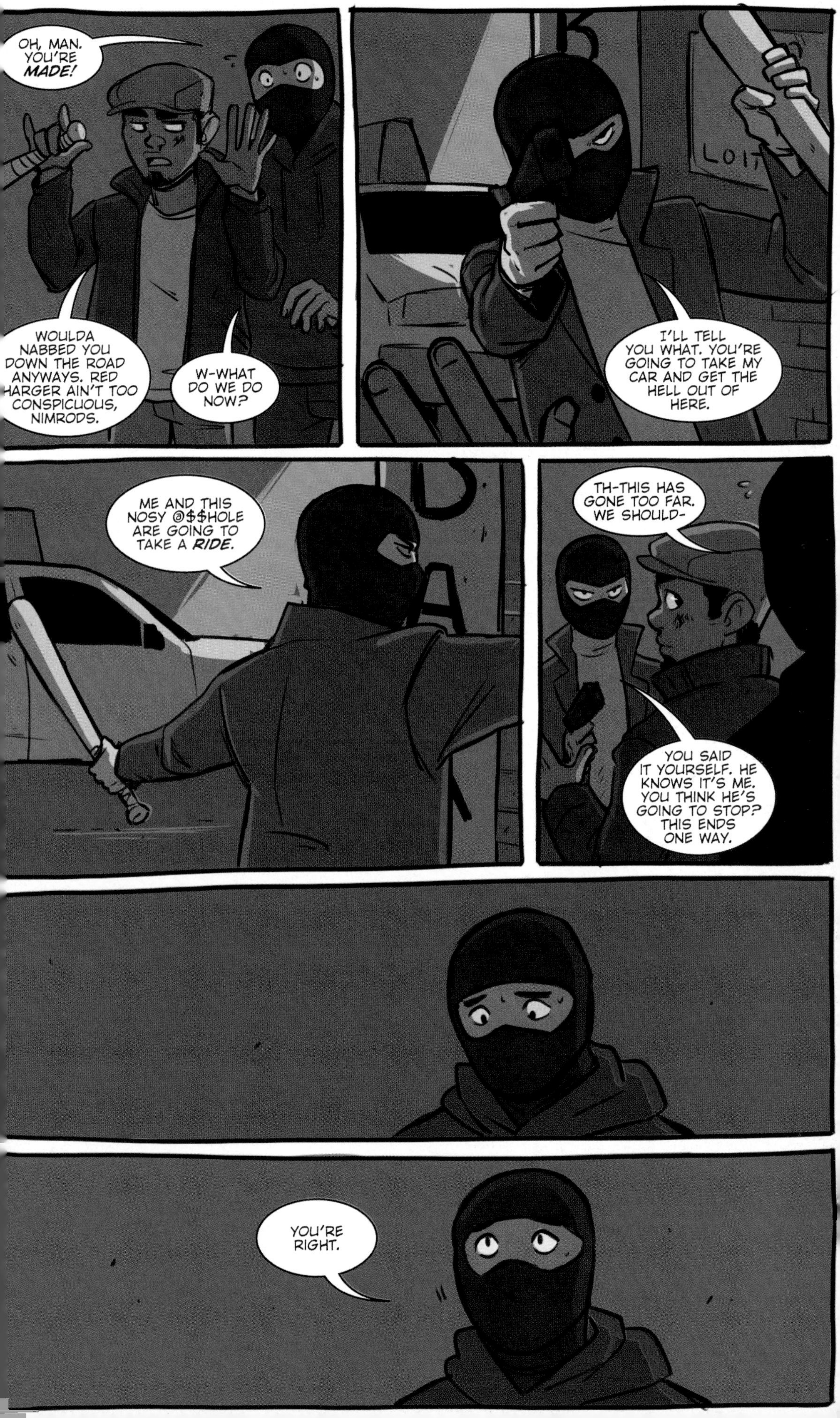
OH, MAN. YOU'RE *MADE!*
WOULDA NABBED YOU DOWN THE ROAD ANYWAYS. RED HARGER AIN'T TOO CONSPICUOUS, NIMRODS.
W-WHAT DO WE DO NOW?
I'LL TELL YOU WHAT. YOU'RE GOING TO TAKE MY CAR AND GET THE HELL OUT OF HERE.
ME AND THIS NOSY @$$HOLE ARE GOING TO TAKE A *RIDE.*
TH-THIS HAS GONE TOO FAR. WE SHOULD-
YOU SAID IT YOURSELF. HE KNOWS IT'S ME. YOU THINK HE'S GOING TO STOP? THIS ENDS ONE WAY.
YOU'RE RIGHT.

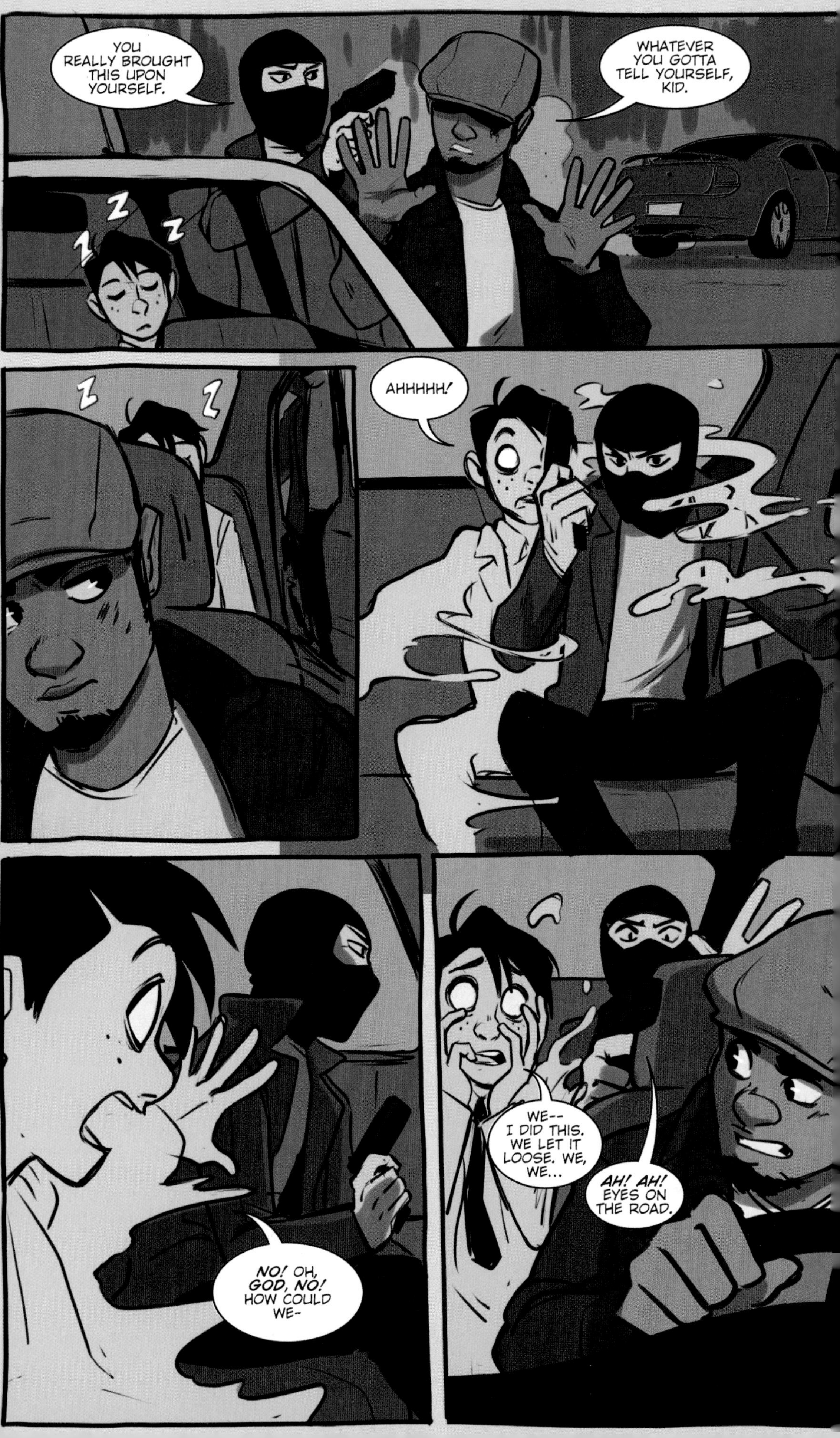
YOU REALLY BROUGHT THIS UPON YOURSELF.
WHATEVER YOU GOTTA TELL YOURSELF, KID.
Z Z Z
Z Z
AHHHHH!
NO! OH, GOD, NO! HOW COULD WE-
WE-- I DID THIS. WE LET IT LOOSE. WE, WE...
AH! AH! EYES ON THE ROAD.

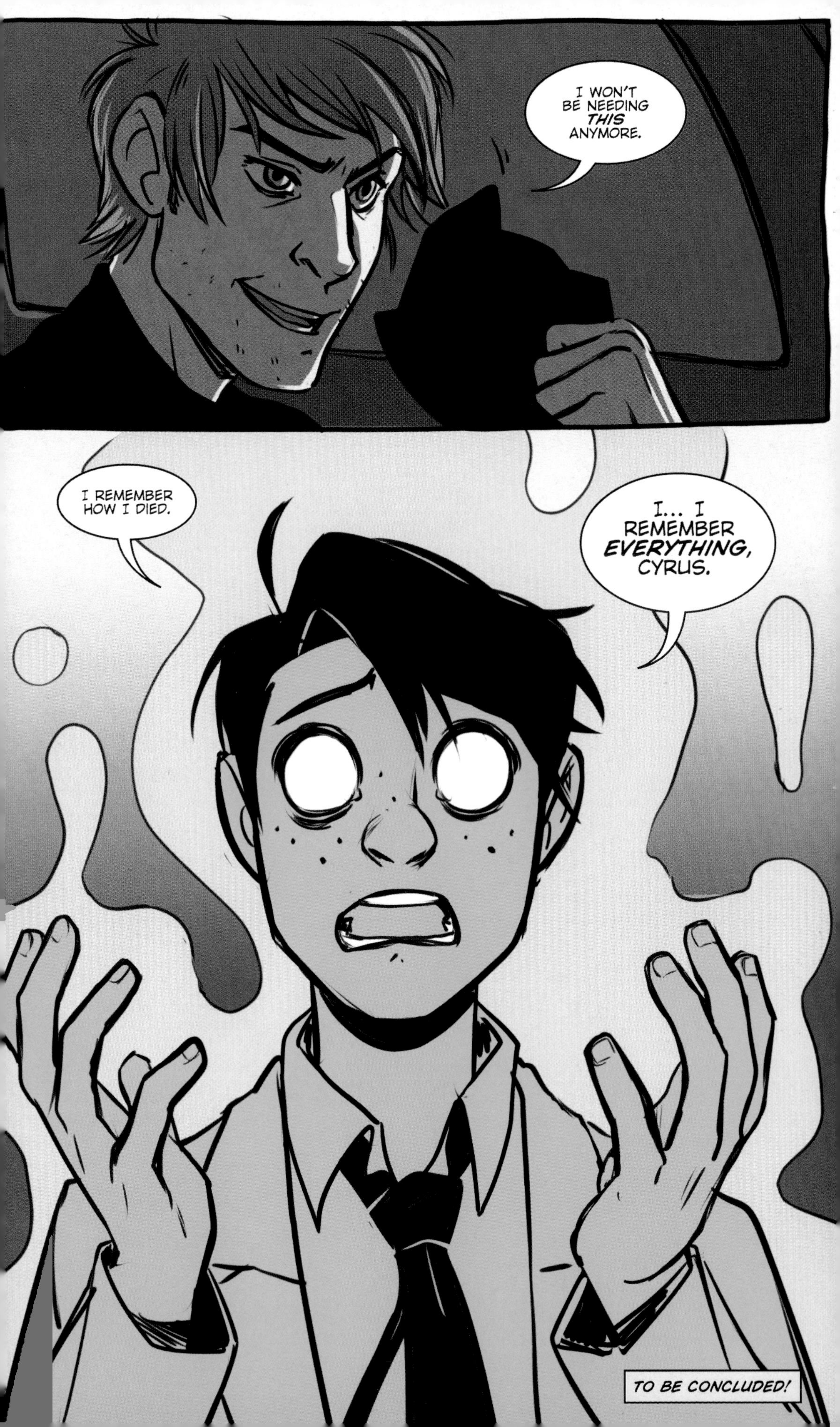
I WON'T BE NEEDING *THIS* ANYMORE.
I REMEMBER HOW I DIED.
I... I REMEMBER *EVERYTHING,* CYRUS.
TO BE CONCLUDED!

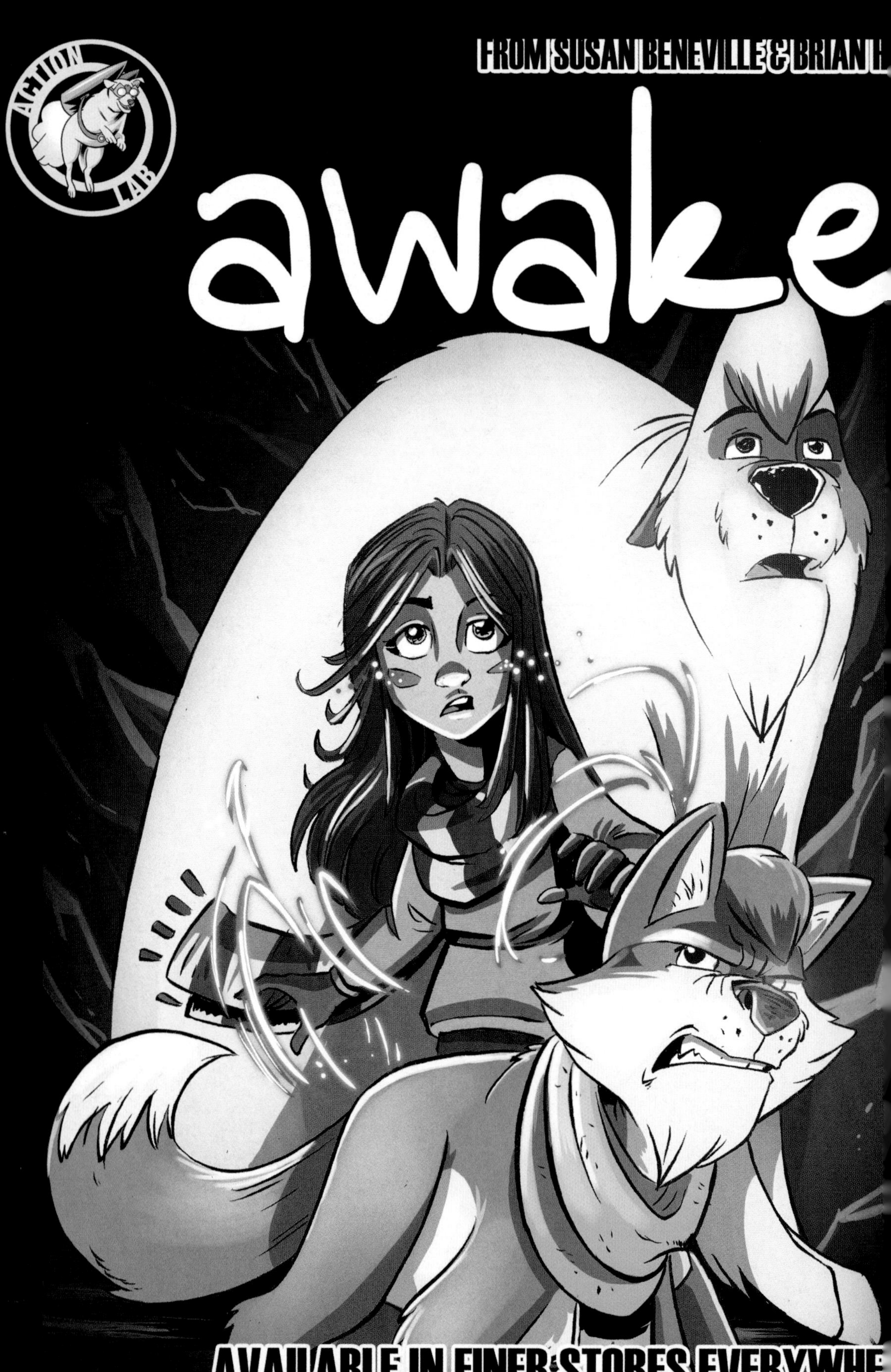
ACTION LAB
FROM SUSAN BENEVILLE & BRIAN H
awake
AVAILABLE IN FINER STORES EVERYWHE

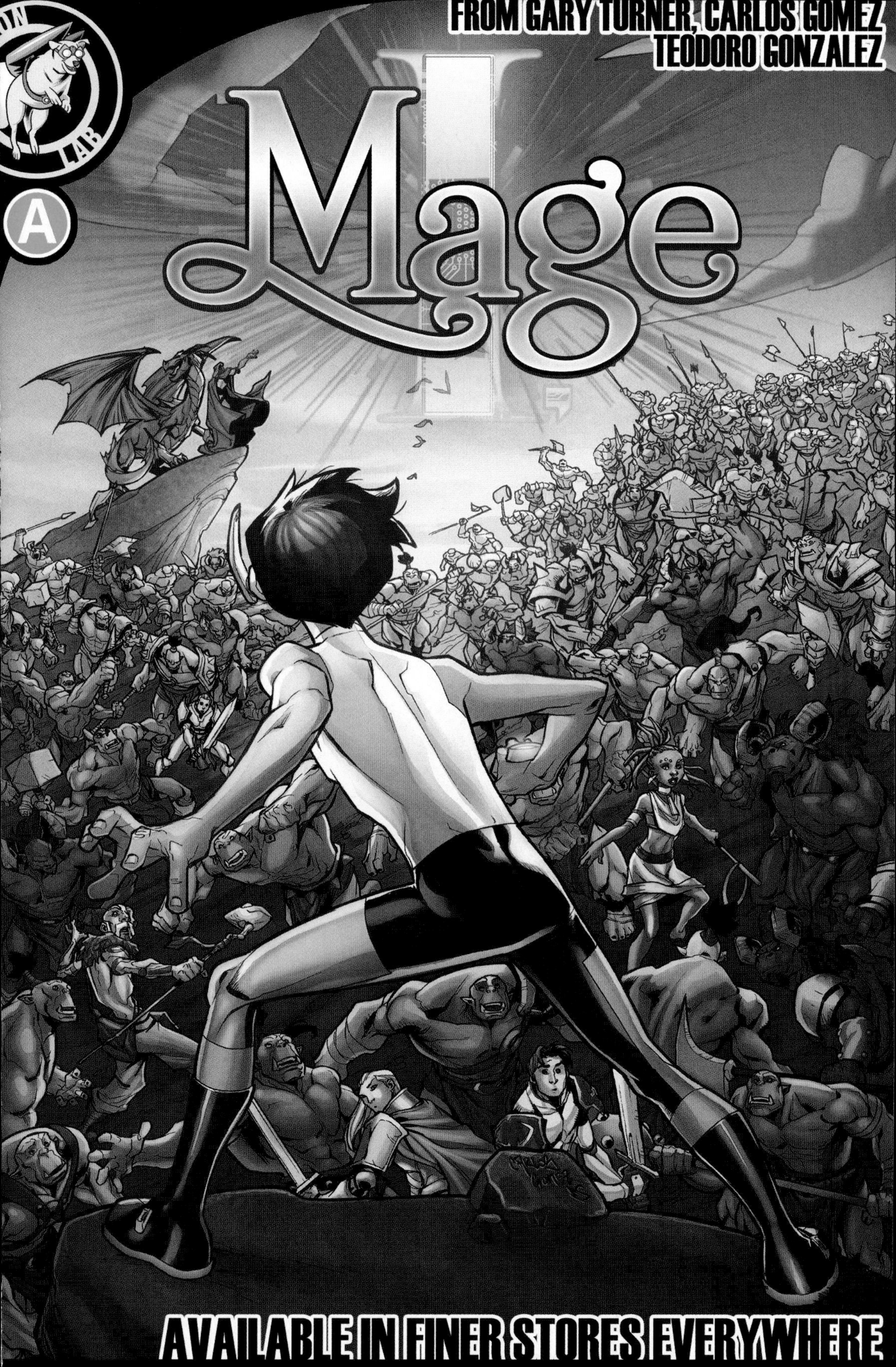
FROM GARY TURNER, CARLOS GOMEZ
TEODORO GONZALEZ
Mage
AVAILABLE IN FINER STORES EVERYWHERE

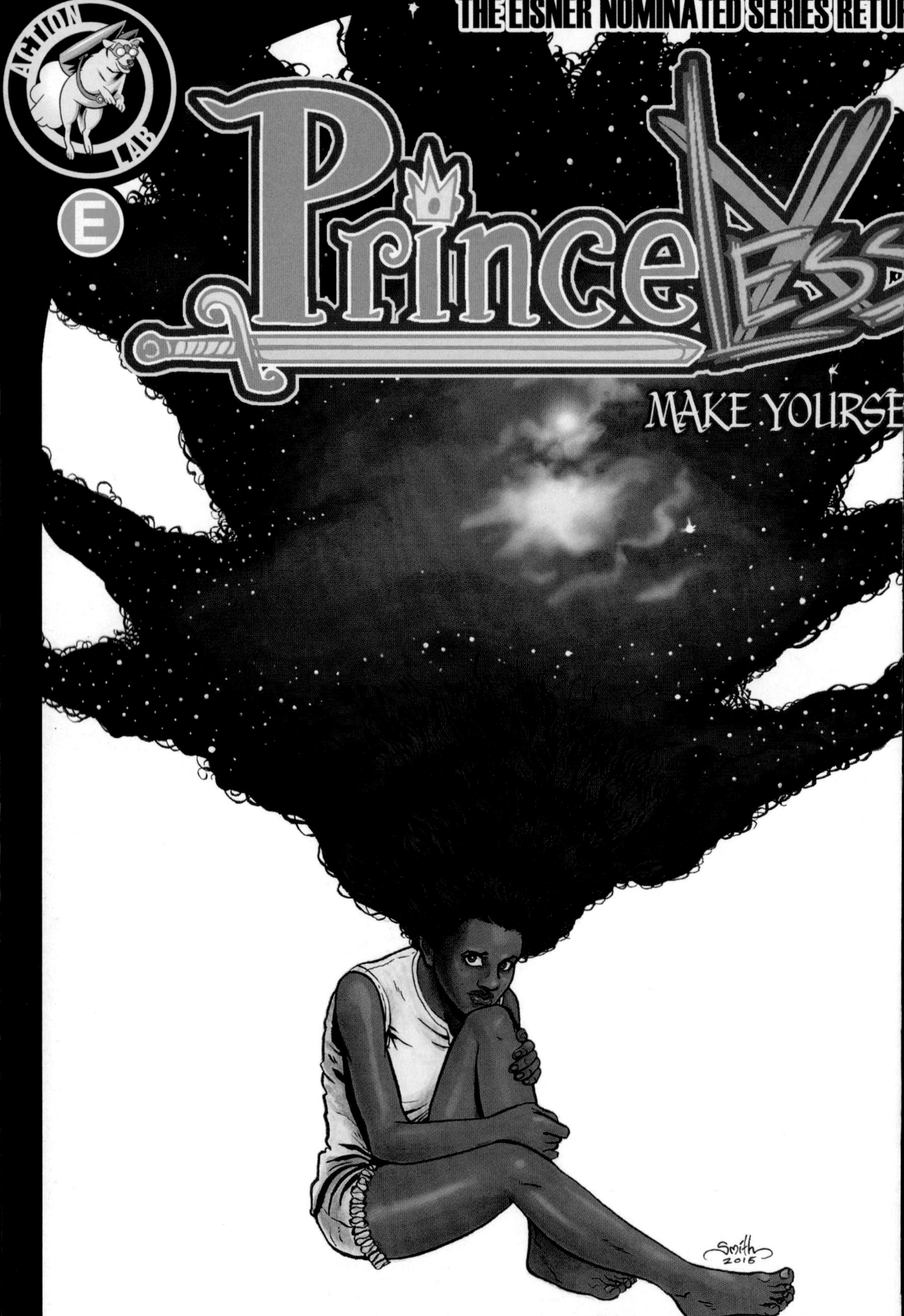
THE EISNER NOMINATED SERIES RETU
ACTION LAB
E
Princeless
MAKE YOURSE
Smith 2015
AVAILABLE IN FINER STORES EVERYWHE

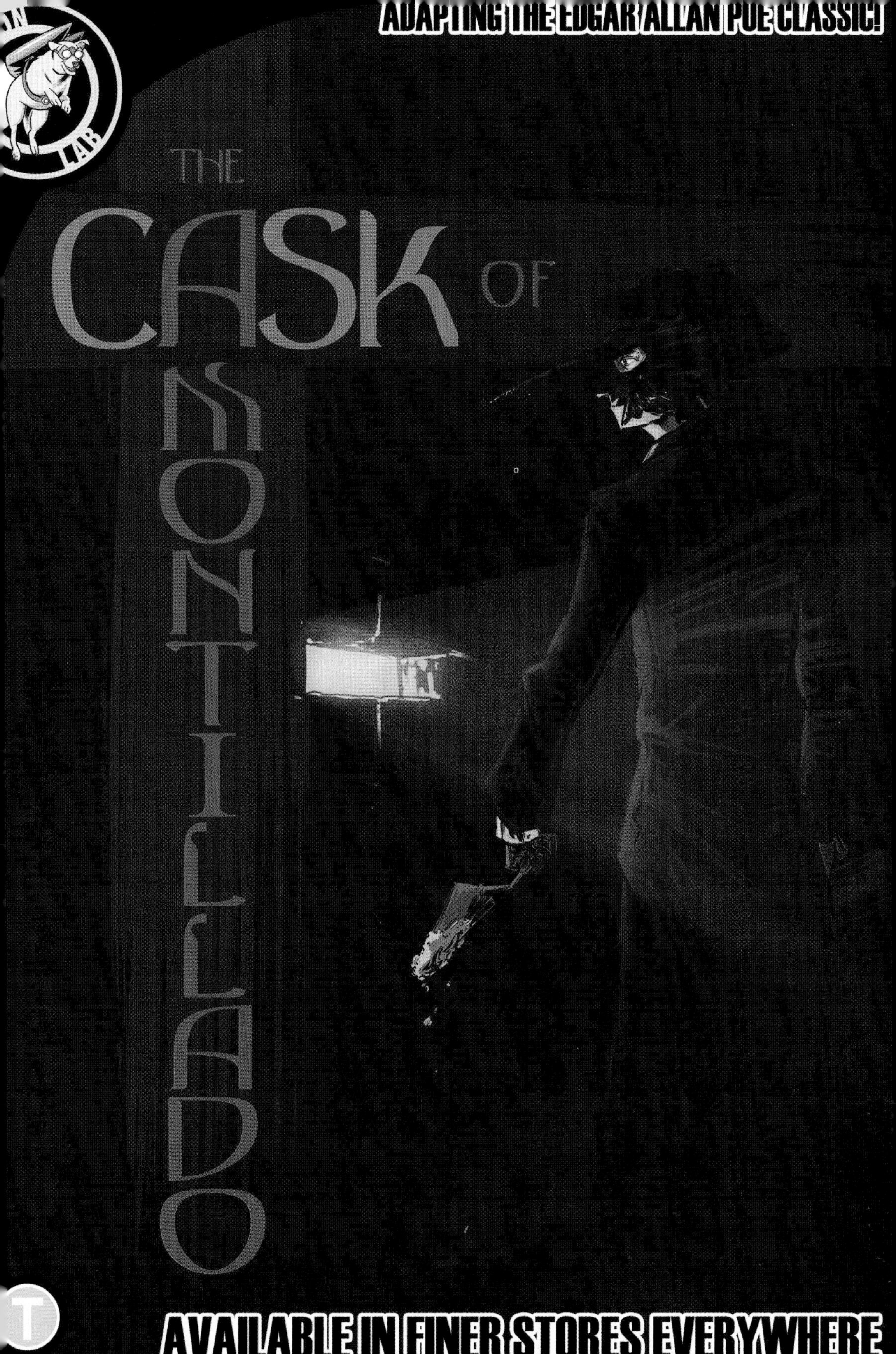
ADAPTING THE EDGAR ALLAN POE CLASSIC!
LAB
THE
CASK OF
MONTILLADO
AVAILABLE IN FINER STORES EVERYWHERE

FROM MAT HEAGERTY & JD FA...

JUST ANOTHER SHEEP

LOVE NOT WAR

STO
TT
E
NO

END THE
VIETNAM
NOW

GREED

suffering
enough
bloodshed.

MORE

AVAILABLE IN FINER STORES EVERYWHE...

In 1969 a timid teen sets out on a road trip. His goal? Find out the origins of his bizarre super human abilities. Always the follower, his trip is derailed when he befriends a grou... of extremist war protesters.

FROM ALL-AGES TO MATURE READERS
ACTION LAB HAS YOU COVERED.

 **Appropriate for everyone.**

 **Appropriate for age 9 and up. Absent of profanity or adult content.**

Suggested for 12 and Up. Comics with this rating are comparable to a PG-13 movie rating. Recommended for our teen and young adult readers.

 **Appropriate for older teens. Similar to Teen, but featuring more mature themes and/or more graphic imagery.**

 **Contains extreme viloence and some nudity. Basically the Rated-R of comics.**

Cyrus Perkins - Action Lab
www.actionlabcomics.com

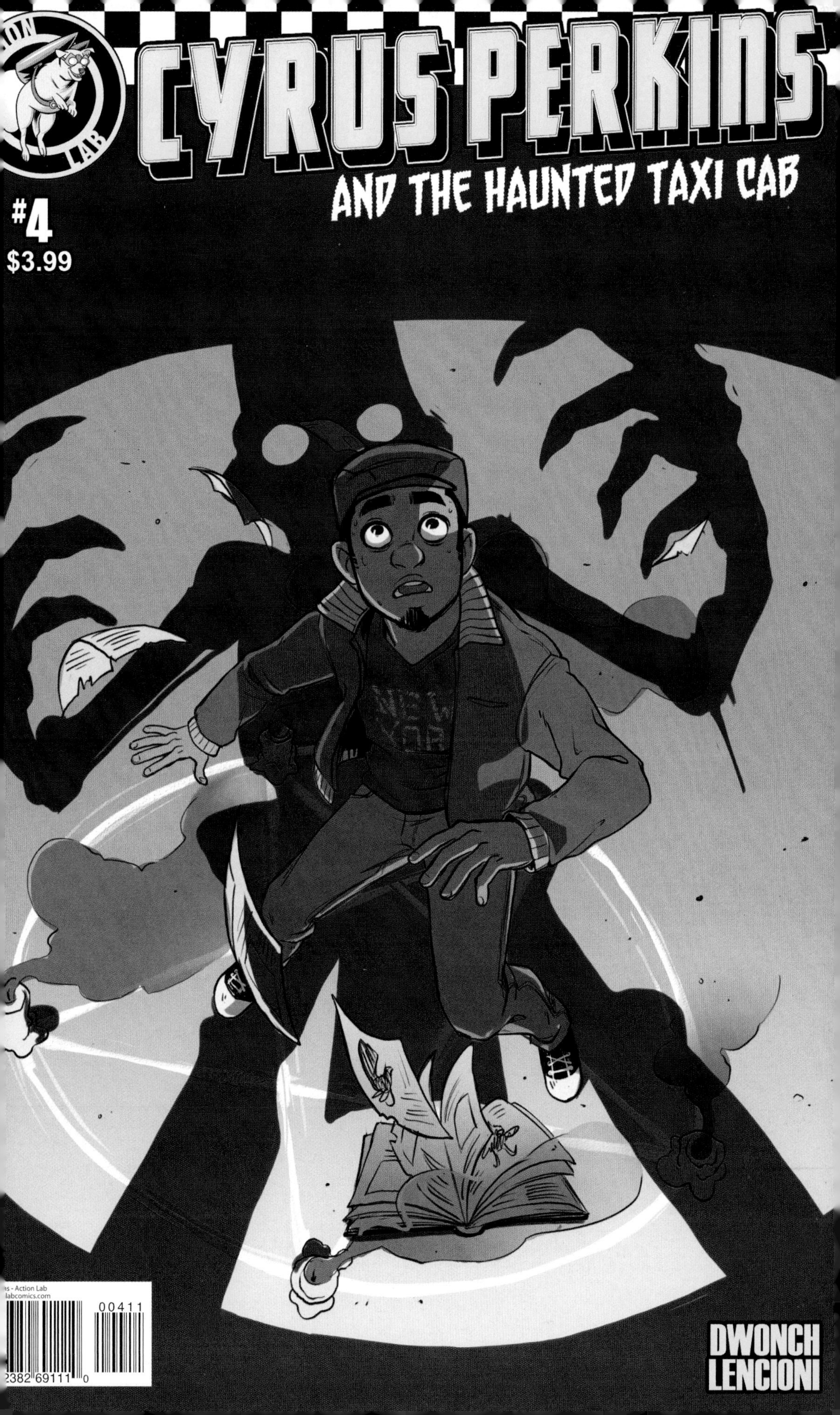
CYRUS PERKINS
AND THE HAUNTED TAXI CAB
#4
$3.99
DWONCH
LENCIONI

CYRUS PERKINS
AND THE HAUNTED TAXI CAB!

DAVE DWONCH
STORY/LETTERS/COLORS

ANNA LENCIONI
ART/TONES

BRYAN SEATON: PUBLISHER
DAVE DWONCH: PRESIDENT/CREATIVE DIRECTOR
SHAWN GABBORIN: EDITOR IN CHIEF   KEVIN FREEMAN: SENIOR EDITOR
JASON MARTIN: EDITOR   JAMAL IGLE: VICE-PRESIDENT OF MARKETING
JIM DIETZ: SOCIAL MEDIA DIRECTOR   CHAD CICCONI: HAUNTS THE OFFICES
VERY SPECIAL THANKS TO LUDWIG OLIMBA

"THE TRUTH?"

"YOU WANT THE TRUTH? WE WERE KID JUST BEING KIDS."

"WE GOT IT ON THE INTERNET. *THE BOOK*."

"IT DIDN'T LOOK LIKE MUCH, JUST A TATTERED OLD THING YOU'D FIND AT SOME OLD LADY'S GARAGE SALE."

"WE DIDN'T KNOW WHAT WE WERE GETTING INTO. HOW COULD WE?"

"NOW ALL WE HAVE IS BLOOD ON OUR HANDS. BLOOD AND MORE BLOOD."

"YOU'RE JUST COLLATERAL DAMAGE, CYRUS PERKINS."

MITCH.

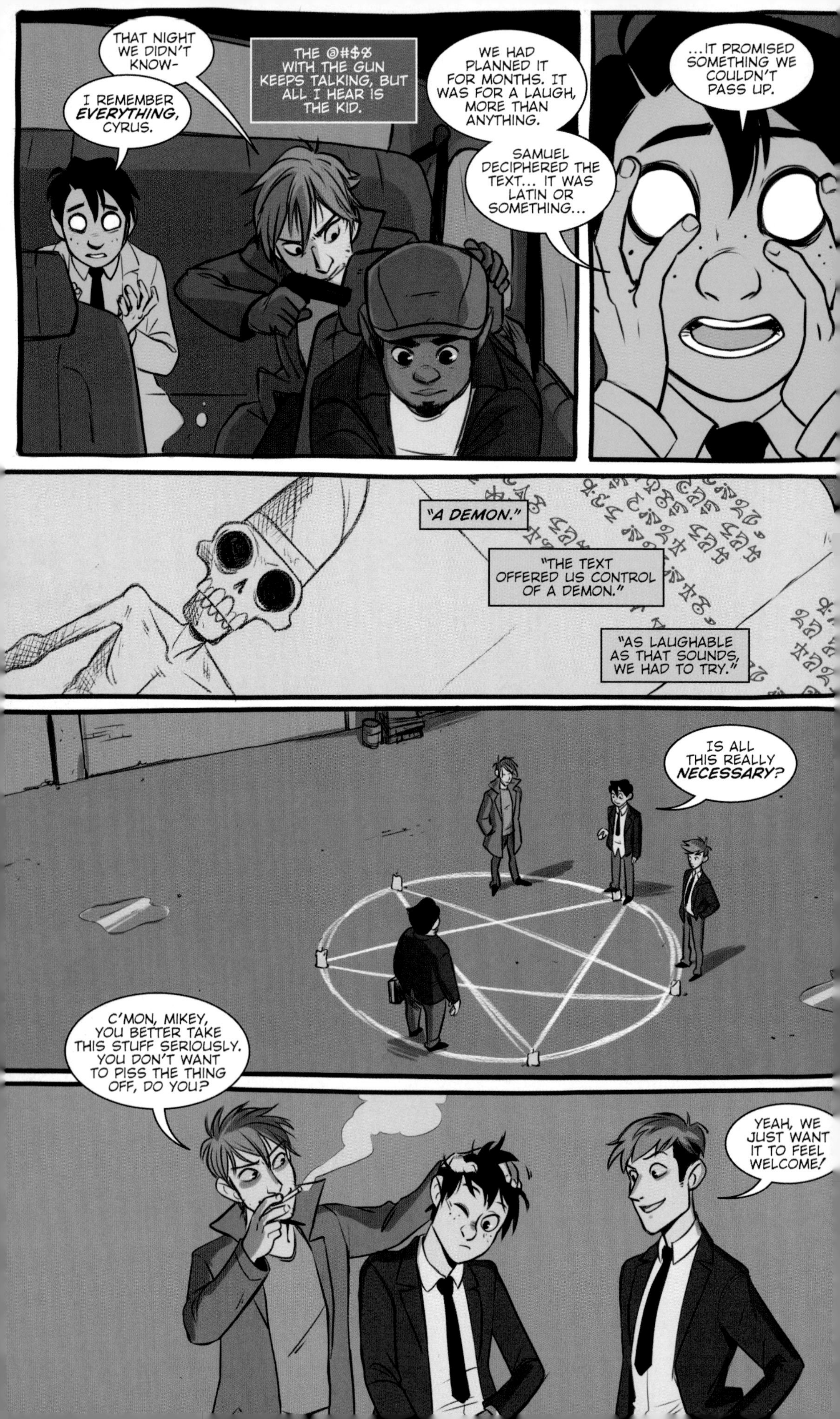

I REMEMBER EVERYTHING, CYRUS.
THAT NIGHT WE DIDN'T KNOW-
THE @#$% WITH THE GUN KEEPS TALKING, BUT ALL I HEAR IS THE KID.
WE HAD PLANNED IT FOR MONTHS. IT WAS FOR A LAUGH, MORE THAN ANYTHING.
SAMUEL DECIPHERED THE TEXT... IT WAS LATIN OR SOMETHING...
...IT PROMISED SOMETHING WE COULDN'T PASS UP.
"A DEMON."
"THE TEXT OFFERED US CONTROL OF A DEMON."
"AS LAUGHABLE AS THAT SOUNDS, WE HAD TO TRY."
IS ALL THIS REALLY NECESSARY?
C'MON, MIKEY, YOU BETTER TAKE THIS STUFF SERIOUSLY. YOU DON'T WANT TO PISS THE THING OFF, DO YOU?
YEAH, WE JUST WANT IT TO FEEL WELCOME!

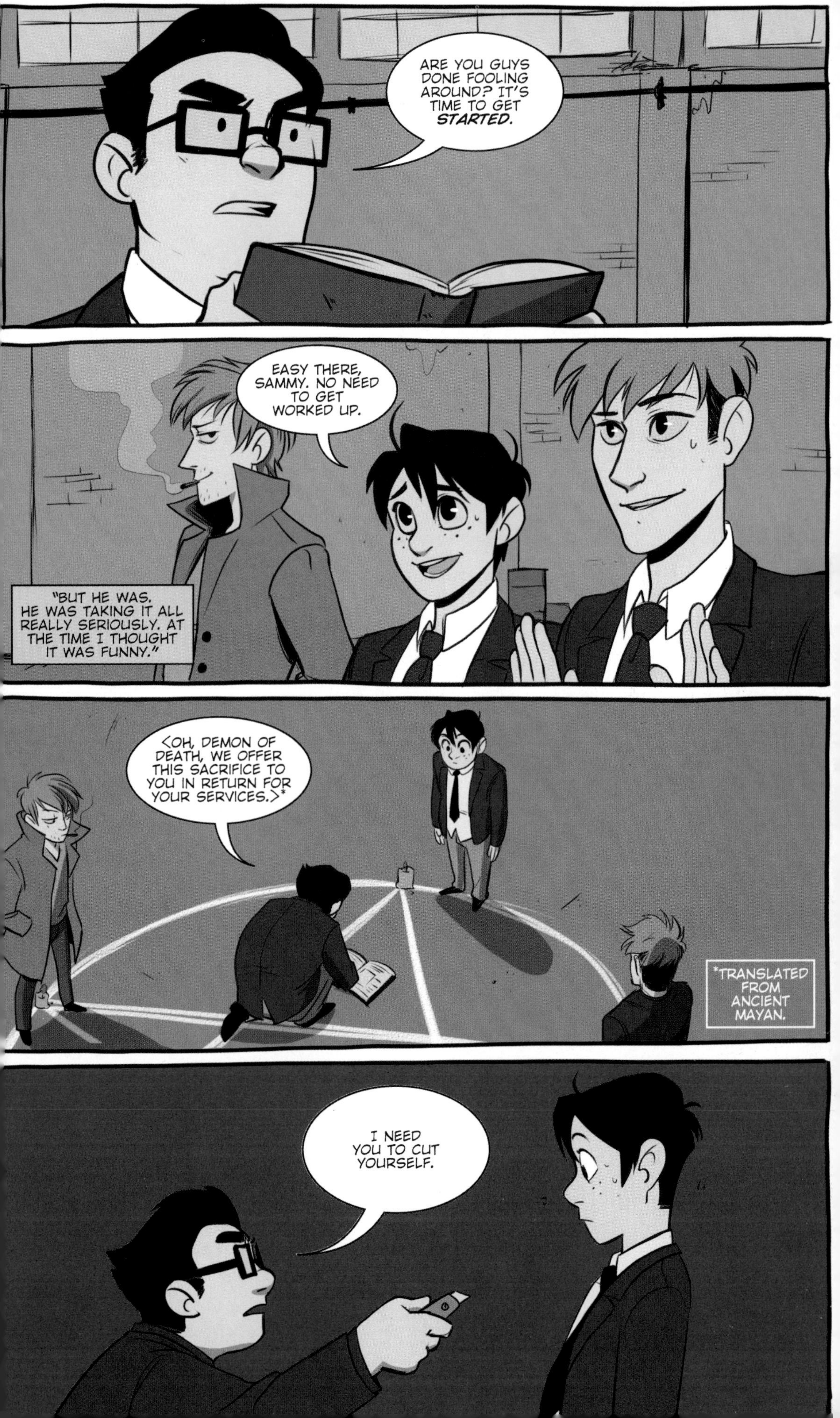
ARE YOU GUYS DONE FOOLING AROUND? IT'S TIME TO GET *STARTED.*
EASY THERE, SAMMY. NO NEED TO GET WORKED UP.
"BUT HE WAS. HE WAS TAKING IT ALL REALLY SERIOUSLY. AT THE TIME I THOUGHT IT WAS FUNNY."
<OH, DEMON OF DEATH, WE OFFER THIS SACRIFICE TO YOU IN RETURN FOR YOUR SERVICES.>*
*TRANSLATED FROM ANCIENT MAYAN.
I NEED YOU TO CUT YOURSELF.

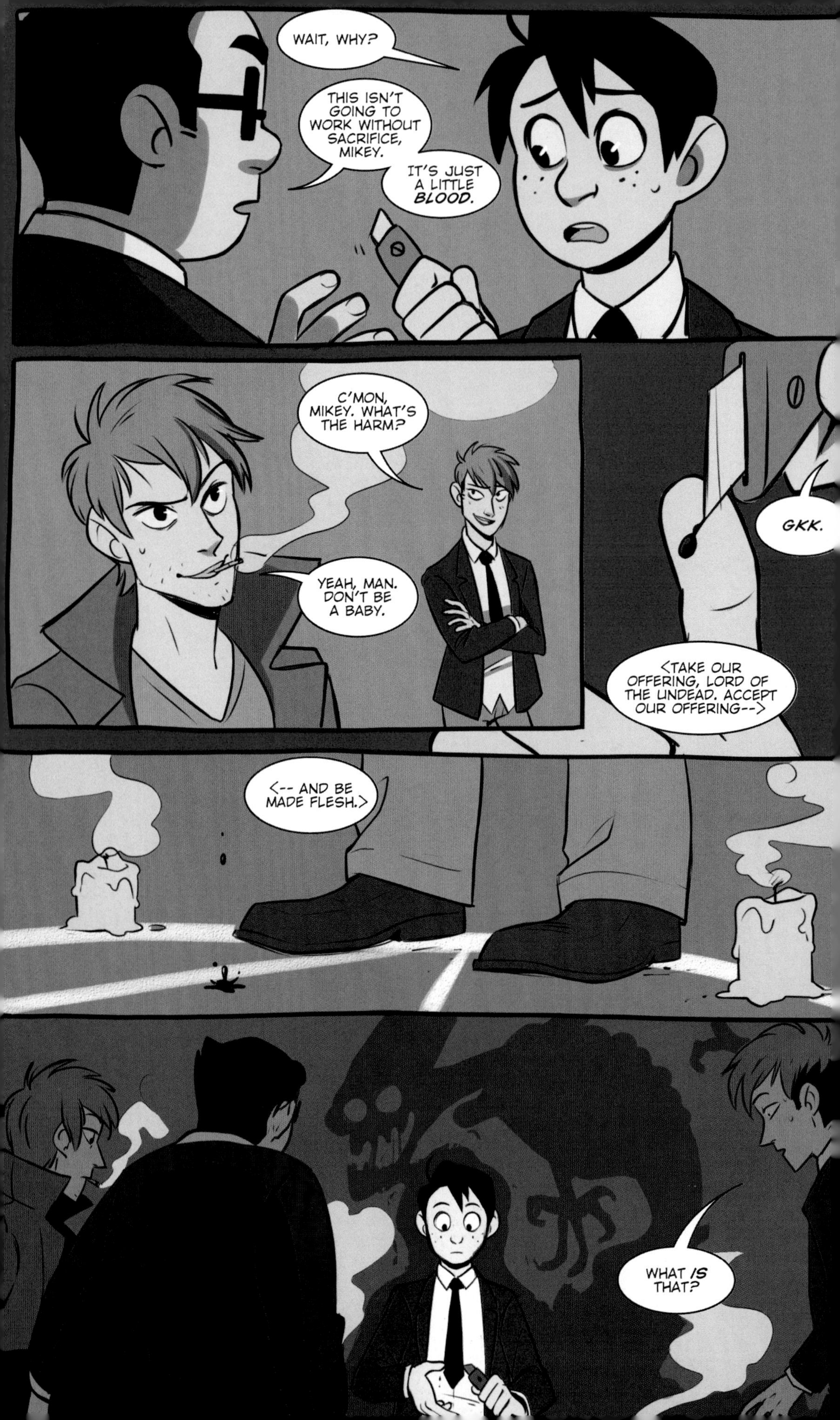
WAIT, WHY?
THIS ISN'T GOING TO WORK WITHOUT SACRIFICE, MIKEY.
IT'S JUST A LITTLE *BLOOD.*
C'MON, MIKEY. WHAT'S THE HARM?
YEAH, MAN. DON'T BE A BABY.
GKK.
<TAKE OUR OFFERING, LORD OF THE UNDEAD. ACCEPT OUR OFFERING-->
<-- AND BE MADE FLESH.>
WHAT *IS* THAT?

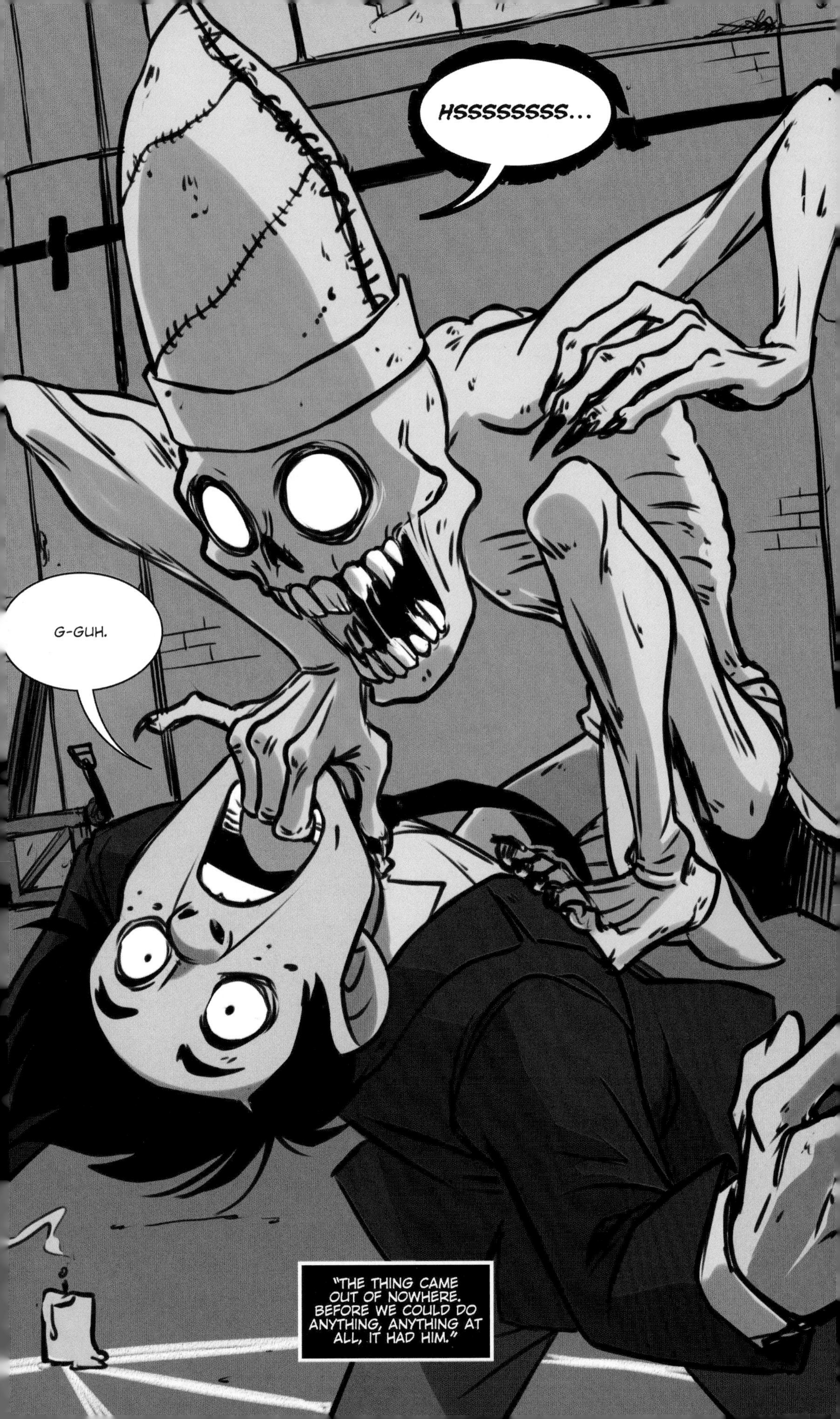
HSSSSSSSS...
G-GUH.
"THE THING CAME OUT OF NOWHERE. BEFORE WE COULD DO ANYTHING, ANYTHING AT ALL, IT HAD HIM."

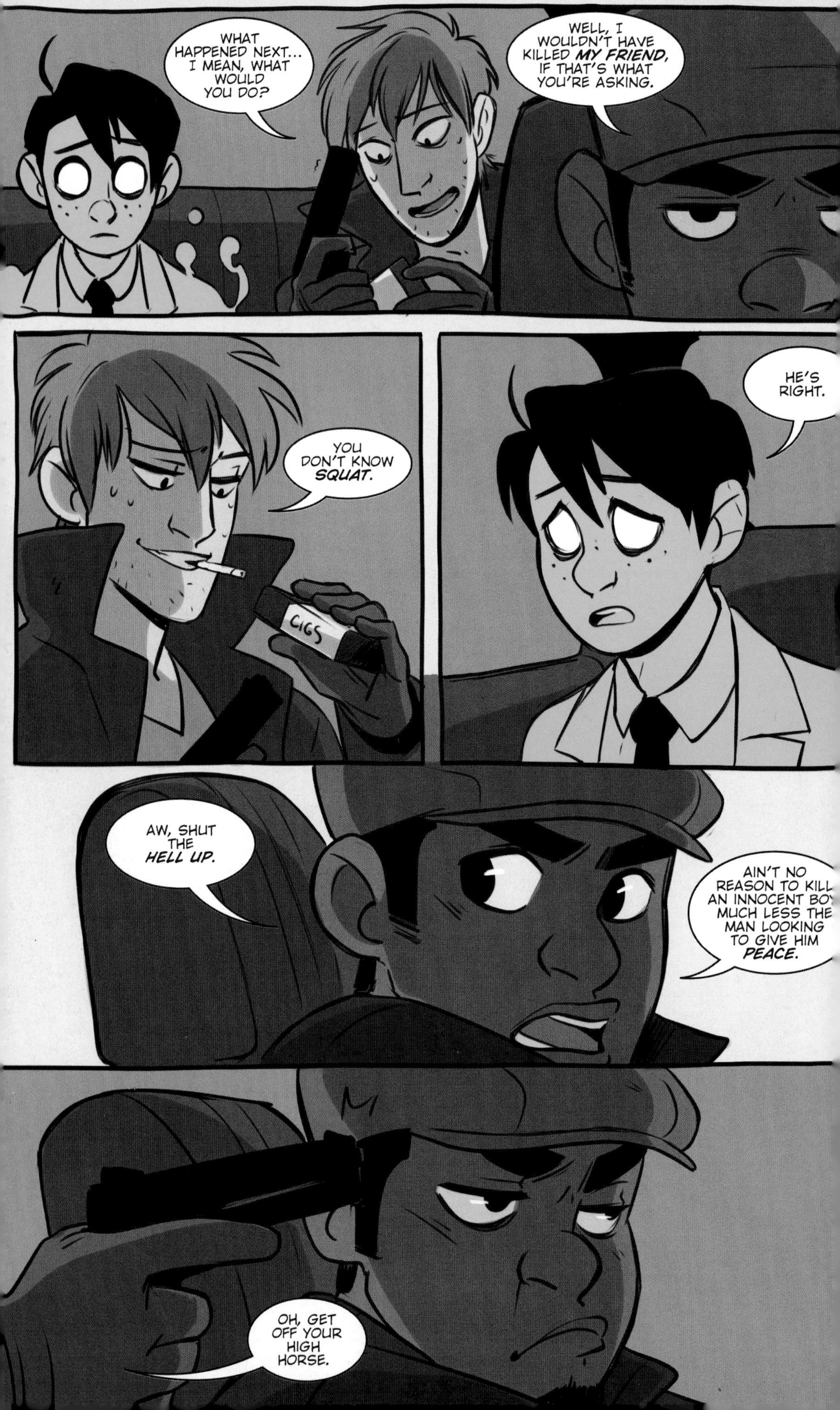
WHAT HAPPENED NEXT... I MEAN, WHAT WOULD YOU DO?
WELL, I WOULDN'T HAVE KILLED **MY FRIEND**, IF THAT'S WHAT YOU'RE ASKING.
YOU DON'T KNOW **SQUAT**.
CIGS
HE'S RIGHT.
AW, SHUT THE ***HELL UP***.
AIN'T NO REASON TO KILL AN INNOCENT BOY MUCH LESS THE MAN LOOKING TO GIVE HIM ***PEACE***.
OH, GET OFF YOUR HIGH HORSE.

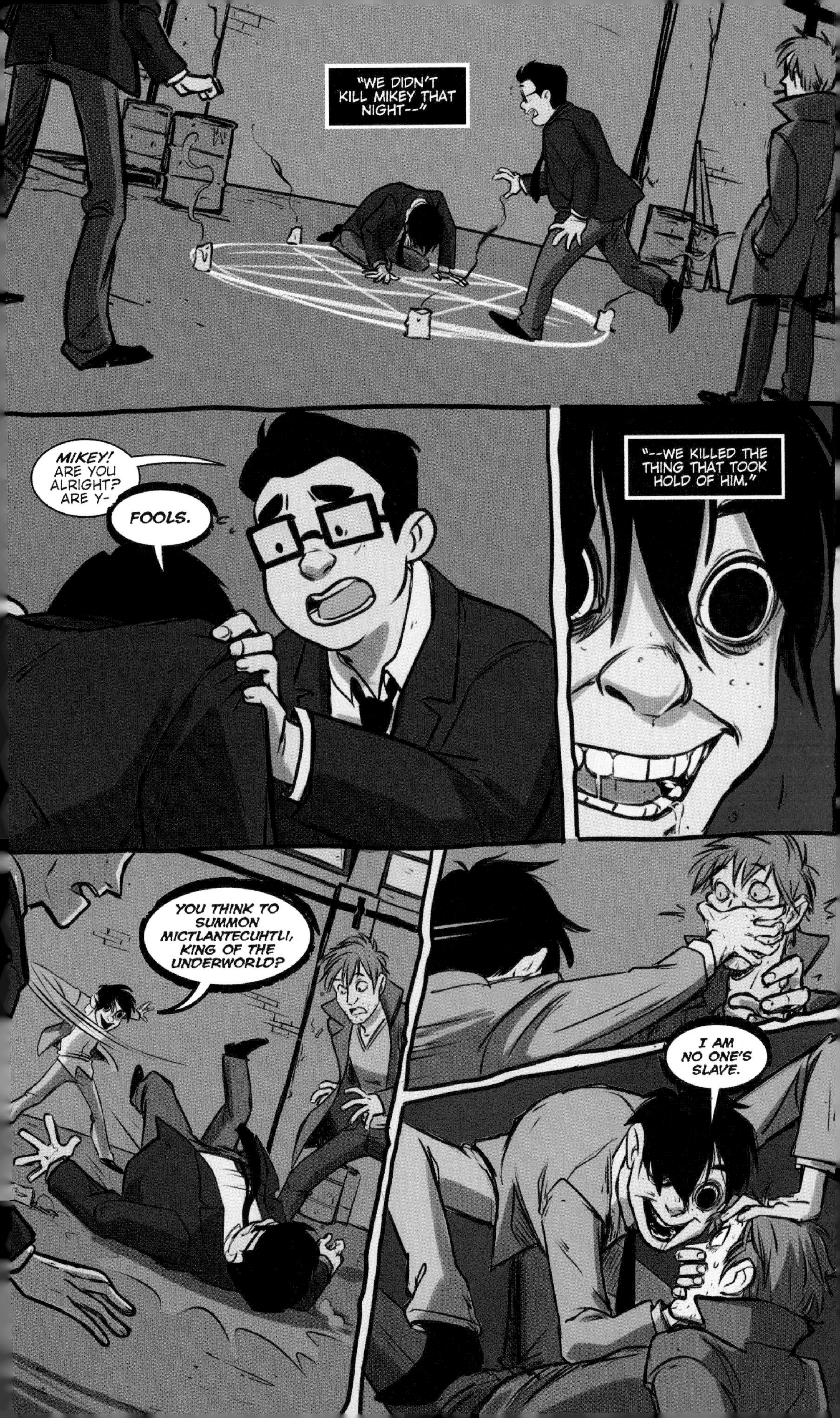
"WE DIDN'T KILL MIKEY THAT NIGHT--"
MIKEY! ARE YOU ALRIGHT? ARE Y-
FOOLS.
"--WE KILLED THE THING THAT TOOK HOLD OF HIM."
YOU THINK TO SUMMON MICTLANTECUHTLI, KING OF THE UNDERWORLD?
I AM NO ONE'S SLAVE.

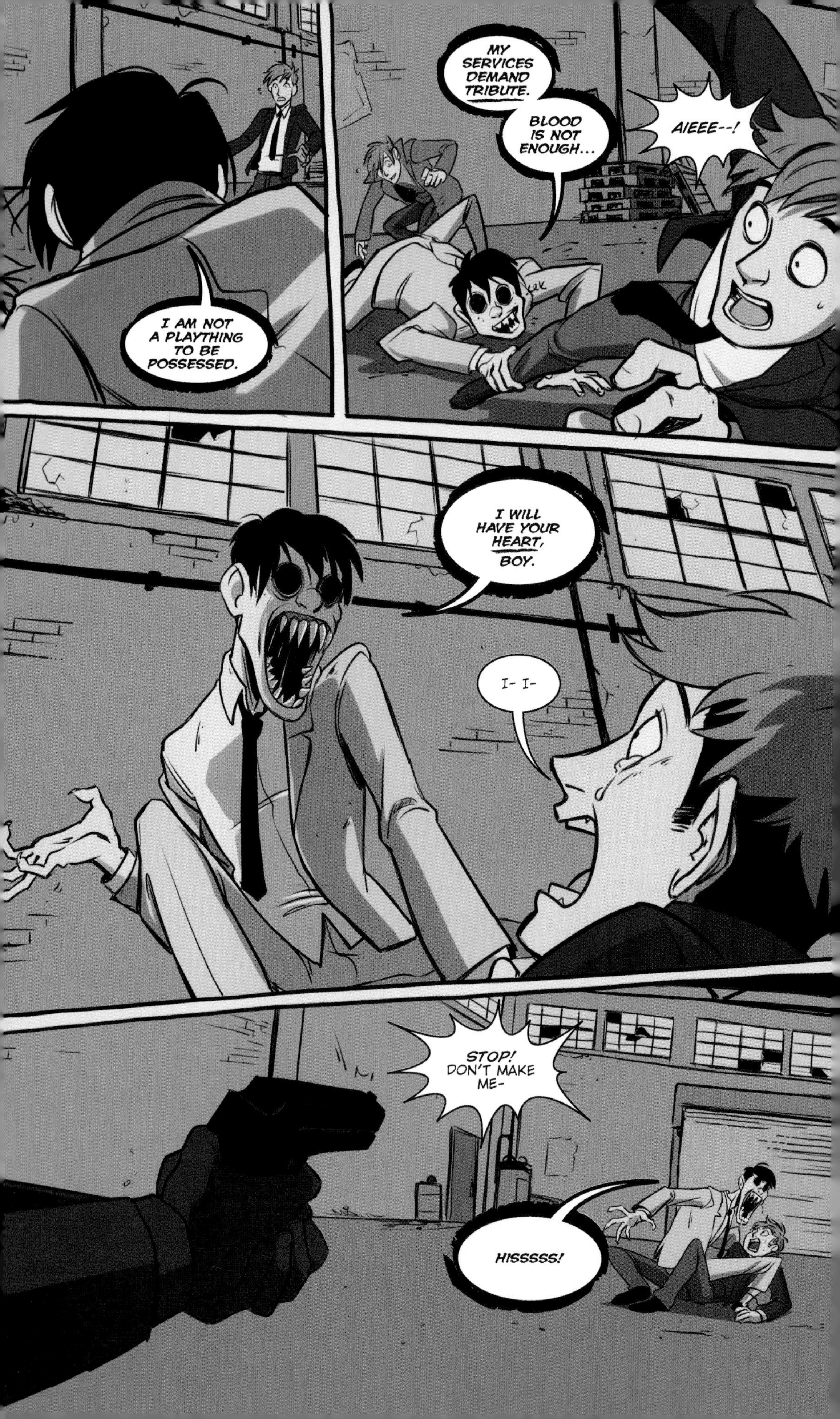
I AM NOT A PLAYTHING TO BE POSSESSED.
MY SERVICES DEMAND TRIBUTE.
BLOOD IS NOT ENOUGH...
AIEEE--!
I WILL HAVE YOUR HEART, BOY.
I- I-
STOP! DON'T MAKE ME-
HISSSSS!

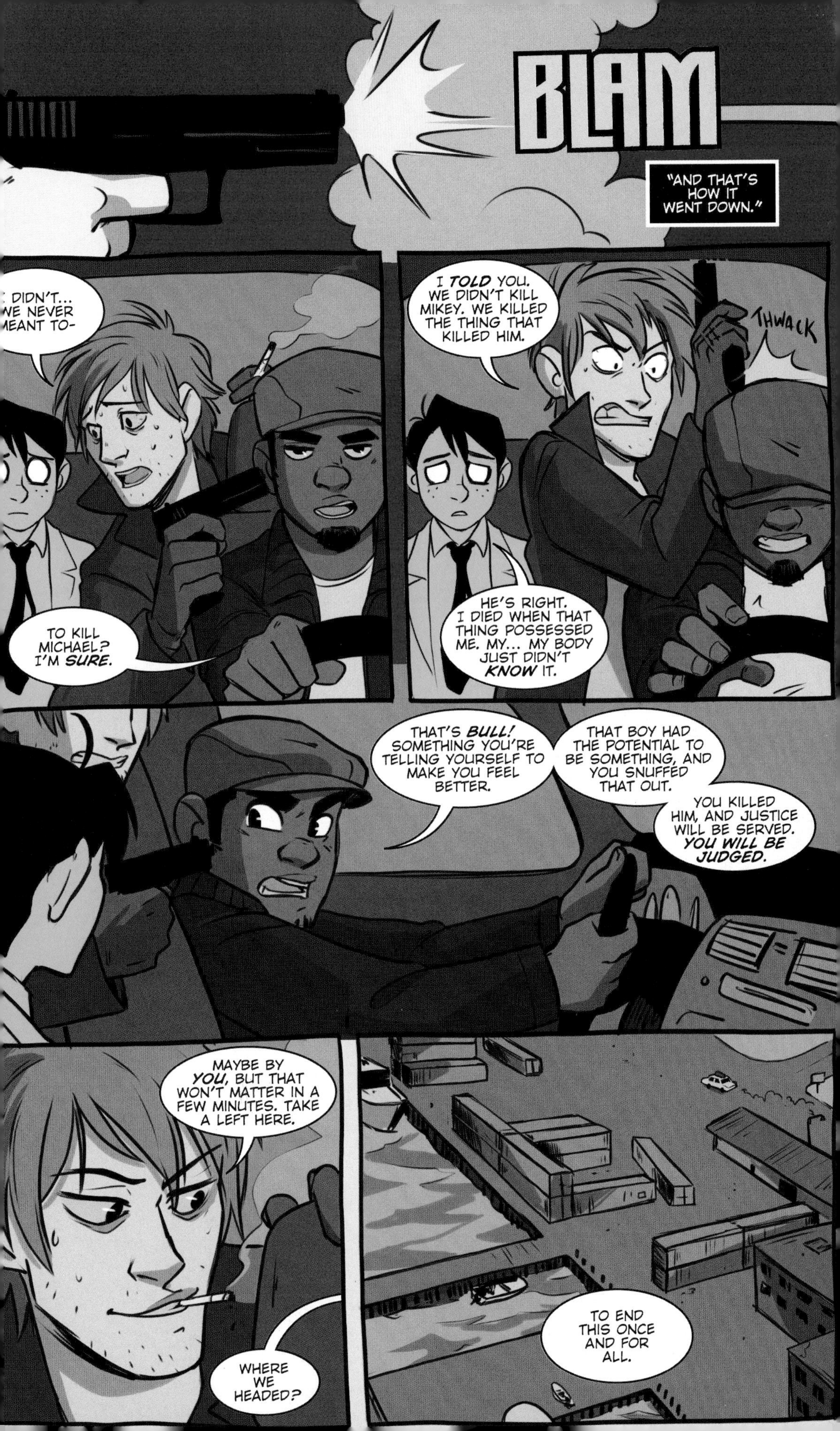
BLAM
"AND THAT'S HOW IT WENT DOWN."
DIDN'T... WE NEVER MEANT TO-
TO KILL MICHAEL? I'M SURE.
I TOLD YOU. WE DIDN'T KILL MIKEY. WE KILLED THE THING THAT KILLED HIM.
THWACK
HE'S RIGHT. I DIED WHEN THAT THING POSSESSED ME. MY... MY BODY JUST DIDN'T KNOW IT.
THAT'S BULL! SOMETHING YOU'RE TELLING YOURSELF TO MAKE YOU FEEL BETTER.
THAT BOY HAD THE POTENTIAL TO BE SOMETHING, AND YOU SNUFFED THAT OUT.
YOU KILLED HIM, AND JUSTICE WILL BE SERVED. YOU WILL BE JUDGED.
MAYBE BY YOU, BUT THAT WON'T MATTER IN A FEW MINUTES. TAKE A LEFT HERE.
WHERE WE HEADED?
TO END THIS ONCE AND FOR ALL.

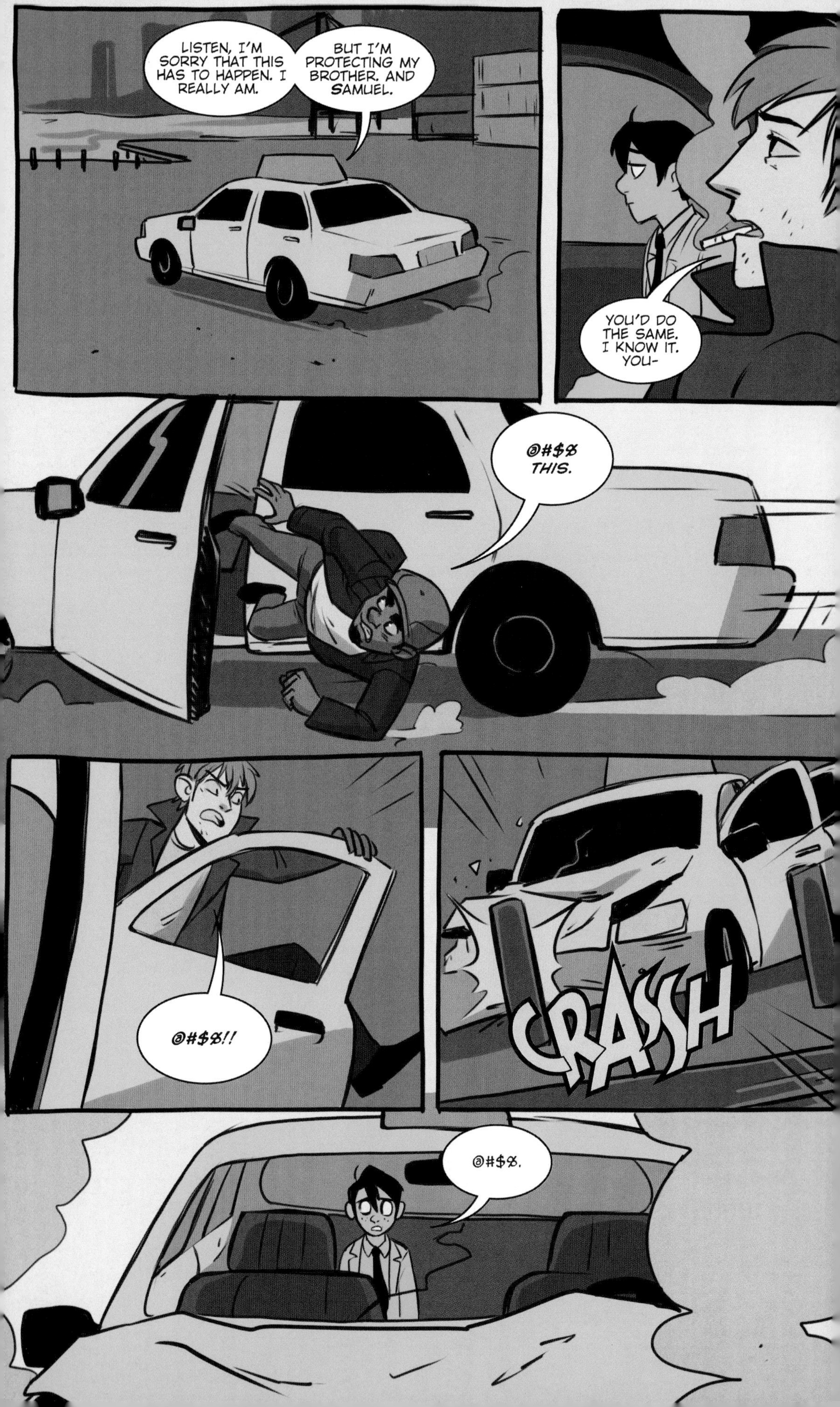
LISTEN, I'M SORRY THAT THIS HAS TO HAPPEN. I REALLY AM.
BUT I'M PROTECTING MY BROTHER. AND SAMUEL.
YOU'D DO THE SAME. I KNOW IT. YOU-
@#$% THIS.
@#$%!!
CRASH
@#$%.

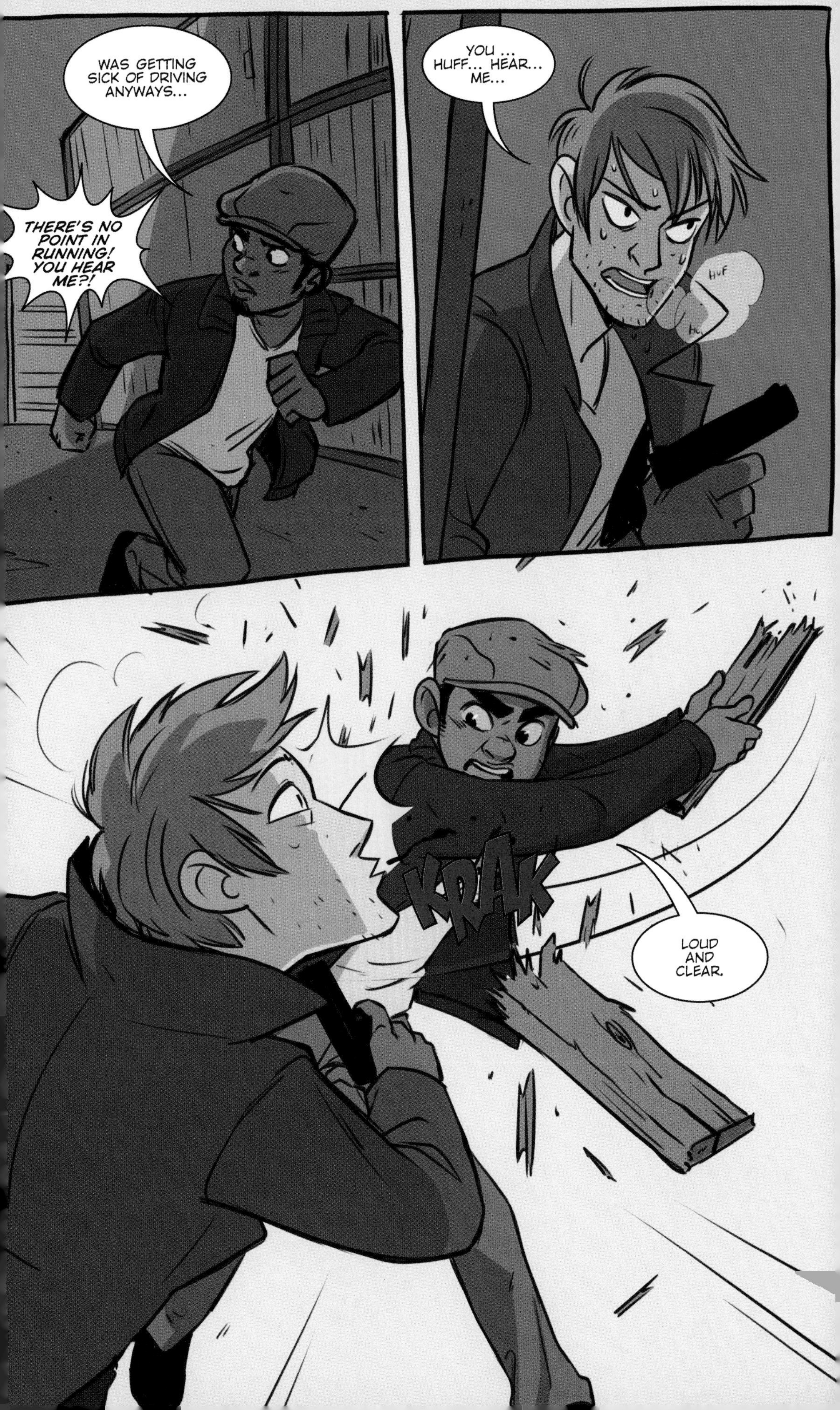
THERE'S NO POINT IN RUNNING! YOU HEAR ME?!
WAS GETTING SICK OF DRIVING ANYWAYS...
YOU ... HUFF... HEAR... ME...
HUF
KRAK
LOUD AND CLEAR.

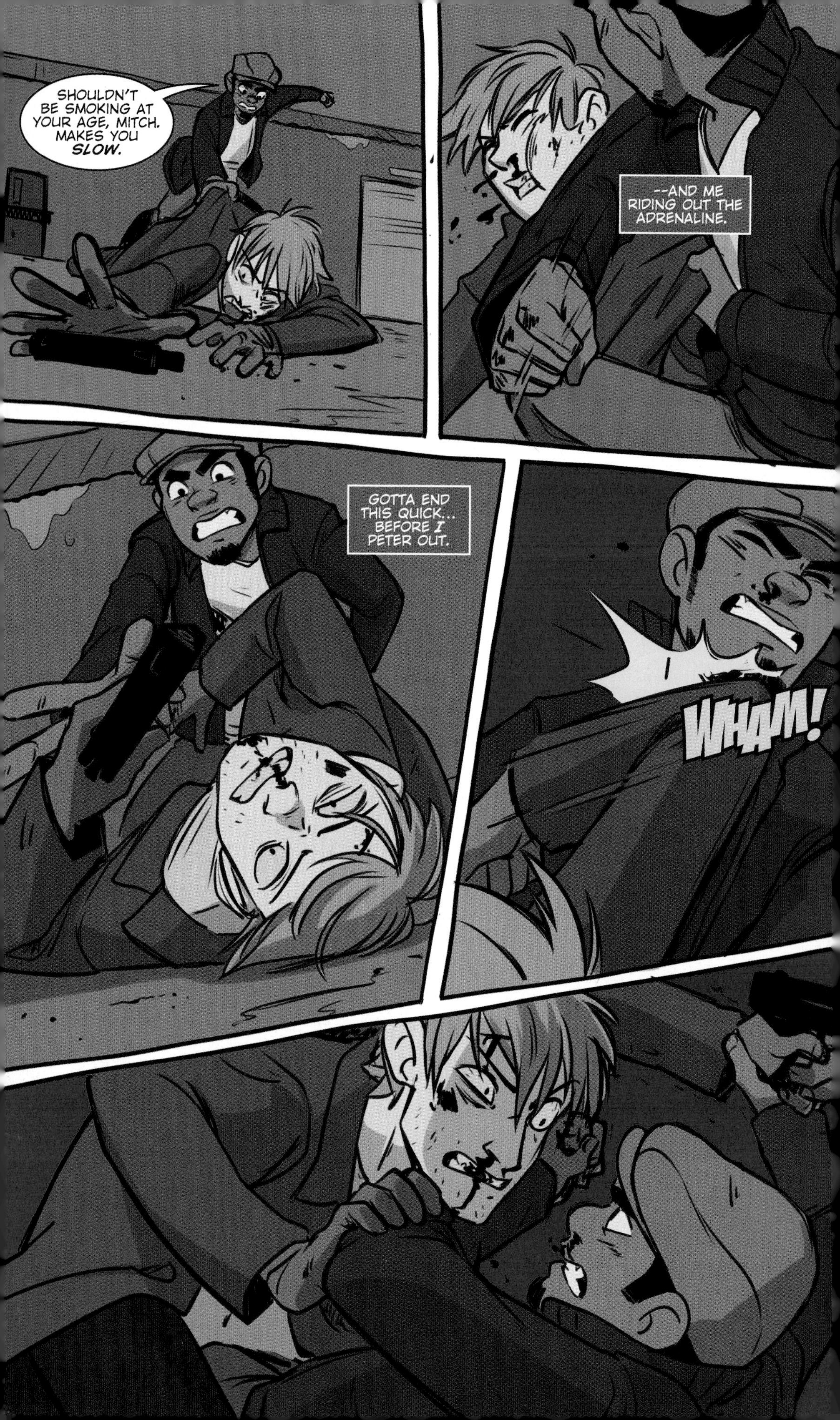
SHOULDN'T BE SMOKING AT YOUR AGE, MITCH. MAKES YOU SLOW.
--AND ME RIDING OUT THE ADRENALINE.
GOTTA END THIS QUICK... BEFORE I PETER OUT.
WHAM!

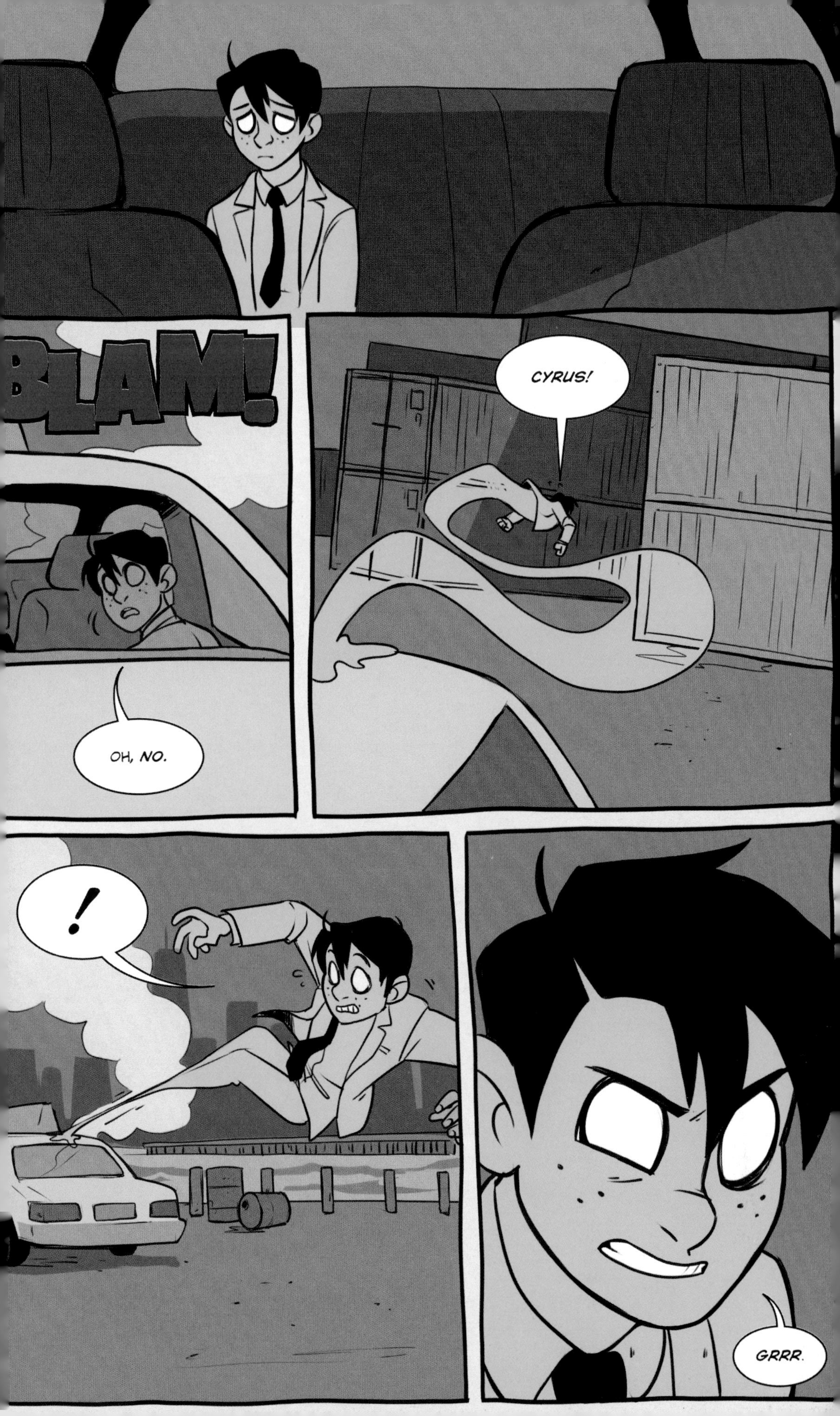
BLAM!
OH, NO.
CYRUS!
!
GRRR.

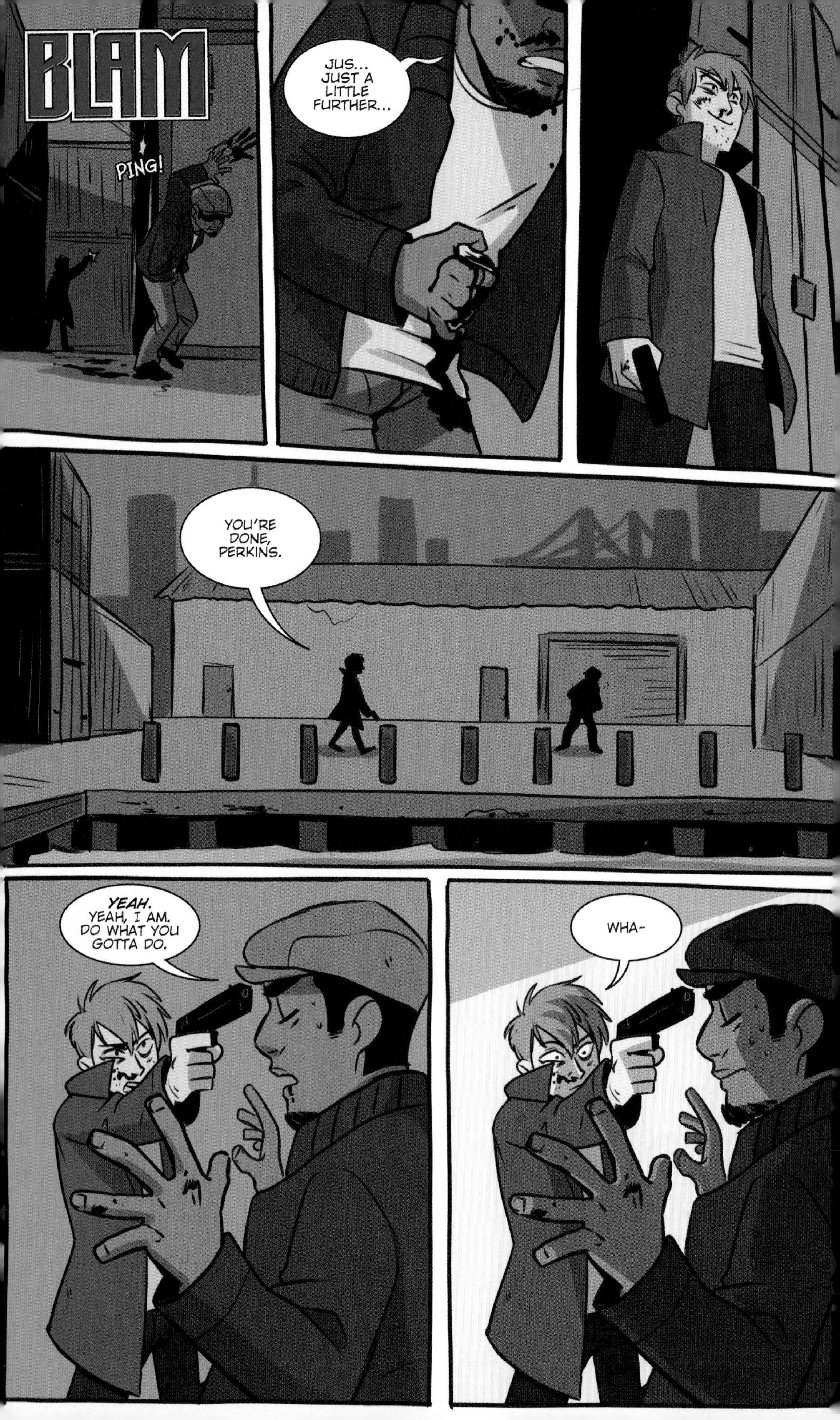
BLAM
PING!
JUS... JUST A LITTLE FURTHER...
YOU'RE DONE, PERKINS.
YEAH. YEAH, I AM. DO WHAT YOU GOTTA DO.
WHA-

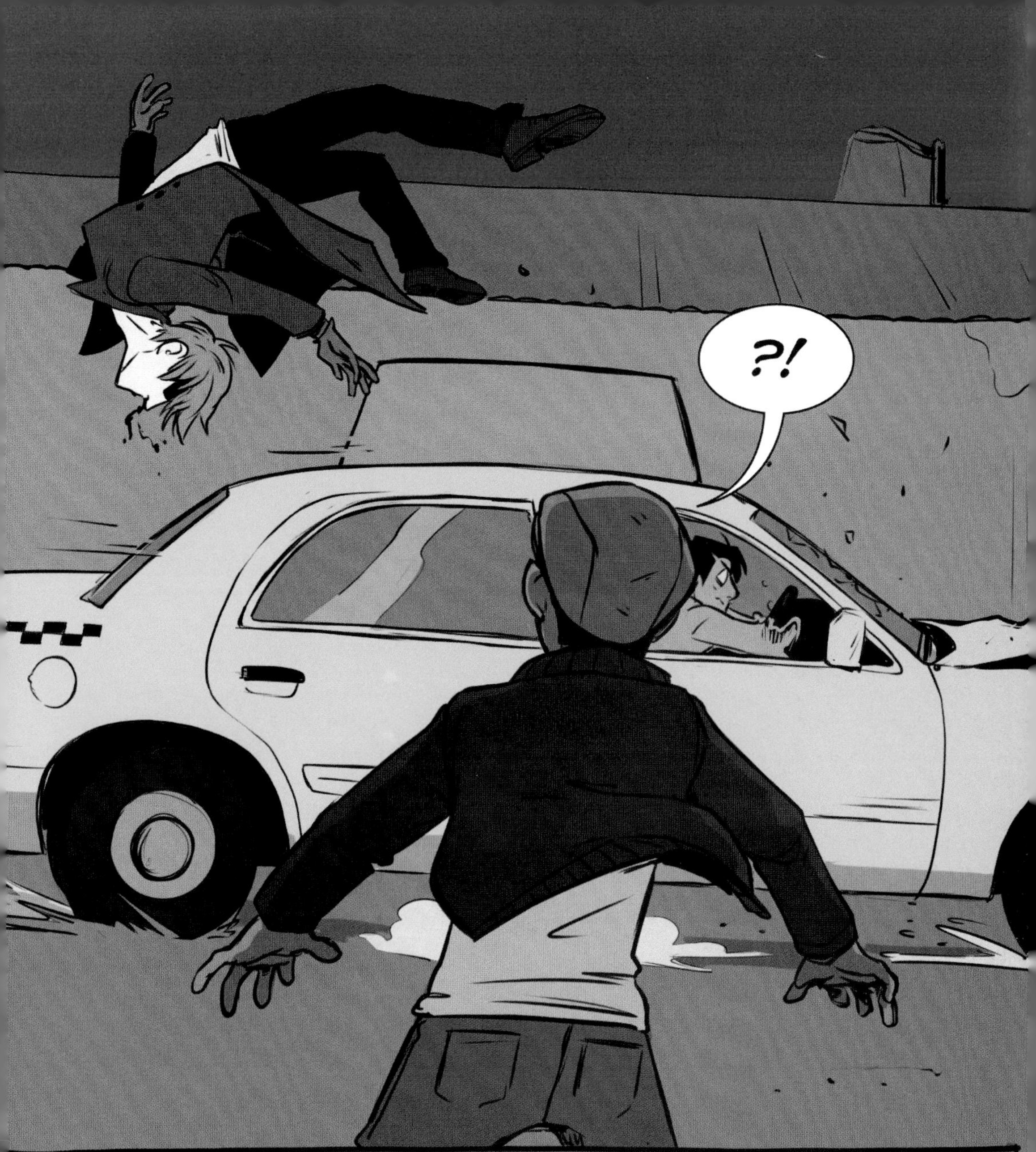
?!

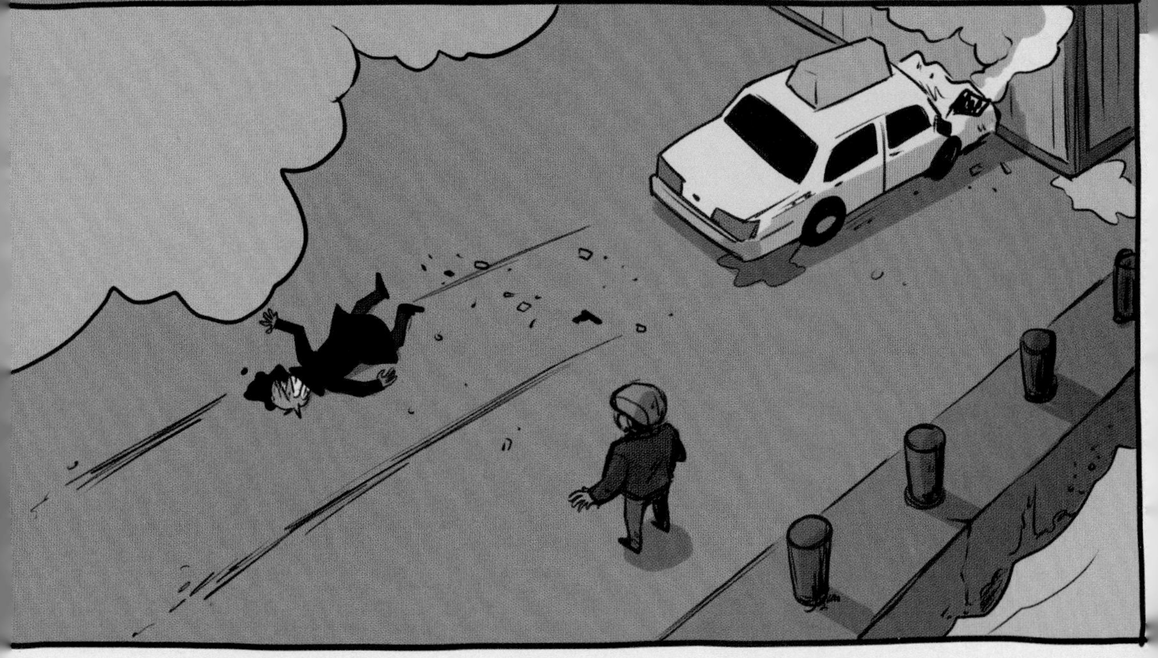

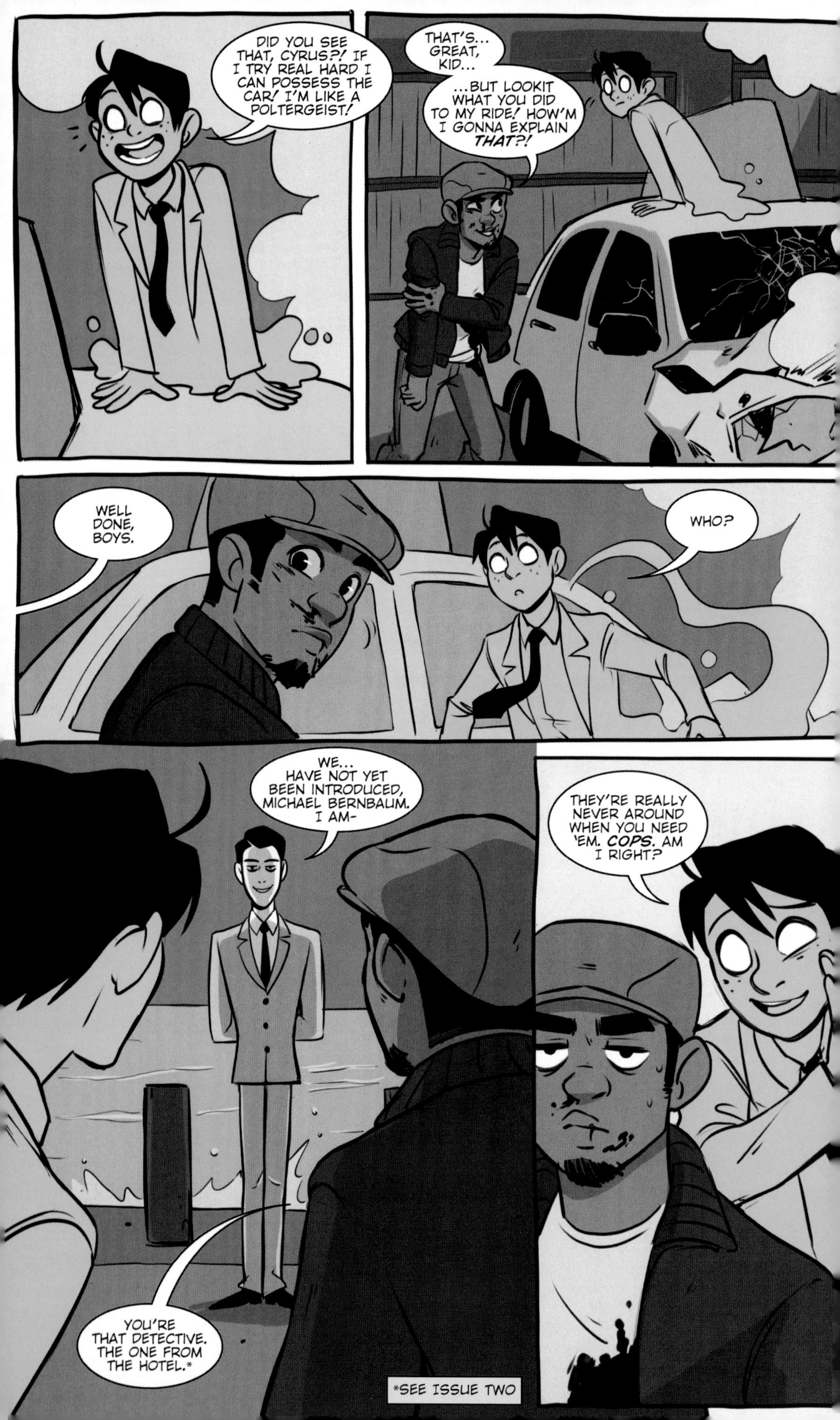
DID YOU SEE THAT, CYRUS?! IF I TRY REAL HARD I CAN POSSESS THE CAR! I'M LIKE A POLTERGEIST!
THAT'S... GREAT, KID...
...BUT LOOKIT WHAT YOU DID TO MY RIDE! HOW'M I GONNA EXPLAIN THAT?!
WELL DONE, BOYS.
WHO?
WE... HAVE NOT YET BEEN INTRODUCED, MICHAEL BERNBAUM. I AM-
YOU'RE THAT DETECTIVE. THE ONE FROM THE HOTEL.*
THEY'RE REALLY NEVER AROUND WHEN YOU NEED 'EM. COPS. AM I RIGHT?
*SEE ISSUE TWO

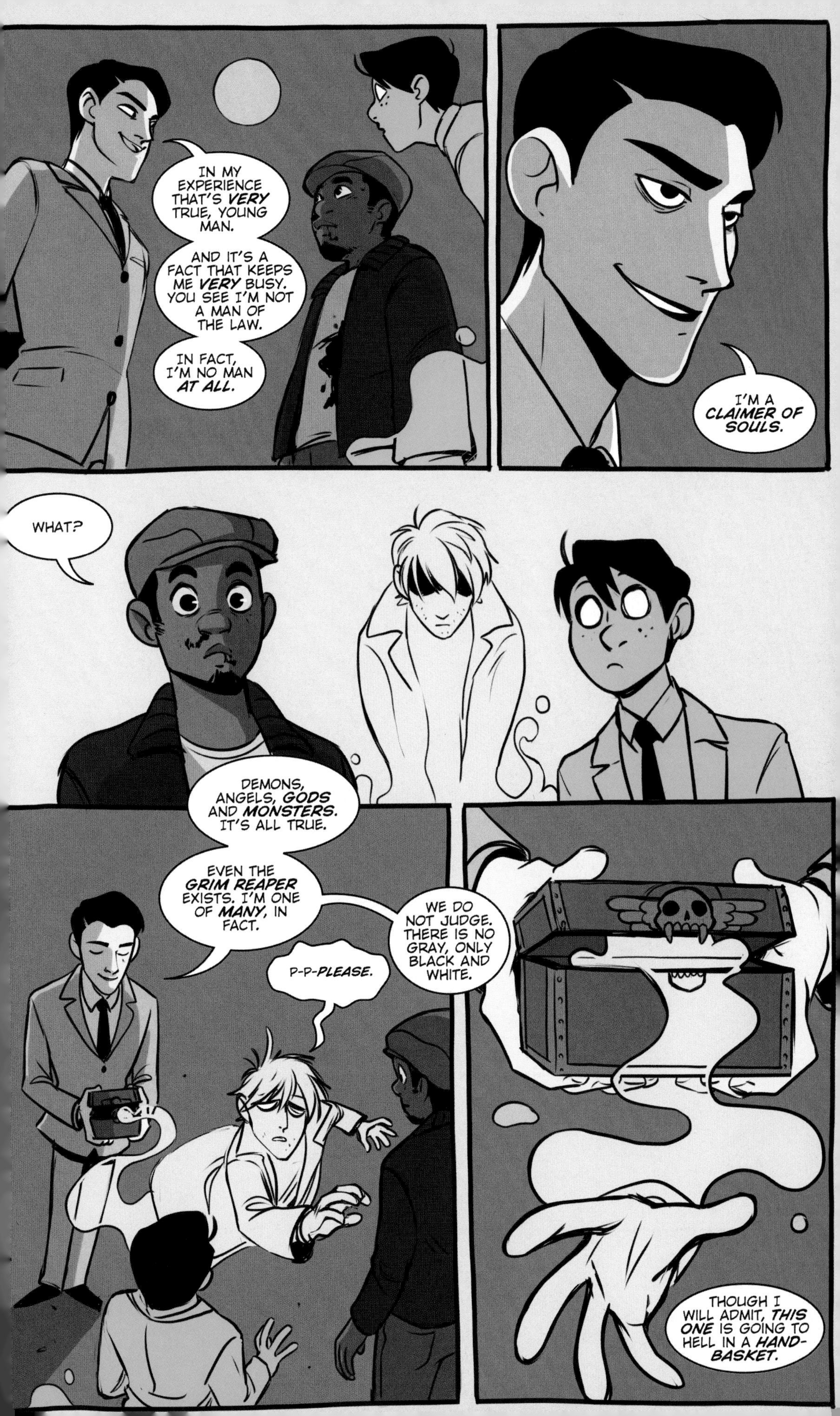
IN MY EXPERIENCE THAT'S VERY TRUE, YOUNG MAN.
AND IT'S A FACT THAT KEEPS ME VERY BUSY. YOU SEE I'M NOT A MAN OF THE LAW.
IN FACT, I'M NO MAN AT ALL.
I'M A CLAIMER OF SOULS.
WHAT?
DEMONS, ANGELS, GODS AND MONSTERS. IT'S ALL TRUE.
EVEN THE GRIM REAPER EXISTS. I'M ONE OF MANY, IN FACT.
WE DO NOT JUDGE. THERE IS NO GRAY, ONLY BLACK AND WHITE.
P-P-PLEASE.
THOUGH I WILL ADMIT, THIS ONE IS GOING TO HELL IN A HAND-BASKET.

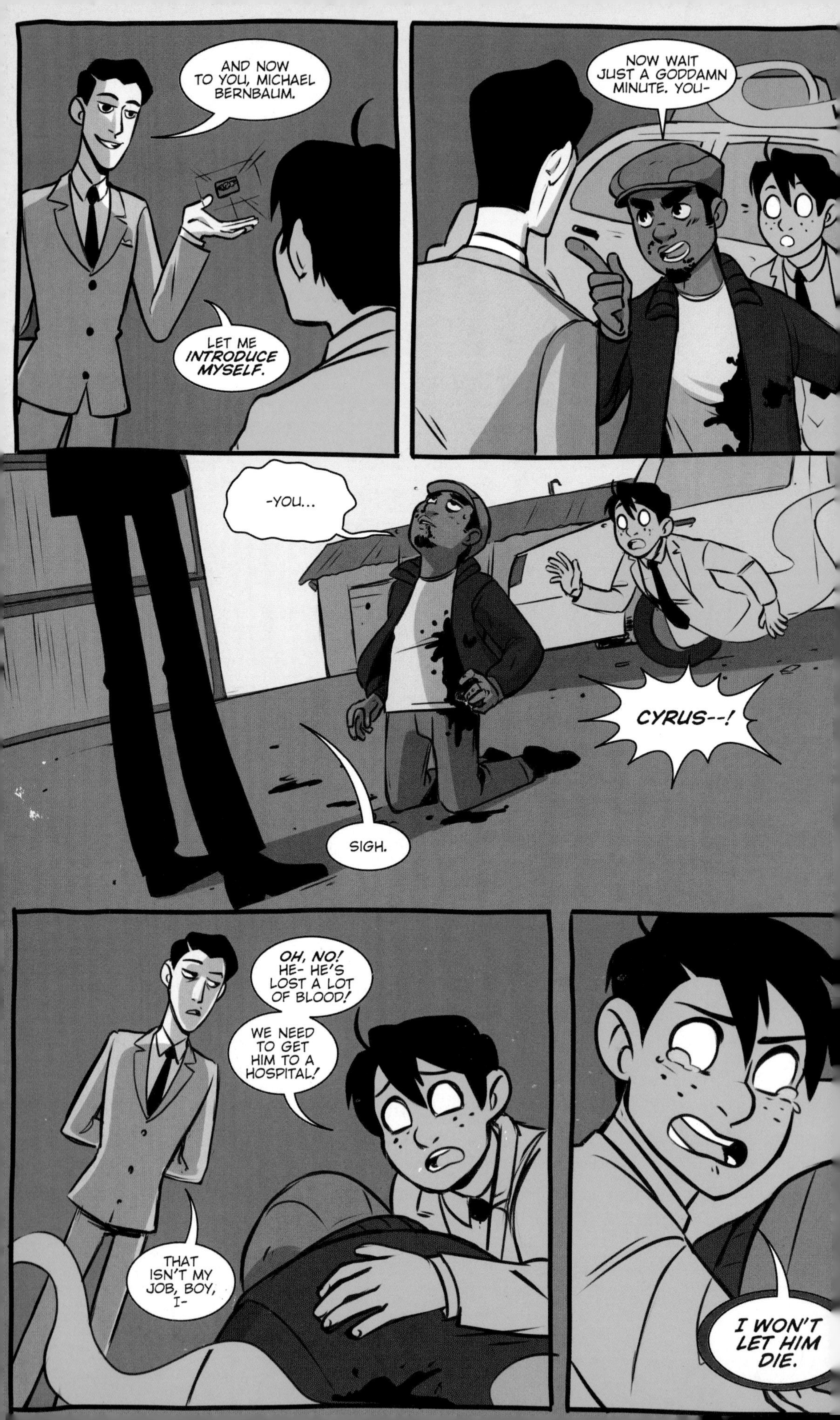
AND NOW TO YOU, MICHAEL BERNBAUM.
LET ME *INTRODUCE MYSELF.*
NOW WAIT JUST A GODDAMN MINUTE. YOU-
-YOU...
CYRUS--!
SIGH.
OH, NO! HE- HE'S LOST A LOT OF BLOOD!
WE NEED TO GET HIM TO A HOSPITAL!
THAT ISN'T MY JOB, BOY, I-
I WON'T LET HIM DIE.

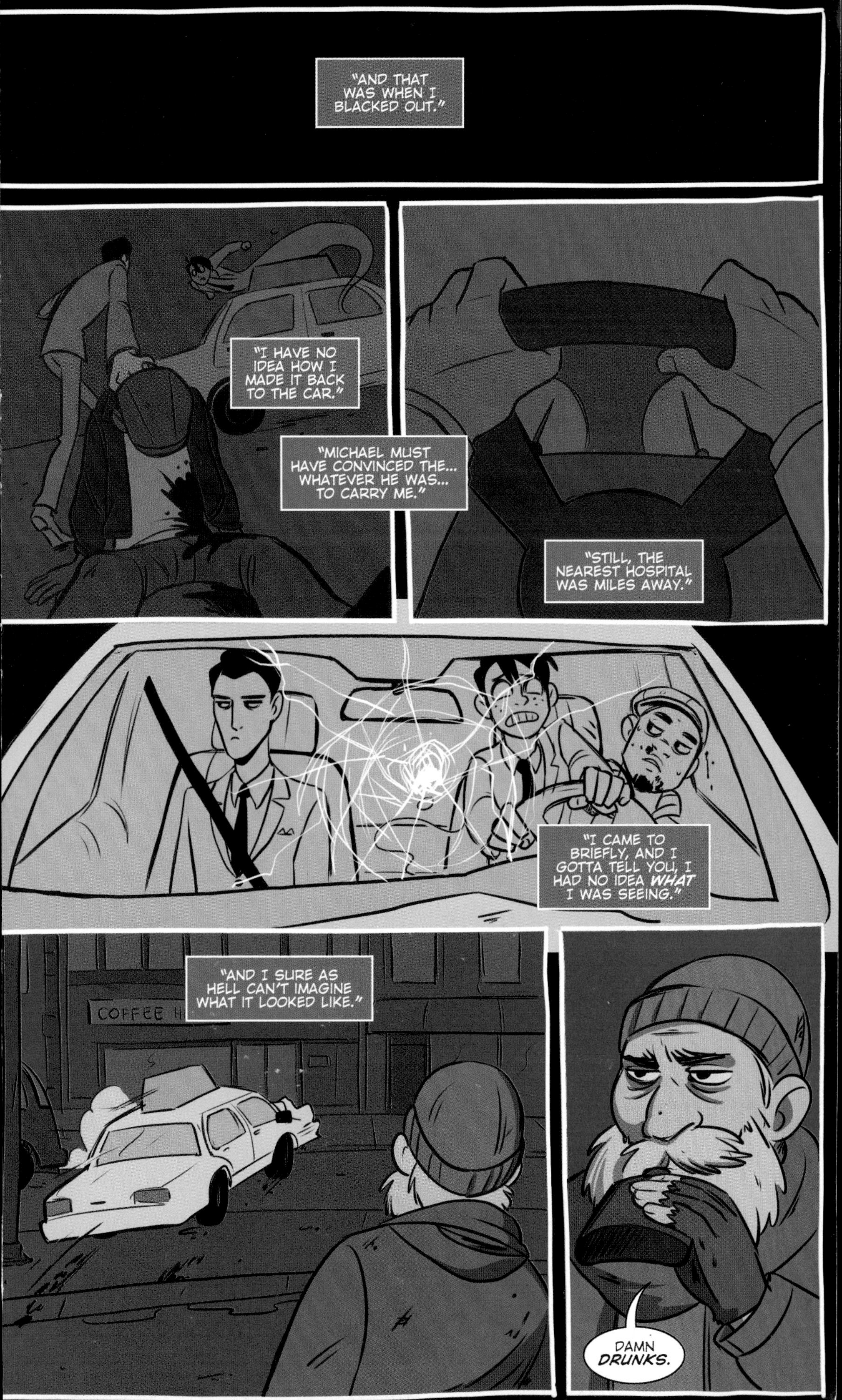
"AND THAT WAS WHEN I BLACKED OUT."
"I HAVE NO IDEA HOW I MADE IT BACK TO THE CAR."
"MICHAEL MUST HAVE CONVINCED THE... WHATEVER HE WAS... TO CARRY ME."
"STILL, THE NEAREST HOSPITAL WAS MILES AWAY."
"I CAME TO BRIEFLY, AND I GOTTA TELL YOU, I HAD NO IDEA WHAT I WAS SEEING."
"AND I SURE AS HELL CAN'T IMAGINE WHAT IT LOOKED LIKE."
COFFEE H
DAMN DRUNKS.

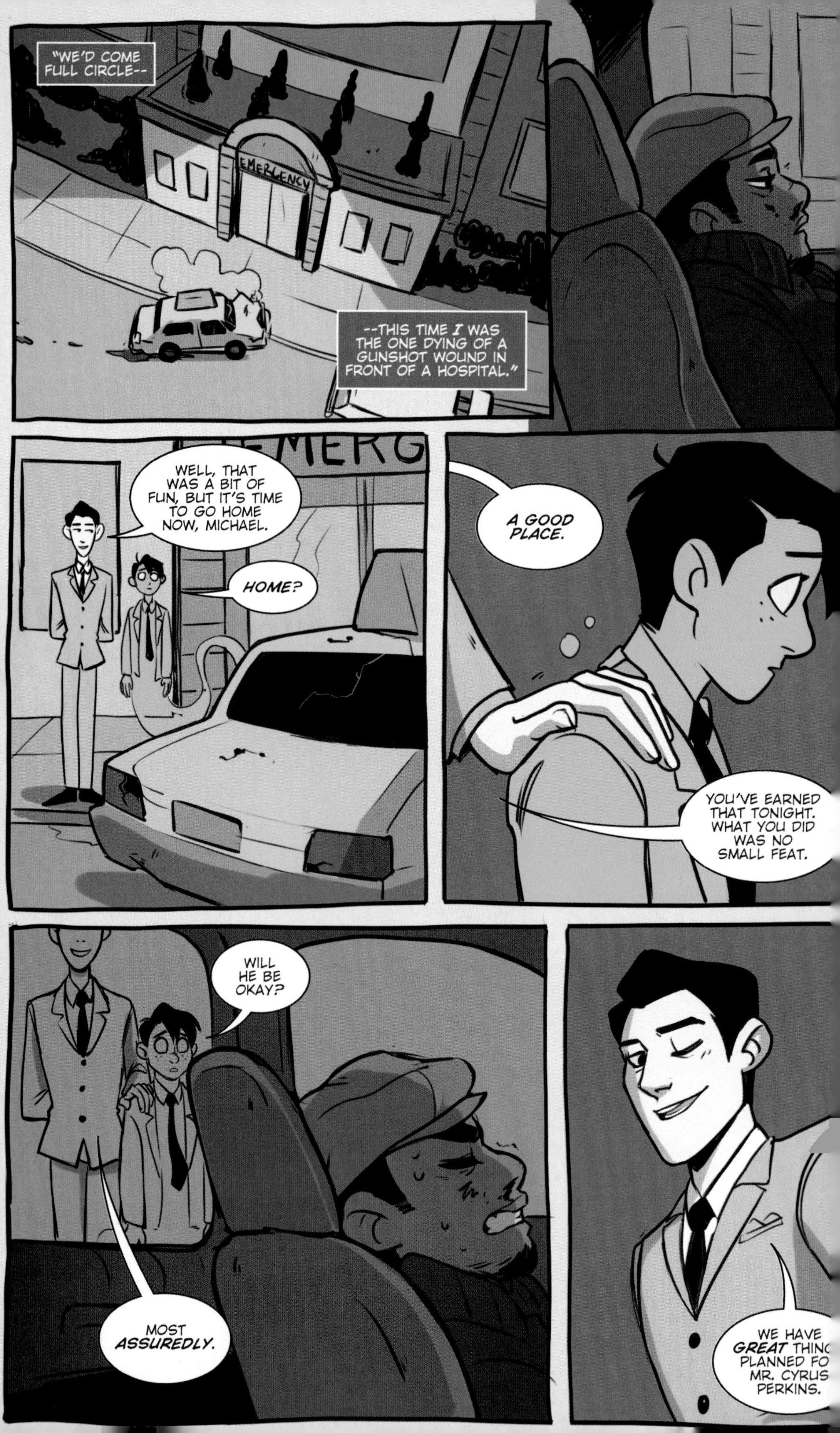
"WE'D COME FULL CIRCLE--
--THIS TIME *I* WAS THE ONE DYING OF A GUNSHOT WOUND IN FRONT OF A HOSPITAL."
EMERGENCY
WELL, THAT WAS A BIT OF FUN, BUT IT'S TIME TO GO HOME NOW, MICHAEL.
HOME?
A GOOD PLACE.
YOU'VE EARNED THAT TONIGHT. WHAT YOU DID WAS NO SMALL FEAT.
WILL HE BE OKAY?
MOST ***ASSUREDLY.***
WE HAVE ***GREAT*** THING PLANNED FO MR. CYRUS PERKINS.

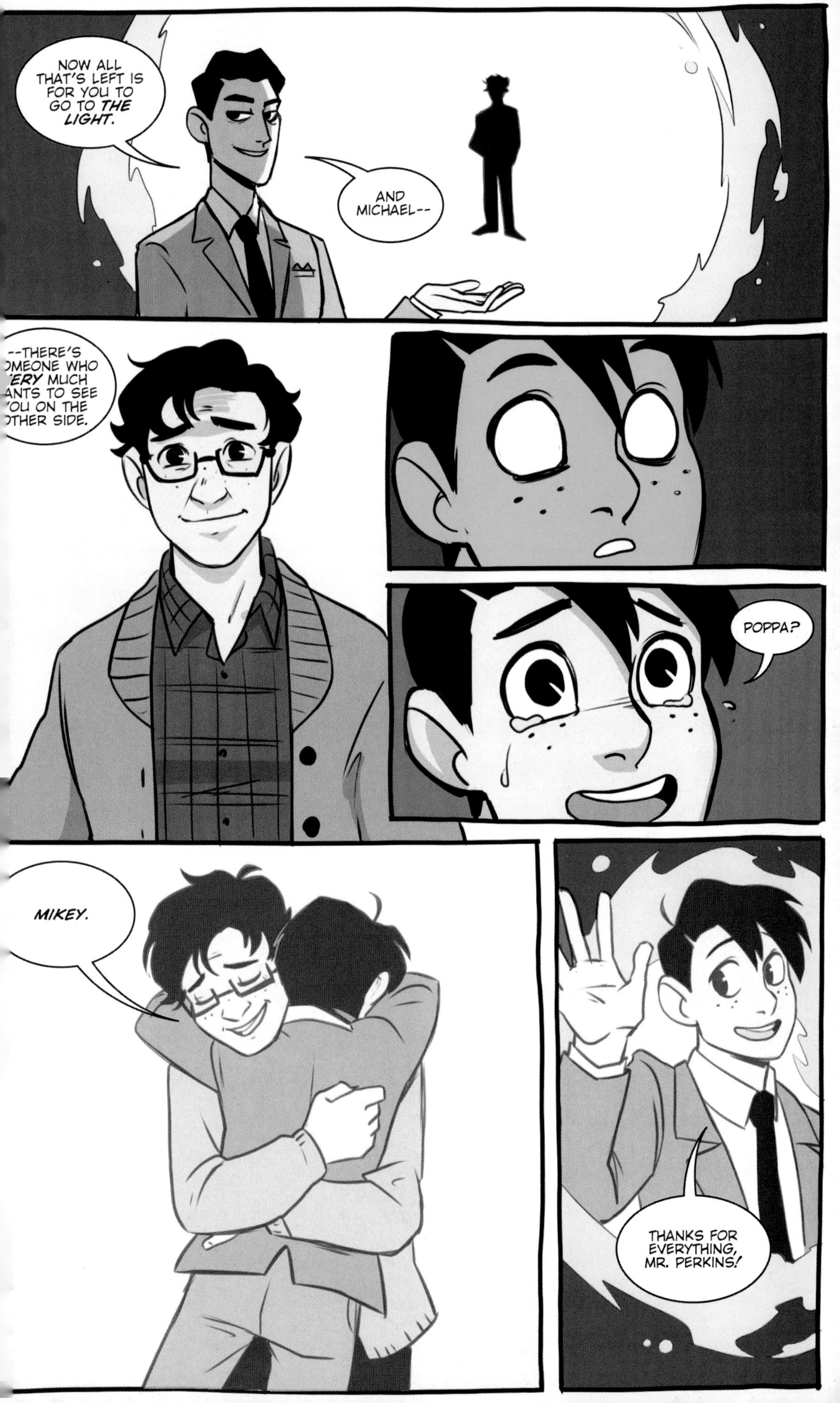
NOW ALL THAT'S LEFT IS FOR YOU TO GO TO *THE LIGHT*.
AND MICHAEL--
--THERE'S OMEONE WHO *ERY* MUCH ANTS TO SEE OU ON THE THER SIDE.
POPPA?
MIKEY.
THANKS FOR EVERYTHING, MR. PERKINS!

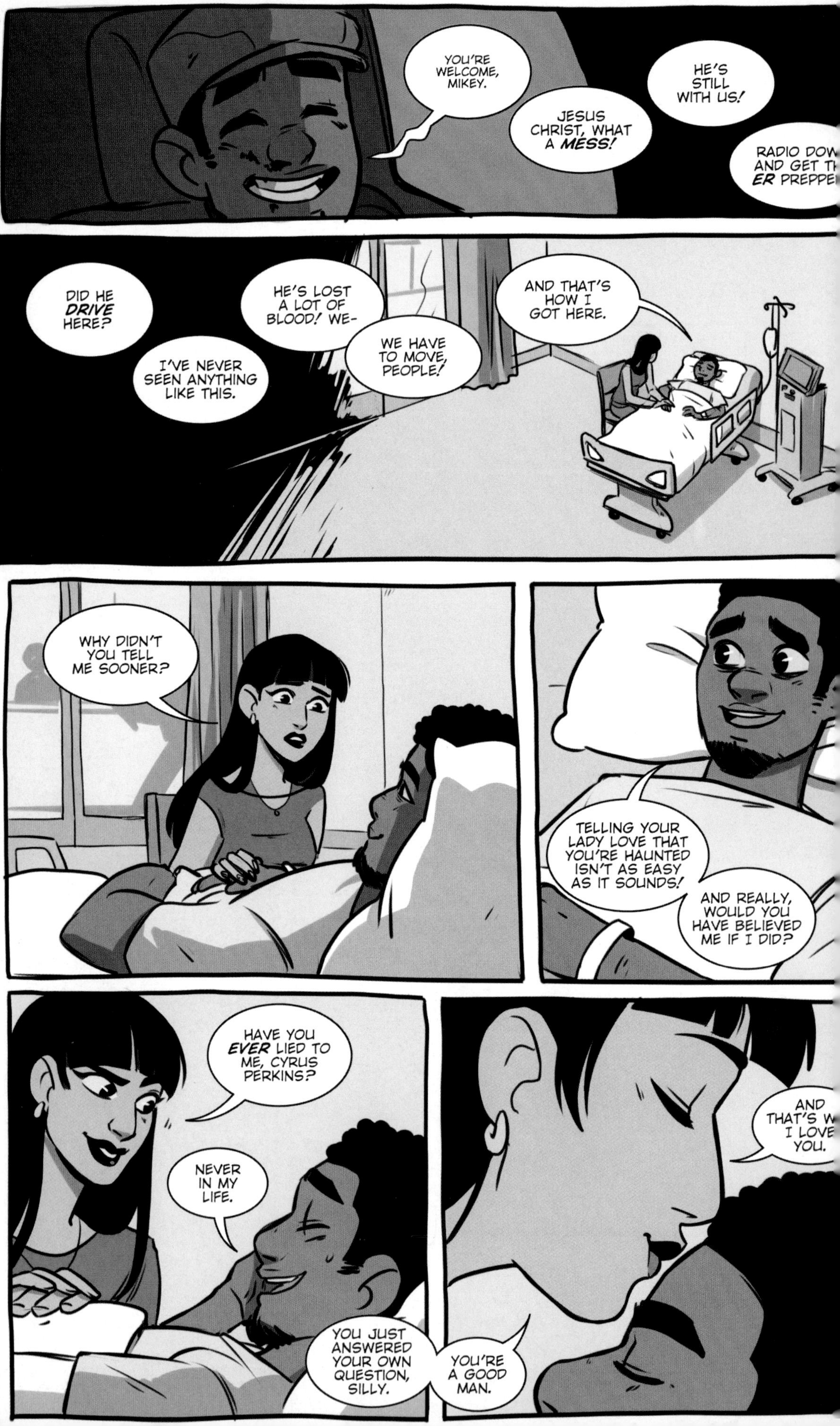
YOU'RE WELCOME, MIKEY.
JESUS CHRIST, WHAT A *MESS!*
HE'S STILL WITH US!
RADIO DOW
AND GET T
ER PREPPE
DID HE *DRIVE* HERE?
I'VE NEVER SEEN ANYTHING LIKE THIS.
HE'S LOST A LOT OF BLOOD! WE-
WE HAVE TO MOVE, PEOPLE!
AND THAT'S HOW I GOT HERE.
WHY DIDN'T YOU TELL ME SOONER?
TELLING YOUR LADY LOVE THAT YOU'RE HAUNTED ISN'T AS EASY AS IT SOUNDS!
AND REALLY, WOULD YOU HAVE BELIEVED ME IF I DID?
HAVE YOU *EVER* LIED TO ME, CYRUS PERKINS?
NEVER IN MY LIFE.
YOU JUST ANSWERED YOUR OWN QUESTION, SILLY.
YOU'RE A GOOD MAN.
AND THAT'S W
I LOVE
YOU.

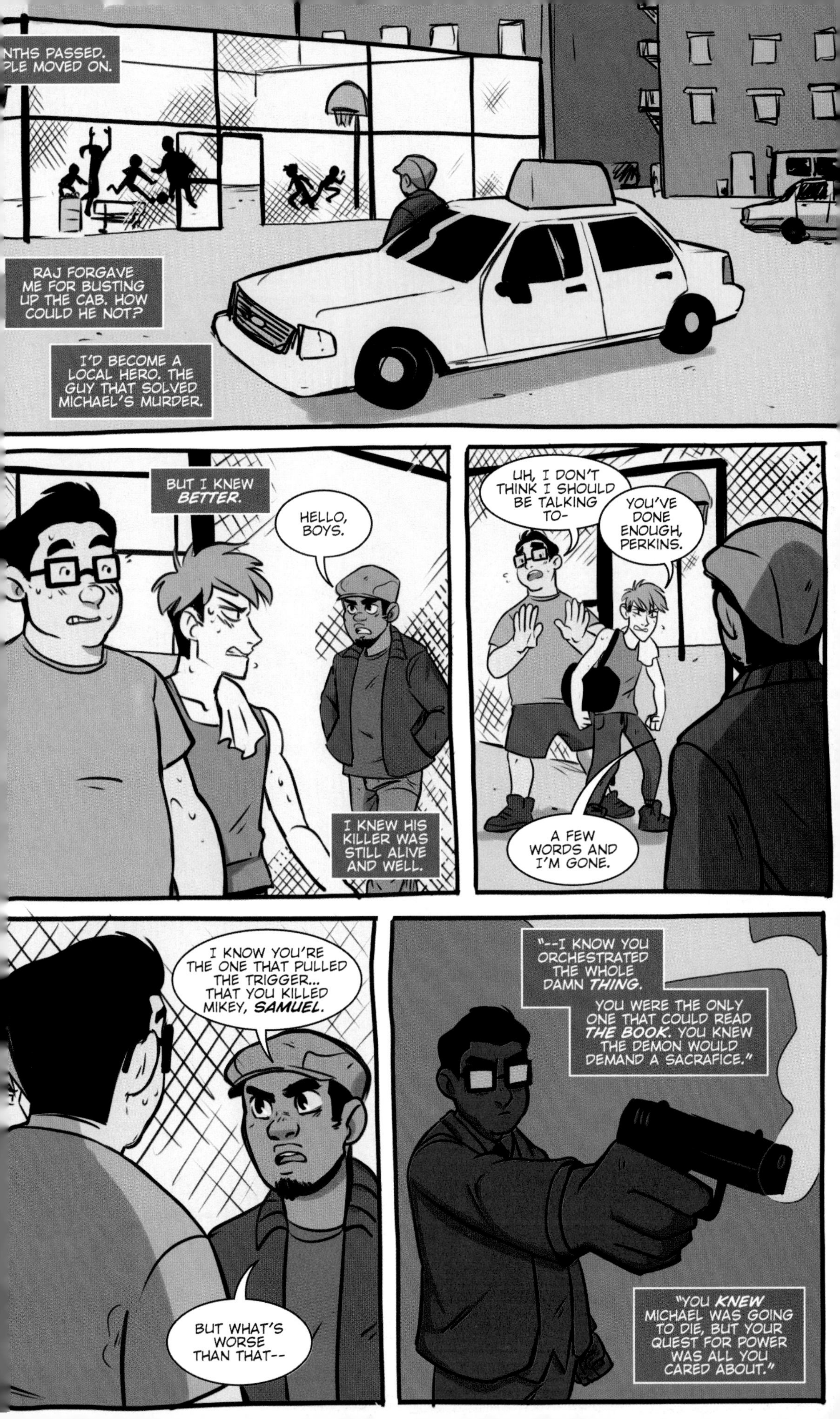
NTHS PASSED.
PLE MOVED ON.
RAJ FORGAVE ME FOR BUSTING UP THE CAB. HOW COULD HE NOT?
I'D BECOME A LOCAL HERO. THE GUY THAT SOLVED MICHAEL'S MURDER.
BUT I KNEW *BETTER*.
HELLO, BOYS.
I KNEW HIS KILLER WAS STILL ALIVE AND WELL.
UH, I DON'T THINK I SHOULD BE TALKING TO-
YOU'VE DONE ENOUGH, PERKINS.
A FEW WORDS AND I'M GONE.
I KNOW YOU'RE THE ONE THAT PULLED THE TRIGGER... THAT YOU KILLED MIKEY, *SAMUEL*.
BUT WHAT'S WORSE THAN THAT--
"--I KNOW YOU ORCHESTRATED THE WHOLE DAMN *THING*.
YOU WERE THE ONLY ONE THAT COULD READ *THE BOOK*. YOU KNEW THE DEMON WOULD DEMAND A SACRAFICE."
"YOU *KNEW* MICHAEL WAS GOING TO DIE, BUT YOUR QUEST FOR POWER WAS ALL YOU CARED ABOUT."

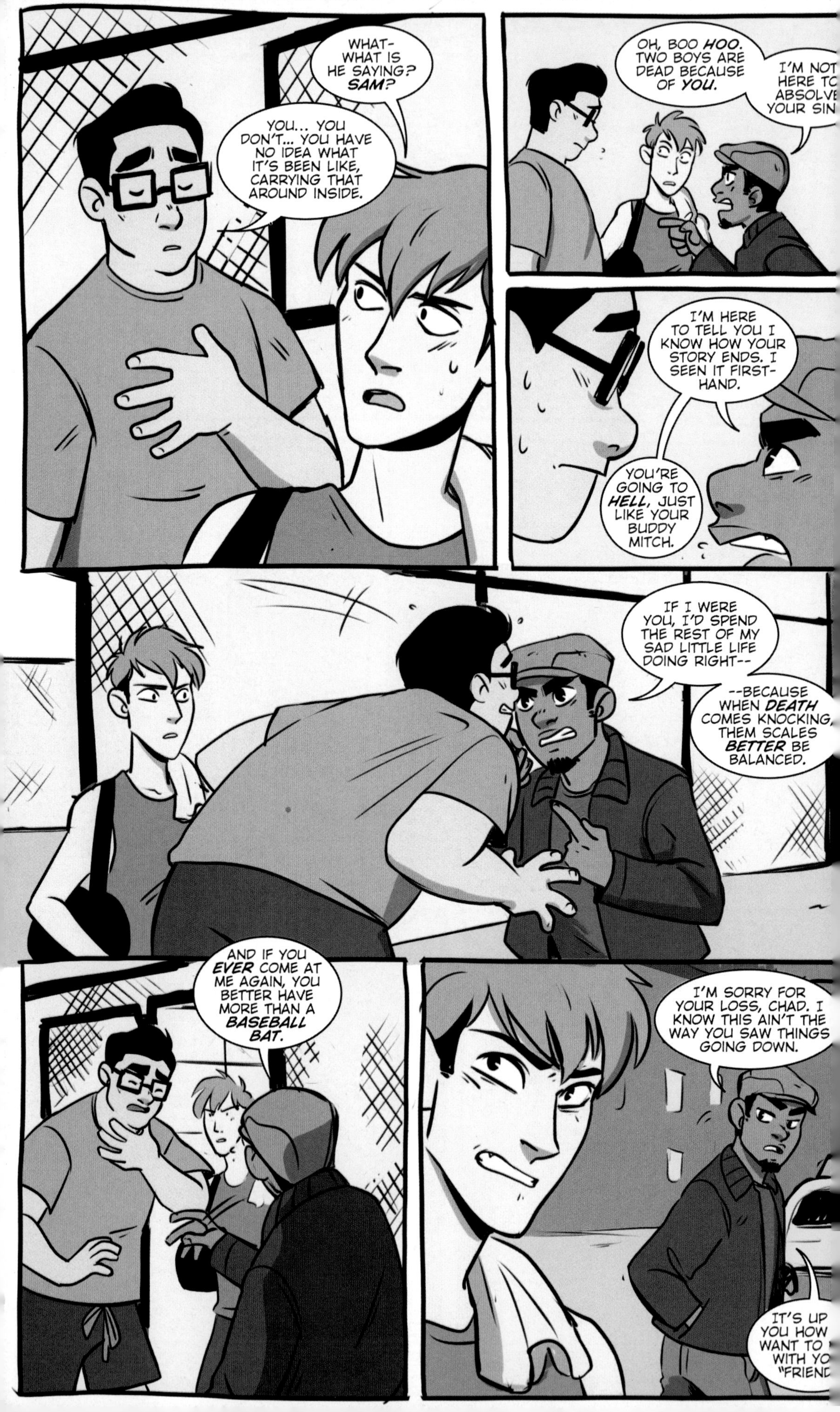
WHAT- WHAT IS HE SAYING? SAM?
YOU... YOU DON'T... YOU HAVE NO IDEA WHAT IT'S BEEN LIKE, CARRYING THAT AROUND INSIDE.
OH, BOO HOO. TWO BOYS ARE DEAD BECAUSE OF YOU.
I'M NOT HERE TO ABSOLVE YOUR SIN
I'M HERE TO TELL YOU I KNOW HOW YOUR STORY ENDS. I SEEN IT FIRST-HAND.
YOU'RE GOING TO HELL, JUST LIKE YOUR BUDDY MITCH.
IF I WERE YOU, I'D SPEND THE REST OF MY SAD LITTLE LIFE DOING RIGHT--
--BECAUSE WHEN DEATH COMES KNOCKING, THEM SCALES BETTER BE BALANCED.
AND IF YOU EVER COME AT ME AGAIN, YOU BETTER HAVE MORE THAN A BASEBALL BAT.
I'M SORRY FOR YOUR LOSS, CHAD. I KNOW THIS AIN'T THE WAY YOU SAW THINGS GOING DOWN.
IT'S UP YOU HOW WANT TO WITH YO "FRIEND

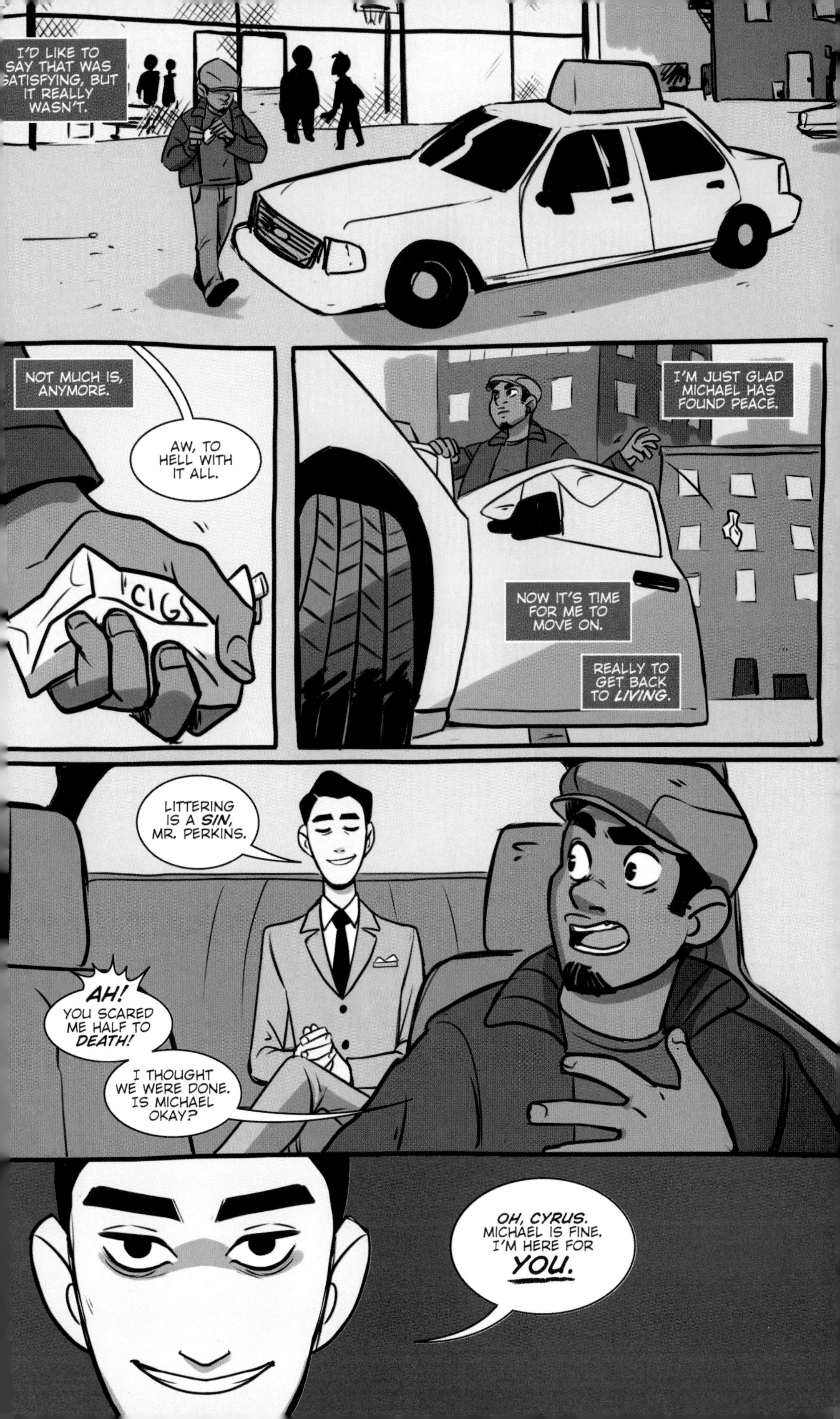
I'D LIKE TO SAY THAT WAS SATISFYING, BUT IT REALLY WASN'T.
NOT MUCH IS, ANYMORE.
AW, TO HELL WITH IT ALL.
CIGS
I'M JUST GLAD MICHAEL HAS FOUND PEACE.
NOW IT'S TIME FOR ME TO MOVE ON.
REALLY TO GET BACK TO *LIVING*.
LITTERING IS A *SIN*, MR. PERKINS.
AH! YOU SCARED ME HALF TO *DEATH!*
I THOUGHT WE WERE DONE. IS MICHAEL OKAY?
OH, CYRUS. MICHAEL IS FINE. I'M HERE FOR *YOU.*

THE ADVENTURE WILL CONTINUE I[N]

CYRUS
PERKINS

AND THE

DEATH
BRIGADE!

WINTER 2016

AVAILABLE IN FINER STORES EVERYWHE[RE]

Into a realm of magic and savagery comes a mysterious boy washed ashore. His is a
lone survivor. Befriended by an apprentice magi, her quirky mentor, and a metal golem
together they are Kai's only hope to stay alive long enough for rescue. Prepare yourse[lf]
for a d20 RPG adventure with an all new twist.

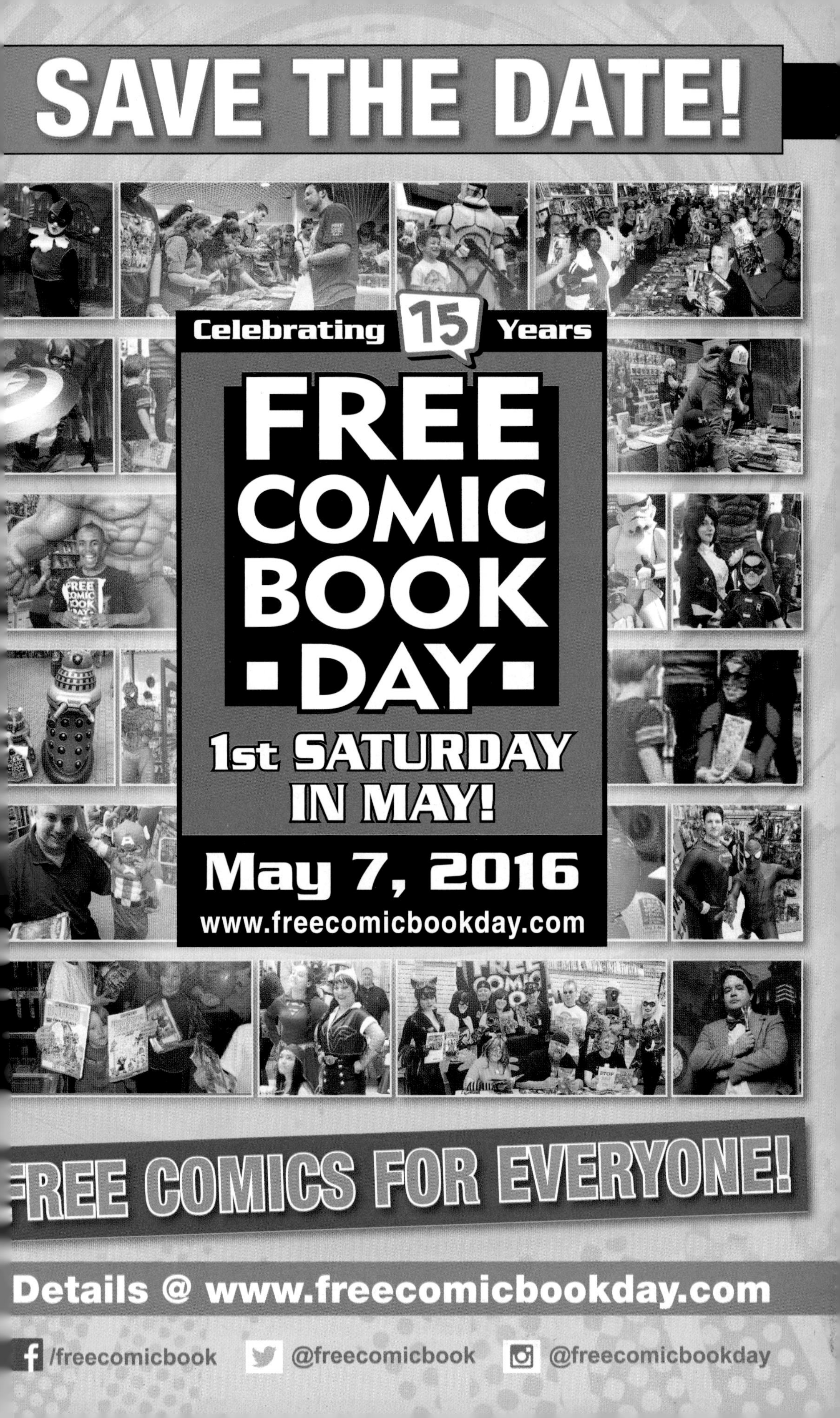
SAVE THE DATE!
Celebrating 15 Years
FREE COMIC BOOK DAY
1st SATURDAY IN MAY!
May 7, 2016
www.freecomicbookday.com
FREE COMICS FOR EVERYONE!
Details @ www.freecomicbookday.com
/freecomicbook
@freecomicbook
@freecomicbookday

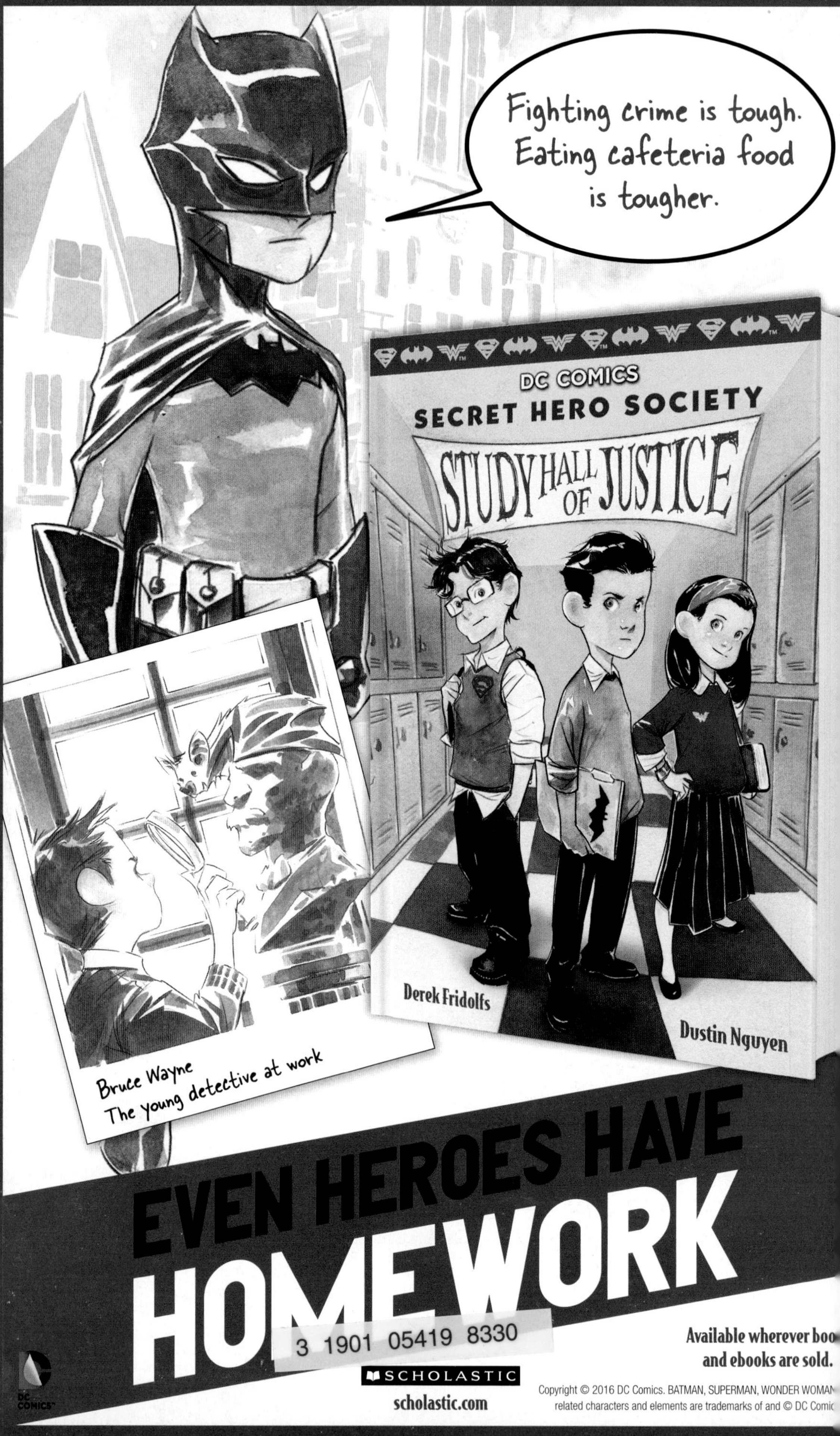
Fighting crime is tough. Eating cafeteria food is tougher.
DC COMICS
SECRET HERO SOCIETY
STUDY HALL OF JUSTICE
Derek Fridolfs
Dustin Nguyen
Bruce Wayne
The young detective at work
EVEN HEROES HAVE
HOMEWORK
Available wherever boo
and ebooks are sold.
SCHOLASTIC
scholastic.com
DC COMICS
Copyright © 2016 DC Comics. BATMAN, SUPERMAN, WONDER WOMAN
related characters and elements are trademarks of and © DC Comic